ROOT TO LEAF

ROOT TO LEAF

A southern chef cooks through the seasons

STEVEN SATTERFIELD

Photography by John Kernick

HARPER WAVE

An Imprint of HarperCollins*Publishers*

FIRST EDITION

Art direction and design by Erika Oliveira

Photographs copyright © 2015 by John Kernick

Library of Congress Cataloging-in-Publication Data has been applied for.

ISBN: 978-0-06-228369-6

15   16   17   18   19   OV/QGT   10   9   8   7   6   5   4   3   2   1

contents

One hour. 23 minutes. 12 seconds. I glanced at the countdown clock on the East Atlanta Village Farmers Market website. It was ticking down to the late-afternoon season opening and I made a point to arrive right on time, knowing it would be swarmed. It was the first warm day of spring and the market was teeming with energy. I ran into an old acquaintance who seemed a little more than disappointed with the spring offerings. "I guess it's just really early in the season?" He shrugged as he disappeared from the scene, empty-handed. I did a quick scan of the market booths and wondered what he meant. Where my friend saw nothing, I saw possibility.

I picked up a few bundles of greens, some spring garlic and leeks, some fresh pasta, a pint of berries, a young cheese, and a little basket of tender mushrooms. The wheels in my head were turning and I already had dinner figured out: melted leek ravioli with mushrooms and green garlic; a salad of tender baby chard and dandelion greens; a hunk of artisanal bread; some macerated strawberries with a delicate sheep's milk cheese; a chilled bottle of rosé. Later that evening, as some friends and I enjoyed this delightful spring meal, I kept thinking about the disappointed fellow at the market. His mind-set is all too common. Even regular market goers who aspire to cook fresh produce–driven meals are often stumped when they have to decide what to put on the table.

Americans have been conditioned to believe that more is better. It is a first-world problem to have everything you want, anytime you want it, and this type of thinking has done some serious damage to our food systems and collective health. Unlimited options clutter our minds and stifle our imagination. We are out of touch with the earth's rhythms and we do not allow ourselves to appreciate the anticipation of the natural cycles of the seasons. I use these seasonal variables as guidelines, rather than limitations, when I buy fresh produce.

I've learned that if you are able to show up with an open mind and some empty bags rather than a shopping list, you can respond to what is available. Allowing the fresh produce to guide you is true seasonal cooking. It's what this book is all about. Yes, I have the advantage of many years in professional kitchens, and this has honed my skills for thinking on my feet. But I still remember the growing pains of making mistakes and learning from them. In writing this book, I am distilling the lessons I've learned to empower you to shop for, select, and create delicious meals regardless of where you may reside. I am fortunate enough to live and work in a locale with extraordinarily rich diversity, and while

I realize every region has different climates with varying access to fresh food, with the right information, you can cook like this too.

When I am deciding how to use a fruit or vegetable, I consider several things:
Texture: Is it crisp, tender, starchy, juicy, seedy, or stringy?
Flavor: Does it taste sweet, chalky, grassy, bitter, or sour?
Shape and Size: Is it large, petite, round, oblong, heavy, or flat?
Color: Is it bright green? Will the color deepen? Does it look fresh? Will it turn brown if I cook it?
Challenges: Is it thick-skinned, hard-shelled, thorny, gooey, time-consuming? Do I know how to cook it? Do I know how to get started?

One bit of advice that I often give people when they are working with fresh produce is to taste it in different stages of cooking. Try it first raw. If you are blanching green beans for instance, taste them several times while they are cooking. You will notice that they go from a dull green with a chalky taste to a tender crunch with a lot of sweetness and a bright green color. That's the moment when you want to pull them from the water and plunge them into an ice bath. Think about the advantage you have that you *can* actually taste vegetables when they are raw. You can't do that with your chicken dish from start to finish, can you?

When I first started cooking professionally, vegetables were more or less an afterthought and most of the focus was on the protein. The idea of Southern food as something noble and respectable was just catching on. And as I grew more and more interested in the local farming community, I thought to myself: why not start a restaurant where we can react to everything that is in season and incorporate all that is harvested? Miller Union was born from this idea, and even though we serve plenty of meats, our focus is on the world of seasonal produce. When we write the menu or test ideas, we are always referencing the farmers' current availability lists.

But before I began my culinary career, I was on a different trajectory. I grew up on the Georgia coast in Savannah, America's first planned city. I was never afraid to cook, and in fact was quite comfortable in the kitchen. I used to rummage through drawers and cabinets, playing with the spice containers and sniffing each one, memorizing the smells. When I was a teenager, I would volunteer to make dinner for the family, opening up some cans or packages from the freezer and heating them up, and doctoring them, to suit my taste.

I moved to Atlanta in the late 1980s to attend architecture school at Georgia Tech. It was there that I got my first taste of living on my own. If I had enough money to go to the store, I would make my own food. My roommate at the time was always happy when I did because I usually made too much. I spent my final year abroad studying in Paris, France, and fell in love with the Parisian lifestyle of shopping on the streets of the *marché* with all of its specialized little storefronts. You simply walk from shop to shop on your way home and pick up what you need for the next day: bread, cheese, vegetables, fruits, and wine. I couldn't afford to purchase meat, and the markets there inspired me to cook simple but satisfying vegetable-based meals on the single electric burner in my tiny one-room apartment.

From Paris, I returned to Atlanta, only to realize that my heart was not in the field of architecture. So I did what any twenty-one-year-old would do on his first summer off after sixteen years of schooling. I checked out. I picked up a guitar for the first time and started learning how to play and write songs. Just over a year later, I formed a band called Seely with some friends from college and we quickly and strangely became widely known and started climbing the college charts. We had the opportunity to play live shows all over the country and lead a fantastic life. But it wasn't lucrative, so I turned to restaurants for supplemental income. I was working in short-order kitchens, but as we matured and took more time off between records, I sought out better food. I was lucky enough to land a job at local chef Anne Quatrano's Floataway Café, one of the first real farm-to-table restaurants in the city. After that I started working under acclaimed Southern chef Scott Peacock at Watershed in Decatur, Georgia. Scott focused on traditional Southern cooking with seasonal flair and it was there that I planted my roots. I worked every station and eventually ended up running the kitchen. After nine years, I decided to go out on my own. With the help of my trusty friend and soon-to-be business partner, Neal McCarthy, I started Miller Union. I was beginning to realize that I had a knack for coaxing flavor out of just about any fruit or vegetable, and I wanted to explore it.

All plants are living things, with life forces and energy that we need to survive. Our earth is covered with edible plant life that changes and evolves throughout the year, following a somewhat predictable and seasonal course. It is the job of gardeners and farmers to navigate the many factors that affect this fresh produce as they seed, irrigate, prune, and harvest. I see it as the cook's duty to acknowledge their hard work by respecting the vegetable. I truly believe that if a fruit or a vegetable is prepared with care, its very best features can be enhanced by the thoughtful cook.

There were many thoughtful cooks here before we were around. Think about a family that lived off of the farm, before industrialized food systems. If they harvested a pig, every single part of that animal would be used for something: pickled trotters, brains and eggs, liver pudding, chitterlings, breakfast sausage, pork chops, country ham, picnic shoulder, bacon, fatback, and so on. The same applies to the crops. If collards were being harvested, they might eat collards every day for weeks. The corn that was grown would be dried and then ground into cornmeal and later mixed with cultured buttermilk and chicken eggs and some hot fat from that pig. The term "nose to tail" was coined much later to describe this idea of using every part of an animal. Now I am proposing that we look at all food this way. Using every edible part of the plant, utilizing scraps, and composting are just as important. This is what I call *Root to Leaf* cooking.

We all need to eat more fresh produce. Plants are nature's original vitamin supplements. Everything we need is there, if we pay attention, and eat what's in season. Although I have always been healthy and active, in 2012, I was suddenly hit with a devastating diagnosis of cancer while writing the proposal for this book. I had to break away from all of my work at the restaurant, undergo surgery, cancel appearances, and endure chemotherapy for twelve weeks. During my treatment, I found solace in food. At a time when most people struggle to eat, I was drawn even more to cook for myself with local produce from the markets in order to heal more quickly. I ate as much fresh fruit and vegetables as I could get down, and continued to do so post-chemotherapy. This farm-fresh nutrition, coupled with herbs, probiotics, and positivity, helped me immensely. I cannot explain how this may have improved the healing process medically, but within two weeks of finishing chemotherapy, I was working a full-time schedule again and I haven't stopped since.

I'm thankful for my health and full recovery and I feel I owe a lot of it to the world of fresh produce. Seasonal cooking begins with the harvest. And what I've come to learn is that there is little that changes so distinctly throughout the course of any year as the diverse world of fruits and vegetables.

SPRING

Springtime brings renewal. Ephemeral young buds, tender shoots, and pastel green leaves emerge. They disappear as quickly as they come when temperatures rise. The fleeting treasures of spring stay cool longer in the mountains, just a few hours away.

ASPARAGUS

As soon as daylight saving time begins, I start texting my produce guy. "Have you seen any asparagus at the market yet?" I ask. "No, maybe next week, still waiting," he replies. Later that week, I prompt him again. "Asparagus? Green garlic? Peas?" By this time, I've had my fill of turnips and rutabagas. I'm prodding him for something fresh and green that screams spring, and I know that asparagus will be one of the first to rear its royal crown. When it does finally appear, we work those spears into the menu every way we can: diced in creamed rice, sautéed in fish dishes, pickled in jars, grilled and chilled as the centerpiece of the plate. I'll shave asparagus into salads or peel it into thin ribbons and toss it with olive oil and garlic like a pasta.

Asparagus is one of the most recognizable symbols of spring. Its season is fleeting, with an average healthy patch yielding for only six to eight weeks. These tender shoots are one of the first things to emerge from the ground as the sun rises earlier each day. But it's not just the warmth that brings these springtime treasures from their underground dwellings. This perennial, related to the lily, needs a cold winter to thrive. If the ground doesn't freeze, it is difficult for the plant to go dormant and regenerate. Asparagus takes three to four years to begin producing from seed, but it can regenerate itself for fifteen years or more. It's an old joke among homeowners who garden that a productive asparagus bed is a good reason to renovate rather than move.

These luxurious spears have always been a delicacy. Before asparagus was cultivated, it only grew wild in sandy maritime soils. Roman emperors would send out ships for the sole purpose of bringing it back for royal feasts. Nowadays, the demand for asparagus is so great that it is produced in and shipped from other parts of the world, so it is available in supermarkets nearly year-round. In the United States, the harvest is primarily from the chilly climates of Northern California, Washington State, and Michigan. Luckily, I can get asparagus in good supply from some of the local farms in Georgia as well as the mountainous regions of North Carolina.

Chlorophyll accounts for the distinctive green hue of asparagus, and it tinges the purple asparagus, too. The skin of the purple varieties contains anthocyanin, the antioxidant that is responsible for red, blue, or purple pigment in food. There is a farming process called blanching that inhibits chlorophyll development: it involves covering the spears with dirt and shielding them from the sun. This results in altered colors and less grassy flavors. Blanched purple varieties never darken beyond pink, and the blanched green varieties never actually turn green, but grow white. While there are minor flavor differences, they are basically interchangeable, and if you happen to find some of these less common colors, they make a stunning presentation.

Asparagus is marketed in specific sizes: pencil, standard, large, and jumbo. All have a similar flavor, but they benefit from different treatments in the kitchen. The smaller sizes need the least cooking, if any, and don't require peeling. The larger, meatier ones may require peeling, especially toward the bottom of the spear. The best way to test is to slice off a piece near the bottom and eat it raw. If the skin is woody or stringy, peel the bottom third or so away. The skin nearest the top will be the most tender.

Whatever the color or size, look for firm, unblemished spears with bright color. The cut ends should not be too hard, although a little woodiness at the base prevents the stalk from drying out. Store asparagus like cut flowers—make a fresh cut at the bottom and set the spears in a vertical container filled with about 1 inch of water. Place a damp towel over the tips to keep them from drying out, until you are ready to use them.

ROASTED ASPARAGUS WITH GREEN GARLIC AND RADISHES

This vibrant side dish pairs asparagus with radishes quickly roasted together. Perfect with an Easter ham, the recipe also fits into a Mother's Day brunch menu or adds seasonal flair to any weekday meal.

4 servings

1 pound standard or large asparagus
1 bunch radishes (reserve tops for another use)
1 stalk green garlic, thinly sliced (or 1 small garlic clove, finely chopped)
Kosher salt
Freshly ground black pepper
1 to 2 tablespoons extra virgin olive oil

Heat the oven to 400°F. Wash the asparagus and trim away the base if woody. Pat dry. Slice the spears into 1-inch pieces and place in a large bowl. Wash the radishes and trim off the taproots. Quarter the radishes and add to the bowl. Add the green garlic, season with salt and pepper, drizzle with olive oil, and toss to combine. Transfer the mixture to a wide baking dish or baking sheet and spread out in a single layer. Roast on the middle rack of the oven until just tender, 10 to 15 minutes. Serve hot or at room temperature.

GRILLED ASPARAGUS WITH BREBIS AND BREAD CRUMBS

Temperature plays a critical role not only in cooking but also in eating. Consider what happens to asparagus when it briefly meets hot wood smoke and then is chilled before serving. The spears become refreshingly crisp, with a deep meaty flavor that tastes even better over a thick smear of creamy brebis, the sheep's milk equivalent of fresh chèvre. Olive oil bread crumbs add a layer of savory crunch to the cheese in the same way that a graham cracker crust complements a cheesecake.

4 servings

1½ pounds standard or large asparagus
2 to 3 tablespoons extra virgin olive oil, plus more for drizzling
Kosher salt
Freshly ground black pepper
¼ cup (2 ounces) brebis (or chèvre)
¼ cup Olive Oil Bread Crumbs (see recipe)
2 medium radishes, halved and thinly sliced
½ teaspoon fresh lemon juice
4 teaspoons loosely packed chopped fresh mint

Grill the asparagus: Heat the grill to high. Wash the asparagus and trim away the base if woody. Pat dry. Lay the spears on a baking sheet or flat surface. Drizzle with olive oil, season lightly with salt and pepper, and toss to coat.

Lay the asparagus spears on the grill, perpendicular to the grill grates so they don't fall through. Do not crowd. Lightly char 30 seconds to 2 minutes per side, depending on the thickness of the spears, turning with tongs. Be sure not to overcook, as the hot asparagus will continue to cook once removed from the grill. Transfer to a plate in a single layer to cool. Cover and refrigerate until ready to use.

Assemble the salad: Place 1 tablespoon brebis in the center of 4 plates. With the back of a spoon, smear it across the middle of the plate. Sprinkle 1 tablespoon bread crumbs across the cheese. Lay the asparagus in a single row across each of the plates. In a small bowl, toss the radish slices with the lemon juice and a pinch of salt. Garnish each portion with some of the radishes and sprinkle with mint. Drizzle each salad with more olive oil if desired.

OLIVE OIL BREAD CRUMBS

I like having these around to sprinkle on salads or add to simple pasta dishes. They taste like well-seasoned garlic bread in the form of a crispy fine crumb.

About 1 cup

½ loaf rustic sourdough bread or a baguette, preferably stale
1 tablespoon finely chopped green garlic (or 1 small garlic clove, finely chopped)
¼ to ⅓ cup extra virgin olive oil (enough to saturate crumbs)
Fine sea salt

Heat the oven to 300°F. Cut the bread into 1-inch cubes and spread in a single layer on a baking sheet. Bake until completely dry but not browned, 10 to 15 minutes. Remove from the oven and let cool. Working in small batches, transfer the toasted bread to a blender and blend into fine bread crumbs. Do not fill the blender pitcher more than one-fourth full. Transfer the bread crumbs to a wide skillet. Add the green garlic and olive oil (just enough to saturate), and season with salt. Turn the heat to medium-low and cook, stirring constantly, until the crumbs are lightly browned. Taste for seasoning and adjust as needed.

CARROTS

Of all the species in the vegetable world, I have the longest history with carrots. They may very well be the first vegetable that I not only agreed to eat but also actually liked. As a kid, I didn't care at all for cooked carrots, which I thought were mushy and overly sweet. But I loved carrots raw and would stand at the refrigerator door eating them straight out of the crisper. "You're going to turn orange if you keep doing that," my mother would warn me.

As a grown-up chef, I am always discovering ways to create the perfect cooked carrot. Its natural sweetness can be balanced with acid or savory herbs, or enhanced with maple syrup, sugar, honey, or sorghum; the texture can be tempered by roasting or braising instead of boiling. In cooking terms, carrots are aromatic plants that add deep flavor and aroma to whatever they are cooked with and are often used in combination with other vegetables for braises, sauces, and stews. Carrots are related to parsley, celery, chervil, cilantro, dill, fennel, and parsnips. They do best in spring and fall weather, but do not grow well in winter and cannot survive hot summer days.

I am a lot pickier about my carrots now than when I was a kid, because I understand the special earthy sweetness of a freshly harvested bunch. The carrots that you might find at a farmers' market will, I guarantee, be some of the best you have ever tried. They are almost like a different vegetable. I have a particular disdain for those bagged "baby" carrots in the supermarket, which are typically regular-size carrots that have been whittled into uniform baby-carrot-size pieces.

Carrots come in many shapes, colors, and sizes. Besides the expected orange, carrots can be purple, pink, red, white, and yellow. Some are indeed naturally tiny. Others are ginormous: the longest recorded carrot measured over nineteen feet. They may be tapered or truncated, elongated or round, straight or gnarled. Imperator carrots are the classic long, tapered shapes that are most commonly seen. The Nantes varieties grow six to seven inches long in a cylindrical shape with blunt tips. Chantenay varieties are shorter and more squat, and usually grow from one to four inches in length. The first domesticated carrots were red, purple, and black and were grown in Afghanistan. Then in the eighteenth century, the Dutch developed an orange carrot and fed it to their cows to produce richer milk and yellow-tinged butter.

Carrots have a special talent for absorbing heavy metals from contaminated soil, so buy organic whenever possible. If they are sold with tops, look for fresh perky greens and deep color. Don't buy carrots that are limp or soft. If they are cracked or green, they could be bitter. Not all carrots need to be peeled. In fact, you need to peel them only if they are very large or especially rough and dirty. Otherwise, just give them a good scrubbing in cool water. Store them in the refrigerator but protect them from the dry air by keeping them in a sealable plastic bag or covered with a damp cotton towel. Once carrots go limp, there is little you can do to revive them.

If you buy carrots with the tops still intact, separate the tops from the roots before refrigerating. Because the tops are trying to stay alive, they will draw moisture, nutrients, and flavor out of the carrots. The tops are edible, but I am not a fan of their strong flavor—unless I'm making Gumbo Z'Herbes (page 79), or blending them with a host of herbs into an à la minute salsa verde.

Mom may have been onto something when she warned me not to eat too many carrots. Because carrots are rich in beta-carotene, overconsumption can cause one's skin to turn yellow or orange, especially on the hands and feet. If this happens to you, try to branch out and eat a few other vegetables, preferably of different colors.

PICKLED BABY CARROTS

These crisp, tangy pickled carrots are easy to make and extremely versatile. You can thinly slice them and add them to a salad, serve them alongside a sandwich, or eat them straight out of the jar for a healthy snack. If you prefer, you can strain off the spices while pouring the hot brine over the carrots. This will make them easier to handle later, as no spices will be floating around in the jar and clinging to the carrots.

1 quart

1 to 2 bunches baby carrots, about ½ inch thick at top
1 cup apple cider vinegar
1 tablespoon honey
4½ teaspoons kosher salt
½ teaspoon mustard seeds
½ teaspoon black peppercorns
½ teaspoon allspice berries
½ teaspoon coriander seeds
½ teaspoon fennel seeds
1 whole clove

Trim off the carrot tops and taproots. Wash and scrub the carrots thoroughly. If thicker than ½ inch in diameter, slice in half lengthwise. Place the trimmed, washed carrots in a clean quart jar. In a small pot over high heat, combine the vinegar, honey, 1¼ cups water, and salt. Add the mustard seeds, peppercorns, allspice, coriander, fennel, and clove. Bring to a rapid boil, and cook about 5 minutes. Pour the hot brine into the jar, leaving ¼ inch of headspace. Place the lid on top of the jar, screw on the band, and refrigerate after cooling. The carrots are best after 2 days and will keep, refrigerated, for up to 3 months.

SORGHUM-GLAZED BABY CARROTS

I like to cook carrots in this flavorful liquid until they are barely tender, and then rescue them from the pan. The starch that the carrots leave behind reduces with the pan liquids to form a glaze that is tossed with the carrots just before serving.

4 to 6 servings

1 cup hard apple cider
½ cup sorghum (honey, molasses, or maple syrup may be substituted)
Juice of 1 lemon
Juice of 1 orange
3 tablespoons unsalted butter
2 bunches baby carrots (about 1 pound trimmed)
Kosher salt
Freshly ground black pepper

Combine the cider, sorghum, lemon juice, orange juice, and butter in a wide skillet. Bring to a simmer, then add the carrots in a single layer. You may need to cook them in batches, depending on the size of your pan. Lightly season the carrots with salt and pepper and cook until tender, about 10 minutes. Remove with a slotted spoon and continue to simmer the sauce until it is reduced to a thin glaze. Before serving, put the carrots back in the pan and reheat them in the glaze.

ROASTED CARROTS WITH RED ONION AND THYME

Carrots can sometimes come across as overly sweet when cooked, but quickly roasting them with strong flavors like red onion and fresh thyme brings out their savory side. This simple, straightforward preparation is delicious with braised rabbit, with duck confit, or in the mix on a vegetable plate. This was one of the first recipes I ever wrote for the Miller Union menu.

4 to 6 servings

2 bunches baby carrots (about 1 pound trimmed)
1 small red onion, diced
3 sprigs fresh thyme
Kosher salt
Freshly ground black pepper
3 to 4 tablespoons extra virgin olive oil
2 tablespoons chopped fresh parsley

Heat the oven to 400°F. Trim away the taproots and carrot tops. Wash and scrub the carrots thoroughly. Slice the carrots on the bias, about ⅓ inch thick and 1 inch long. In a mixing bowl, combine the carrots, onion, and thyme. Season with salt and pepper, and toss with extra virgin olive oil. Spread on a Silpat- or parchment-lined baking sheet and roast until tender and slightly caramelized, 15 to 18 minutes. Toss with chopped parsley and serve.

FENNEL

If sweet corn, field peas, and okra make up my backstory, fennel is part of my new story. In the late 1990s, I was visiting my brother in San Francisco, and while exploring the city, I spotted waist-high stalks of what looked to me like fennel, shooting through the cracks in the sidewalks like a common weed. I rubbed some of the feathery fronds between my fingers to release their aroma, and sure enough, the unmistakable sweet anise scent confirmed my hunch.

It was not so long ago that fennel was practically unheard of in the South. But since that time, fennel has grown in popularity all across the country and even shows up in farmers' markets here in Georgia throughout the cooler months. Now I work with every part of the fennel plant: bulb, stem, fronds, seeds, and pollen from the flowers. It is one of the few garden plants that have three uses: as a vegetable, an herb, and a spice.

Fennel is a hardy perennial and can grow anywhere, but is especially prevalent in the Mediterranean region and in Northern California, and takes to dry soil near seacoasts and riverbanks. Fennel does best in cool weather, with its strongest growing season in spring or fall. It is related to parsley, celery, anise, chervil, cumin, dill, carrot, and lovage.

The bulb is cool, juicy, and crisp when raw and tastes incredibly refreshing on a crudités platter or shaved into a salad. One of my favorite cool-weather side dishes is made by braising the fennel bulb until it is fork-tender and the flavor has mellowed. When cooked in this manner, it takes especially well to Mediterranean flavors like citrus, olives, garlic, dry white wine, and put-up tomatoes. Fennel complements many different fruits or vegetables without overpowering them. It also is an easy, natural pairing with fish or shellfish.

The Greek name for fennel is *marathon*. In 490 B.C., the Greeks fought the Persians in a fennel field in what is now known as Marathon, Greece. When the Greeks won, they sent a runner named Phidippides to deliver news of the victory. He ran exactly 26 miles and 385 yards to Athens, where, supposedly, he dropped dead upon arrival.

Fennel has been a prized ingredient in French, Italian, and other European cuisines for centuries. It also has been used to treat respiratory congestion and is a common ingredient in cough syrup. Fennel seeds, or tea made of fennel, can relieve indigestion, stimulate breast milk production, and freshen your breath.

Fennel seed is a main ingredient in absinthe—just about every European country has its own anise-flavored liqueur. Fennel seed is also part of the traditional Chinese five-spice blend. A light dusting of intensely sweet-flavored pollen can add a heady accent as a garnish for soups, salads, or seafood dishes. The fronds make a beautiful garnish and they are perfect for adding to stocks, braises, or even an ice cream base. The stems can also be used, but need to be crosscut if intended for eating, to break up the stringy fibers that run their length.

There are two main types of fennel. "Florence" or "finocchio" has a rounded white bulb with stalks that resemble celery, and beautiful wispy dark green fronds. The other type, considered "sweet fennel," is left in the ground as mostly foliage used for growing seeds. Though low-maintenance, it does not share its space well with others. If planted too close to dill, for example, it can cross-pollinate.

Look for fennel bulbs that are smooth, compact, and free of cracks. Avoid bulbs that are turning yellow or brown. Fennel from the West Coast tends to be large with white bulbs and thick stems. The fennel that we see in Georgia is a small-bulbed, pale green variety that grows best in fall or spring. Look for perky fronds, if still attached. Store fennel loosely wrapped in the refrigerator. Don't let it get too cold, as its high water content makes it prone to freezing.

BRAISED FENNEL WITH OLIVES AND ORANGES

The classic accents of briny olives and tart oranges balance the mellow sweetness of fennel when it is cooked until fork-tender. I prefer picholine and Kalamata olives when I make this, but feel free to choose your favorite varieties. Note that some of the olive brine is added to the dish instead of salt. Taste the liquid in the pan after all the ingredients are combined to check for seasoning, and adjust as needed before cooking.

6 to 8 servings

4 fennel bulbs, quartered if small, cut into sixths or eighths if larger
2 oranges, quartered, seeds removed
½ cup olives packed in brine; more than one variety is fine
½ cup olive brine
2 stalks spring leeks or spring onions
1 cup dry white wine
2 tablespoons extra virgin olive oil
2 tablespoons unsalted butter
½ teaspoon freshly ground black pepper
Kosher salt, if needed

Heat the oven to 300°F. Arrange the fennel across the bottom of a deep braising pan or ovenproof dish in a single layer. Squeeze the oranges over the fennel, then add the rinds to the pan. Add the whole olives and the measured olive brine. Trim the spring leeks or onions into 1-inch pieces and add to the pan. Add the wine, olive oil, and butter; add pepper and (if needed) salt; and cover the pan with parchment and aluminum foil or a lid. Bake on the center rack of the oven until fork-tender, about 60 minutes. This dish can also be cooked, covered, over medium-low heat on the stove top, until tender.

TROUT FILLETS WITH SAUTÉED FENNEL STEMS AND FRONDS

Most recipes for fennel call for the bulb only. The long stems are flavorful but fibrous, so cooks tend to discard them, feathery fronds and all. To address this problem, I devised an herb sauce that utilizes the fronds, and a quick sauté that features the stems. Note that the cooking method for the trout involves turning the fish at the last minute just before serving. This keeps the flesh moist and tender, and the skin crisp.

4 servings

Stalks and fronds from 2 fennel bulbs
⅓ cup extra virgin olive oil
1 stalk green garlic
Kosher salt
2 spring leeks
4 tablespoons (½ stick) unsalted butter
Freshly ground black pepper
4 skin-on trout fillets
2 tablespoons canola oil

Fennel frond sauce: Separate the fronds from the stalks and set the stalks aside. Measure ½ packed cup of the fronds and put in the base of a blender pitcher. Reserve some of the remaining fronds for garnish. Add olive oil, green garlic, and a pinch of kosher salt. Blend until combined, then place in a shallow container and chill.

Sautéed fennel stalks and spring leeks: Wash and thinly slice enough fennel stalks to measure about 2 cups. Trim the roots and dark green tops from the leeks and thinly slice the white and light green parts into rings. Transfer the sliced leeks to a medium bowl and fill it with water. Agitate to loosen any sand or dirt and then remove the leeks from the water and transfer to a colander to drip dry. In a wide skillet over medium-high heat, melt the butter. Add the fennel stalks and leeks to the pan and season with salt and pepper. Sauté until tender, about 8 minutes.

Pan-seared trout fillets: Season the trout fillets on both sides generously with kosher salt and black pepper. In a wide skillet over high heat, warm the canola oil until shimmery. Carefully add the trout fillets skin side down and cook until the skin is crisp and golden brown, 7 to 10 minutes. The thin fillets will be mostly cooked through, so turn off the heat if not ready to serve. When ready, return the pan to the heat and then turn the fillets over and cook for 1 minute.

To serve: Divide the sautéed fennel stalks and leeks among 4 plates. Place the trout fillets on top and drizzle with fennel frond sauce. Garnish with fresh fennel fronds. Serve immediately.

LETTUCES

People sometimes use the word "greens" interchangeably with "lettuces," but I find that confusing. The tender heads thrive in spring and fall and are related to the sunflower and the daisy. Extremes are hard on their delicate leaves. If there is a drop in temperature, they freeze. If there is too much heat, they wither or turn bitter. Raised right, they are sweet, crunchy, light, airy, and mild—the perfect base for a well-made salad.

While I occasionally use lettuces for other purposes—cooked into a soup, lightly grilled, or blended into a smoothie—the salad bowl is where they shine. Once you understand and appreciate their nuances, and master the art of dressing them, you will always be able to make the distinction between farm-fresh lettuce and a bagged mix at the supermarket. There are seven main types of head lettuces.

LOOSELEAF: Fast-growing open head lettuces with leaves that spread away from the base. The leaves are cut from the base and sold as a mix. Leaves can regenerate for a second cutting, so even though they are labor intensive, they produce well.

BUTTERHEAD: A semi–open head lettuce that has a delicate texture and a savory quality. The dark outer leaves wrap loosely around the center, forming beautiful chartreuse inner leaves where, because sunlight is kept off, the chlorophyll does not develop.

ROMAINE: A semi–open head lettuce that grows upright with dark outer leaves and crunchy textured ribs. The thick ribs provide the structure for its verticality, and it requires plenty of watering to avoid tasting bitter.

BUTTERCRUNCH: A cross between butterhead and romaine, this semi–open head grows more upright with a crunchy rib, but does not spread as wide as butterhead.

SUMMERCRISP: Also called Batavian lettuces, these varieties usually fare well in heat. If temperatures rise above ninety degrees for several days, however, just about any lettuce will either wither or turn bitter.

HEADING: Also called crisphead lettuce, these are the iceberg varieties with leaves that layer over each other into a tight head like a cabbage. They have high water content and less nutrients overall.

CHINESE: Much less popular in the United States, these varieties have crisp, juicy stalks and long, tender leaves. They tend to be strongly flavored and bitter.

To prep head lettuces, cut out the core and trim away any bruised leaves or weathered tops. Trim to large fork-size pieces for ease of eating. Completely submerge the trimmed leaves in enough water to move them around freely. Agitate the leaves slightly to knock off any clinging dirt. Spin-dry in a salad spinner to remove as much water as possible from the leaves. To prevent wilting or drying out, store refrigerated in a resealable bag with a damp paper towel, or cover with a damp cotton towel.

HOW TO DRESS A SALAD: I apply a technique that works in reverse. Rather than dressing the leaves, I dress the inside of the bowl and use a delicate touch to—in effect—paint the dressing onto each leaf. This ensures that the salad will be evenly coated. Place the trimmed, washed, and dried lettuces in a bowl deep and wide enough so that you can easily get your hands in and around them. Spoon a thin film of dressing onto the sides of the bowl, all the way around. Use the back of the spoon to distribute. With clean hands and fingers spread apart, gently lift the lettuces upward from the bottom of the bowl, allowing your fingers to graze the inside of the bowl. This catches small amounts of the dressing and redistributes it evenly. Repeat this motion until the lettuces are lightly and evenly coated.

DRESSINGS

Vinaigrettes are usually my dressings of choice and they appear throughout this book. But when spring lettuces are abundant, and I eat salad every day, I need variety. These three distinctly different dressings are great changeups from the vinaigrette. Think of the lettuces as a blank canvas and the dressing as the paint.

GREEN GODDESS DRESSING

About 1 cup

2 tablespoons each chopped fresh chives, basil leaves, and parsley leaves
2 teaspoons chopped fresh tarragon leaves
1 tablespoon lemon juice
1 tablespoon Champagne vinegar
1 teaspoon kosher salt
½ teaspoon black pepper
1 anchovy fillet
½ cup crème fraîche (store-bought, or see Crème Fraîche, page181)
½ cup Homemade Mayonnaise (see recipe)

Combine everything in a blender. Turn on at low speed and blend until smooth, scraping down the sides of the blender as needed. Transfer the dressing to a storage container, cover, and refrigerate until ready to use.

BUTTERMILK DRESSING

About 1½ cups

1 teaspoon minced garlic—use green garlic when in season
1 tablespoon Champagne vinegar
1 teaspoon kosher salt
½ teaspoon freshly ground black pepper
1 cup Homemade Mayonnaise (see recipe)
½ cup buttermilk
1 tablespoon finely sliced chives

In a medium bowl, combine the garlic, vinegar, salt, and pepper. Whisk in the mayonnaise, buttermilk, and chives. Taste for seasoning and adjust as needed. Transfer the dressing to a storage container, cover, and refrigerate until ready to use.

HOMEMADE MAYONNAISE

About 2 cups

1 whole egg
1 egg yolk
1 teaspoon dry mustard
1 tablespoon lemon juice
1 tablespoon apple cider vinegar
1 teaspoon fine sea salt
1½ cups canola oil

Combine the whole egg, yolk, mustard, lemon juice, vinegar, and salt in a food processor. With the motor running, slowly drizzle in the oil until emulsified. Store covered and refrigerated for up to 2 weeks.

WARM BACON DRESSING

About 1 cup

8 slices bacon
1 cup apple cider vinegar
⅓ cup sorghum syrup
1 teaspoon kosher salt
½ teaspoon freshly ground black pepper
1 spring onion, green part thinly sliced crosswise, white bulb thinly sliced into
    crescents
Salad greens

In a medium skillet over medium-low heat, cook the bacon slices until browned on one side. With tongs, turn the bacon over, and cook on the opposite side until fully crisp. Transfer the bacon to a paper towel–lined plate, chop, and reserve. Raise the heat to medium-high and add the vinegar, sorghum, salt, and pepper to the skillet. Reduce by half and taste for seasoning. Bring to a boil and add the spring onion. Cook for 1 minute, then spoon just enough of the boiling dressing around the sides of the bowl and toss the salad greens to lightly wilt and coat them. Garnish with chopped bacon and serve immediately. Reserve any remaining dressing for future use.

ONIONS AND GARLIC

Onions and garlic are year-round staples in any cook's pantry, but their initial season is spring. All members of the allium genus start with green shoots that emerge from the ground after a winter planting. The green tops will eventually wilt and die, if not harvested, and full-size onion or garlic bulbs form under the ground. In the spring, both the white bulbs and the tender green tops can be used, imparting a sweeter, milder flavor than their shelf-stable, cured counterparts. The tougher ends of the tops and the root are great for flavoring stocks.

ONIONS: The early emergent onion grows long, hollow green tops. Every onion starts out this way, and the bulb widens as it matures. It is up to the farmer to harvest onions early and sell them as SPRING ONIONS or wait until they are fully grown and cure them for a later sale. The many varieties of onions include the torpedo onion, which is great for grilling because it has a uniform shape with very little taper. The cipollini onion has a round, wide, squat bulb with a mild sweet flavor. Georgia's terroir onion, the Vidalia, shows up as early as January and is sugary sweet. Any onion that is left to mature and harvest once the greens have died will eventually get cured or dried to make it shelf stable. This is the cured onion that we all recognize—red, yellow, or white. Its thin papery skin is a result of the drying. SCALLIONS, also called green onions or pencil onions, are delicate enough to be thinly sliced raw as a garnish and sturdy enough to be cooked quickly. A scallion is a bunching onion that does not form a bulb. The term "bunching onions" comes from the fact that they are sold by the bunch. CHIVES are thin, wispy, sharp-flavored green shoots used as an herb. They look like tall tufts of grass. A hardy perennial, chives are in fact closely related to grass. Chives can be clipped with scissors to use straight from the garden. RAMPS are a leek found only in the wild, with a leaf that fades quickly in heat. They add depth and complexity to any dish when cooked and impart a strong umami flavor. The long, slender bulbs are great for pickling, and can be put up for months. I use ramp tops in different ways from the bulb. I might toss them whole into sautés at the last minute, blend them with lemon and olive oil for a zesty sauce for fish or vegetables, or chop them up and add them to salsa verde or vinaigrette. SHALLOTS have a distinctive tapered shape that sets them apart from other members of the onion family. Their bulbs grow in clusters like garlic cloves, but the insides are structured like the concentric rings of an onion. Most often copper brown, they may also be reddish or gray. Their flavor, sometimes described as a blend of sweet onion and garlic, makes them a favorite of chefs. LEEKS are the largest member of the allium genus and look like giant scallions. They may grow up to two feet long and two inches thick, and they do not form a bulb. The layers within their stalks collect sand, so it is important to wash them carefully. I often prep the leeks first, then wash them to be sure to get all the dirt that may be trapped in the layers.

GARLIC: This has the strongest flavor of all the alliums, and has been prized for both culinary and medicinal use. This hardy perennial grows as bulbs, which are made up of cloves. Hardneck varieties have thick, fibrous, woody stems, and they form shoots called GARLIC SCAPES that taste like a cross between asparagus and garlic. Blanch them, lightly roast or grill them, and they are ready to eat. The softneck varieties are used to make garlic braids after their long green tops have been dried. GREEN GARLIC is simply young spring garlic that is harvested with the long green tops and undeveloped bulbs. It resembles a young leek or a scallion. Green garlic can be used in place of cured garlic while it is in season. Because it is milder, you can use an entire stalk in place of a couple of cloves of cured. Cured garlic should always be stored at room temperature. If refrigerated, it will quickly sprout, becoming soft and unusable. GARLIC FLOWERS AND BLOSSOMS are also edible and have a pungent herbal flavor. The little flowers can be sprinkled over a salad, and the whole blossoms can be sautéed or roasted.

SPRING GARLIC
BAGNA CAUDA

Bagna cauda in Italian literally means "warm bath" and refers to a mixture of garlic, anchovy, and fat served in the Piedmont region of Italy. It is always heated to temper the overpowering raw garlic flavor and is traditionally served warm, like a fondue, with crudités as an appetizer. Here, I highlight the milder, sweeter green garlic of spring to show how vegetables that grow in this season can make this dish fresh and modern.

12 servings

8 tablespoons (1 stick) unsalted butter
1 cup sliced green garlic
12-ounce container anchovy fillets packed in olive oil,
   drained and mashed with a fork
½ cup extra virgin olive oil
½ teaspoon flaky sea salt
¼ teaspoon freshly ground black pepper
⅛ teaspoon cayenne pepper
Zest of 1 lemon
Juice of 2 lemons
Selection of crudités (see Note)

In a small saucepan on medium-low heat, warm the butter until foamy. Reduce the heat to low and continue to cook the butter until the foam subsides and milk solids separate and begin to brown on the bottom of the pan, about 12 minutes. Swirl the pan to incorporate the solids, and when the butter begins to turn a blond caramel color, about 2 minutes more, remove from heat and add the green garlic and mashed anchovy. Off the heat, the garlic and anchovy will continue to cook gently without browning or burning. Add the olive oil, salt, pepper, cayenne, lemon zest, and lemon juice. Return to the heat and bring to a low simmer. Serve warm with crudités.

Note: I think five is a good number of crudités for variety. Choose vegetables that contrast in color, texture, and flavor. Pictured here are scarlet turnips, baby fennel, sliced carrots, whole radishes, and blanched garlic scapes.

PICKLED RAMPS

If you can get your hands on a good supply of ramps, this is a smart way to maximize the opportunities to enjoy them beyond their fleeting season. When they are raw, their flavor can sometimes be jolting, so I actually prefer pickling them for most uses. They add a sharp zing anywhere you might use pickled onions or garlic. When you get to the bottom of the jar, don't toss the liquid. Use it as you would pepper vinegar on greens or other vegetables or as the base of a vinaigrette.

1 quart

1½ to 2 pounds ramps
2 cups Champagne vinegar or apple cider vinegar
½ cup granulated sugar or honey
3 tablespoons kosher salt
2 teaspoons coriander seeds
1 teaspoon black peppercorns
1 teaspoon fennel seeds
1 bay leaf

Clean the ramps under running water and slice off the root base on each. Separate the green leaves by pinching them off at the base of the taper. Rinse the greens well and set aside for another use (see Spring Onion Soubise). Gather all of the cleaned ramps and stuff them tightly into a sterilized wide-mouth quart jar.

To make the brine, in a small saucepan over high heat, combine the vinegar, sugar or honey, salt, coriander, black pepper, fennel, and bay leaf with 2 cups water.

Place a canning funnel over the mouth of the jar. Position a small strainer over the funnel. When the brine comes to a boil, immediately pour it through the strainer, catching the spices and filling the jar with brine. Leave ½ inch of headspace at the top of the jar, wipe off the rim, and place the lid on top and screw on the band. Turn the jar over for 5 minutes to cool, then turn it right side up and check the seal. Pickled ramps can be stored in the refrigerator for up to 1 month or processed following standard canning procedures for pickles.

SPRING ONION SOUBISE

Traditionally this classic French onion cream sauce is thickened with rice or enriched with beef stock. My lighter, meat-free version highlights the spring onion flavor and utilizes the green tops for color. This velvety sauce is perfect with any protein or with roasted spring vegetables.

About 1½ cups

2 tablespoons unsalted butter
2 spring onions, washed and roughly chopped, green tops reserved
1 teaspoon kosher salt
½ teaspoon freshly ground black pepper
1 cup dry white wine
1 cup heavy cream
1 sprig thyme

In a wide skillet over medium heat, warm the butter until foamy. Add the onions and season with salt and pepper. Cook until the onions are translucent, about 4 minutes; then add wine, cream, and thyme. Cover, reduce the heat to low, and cook until the onions are completely wilted, about 15 minutes. The cream may curdle from the acid in the wine, but that's OK. Remove the thyme sprig. Stir in the reserved green tops. Transfer the mixture to a blender and blend until smooth. Taste for seasoning and adjust as needed.

GRILLED TORPEDO ONIONS WITH GREEK YOGURT

Torpedo onions do not form round bulbs like their cousins, so their tapered bases and tops are nearly the same thickness. This uniform shape allows for even cooking. When grilling onions, think of them as like a steak. Season well and let the flame and hot smoke do the rest.

8 servings

8 torpedo onions, halved, washed, and trimmed
2 teaspoons kosher salt, plus more for yogurt sauce
½ teaspoon freshly ground black pepper, plus more for yogurt sauce
3 tablespoons extra virgin olive oil
1 cup whole-milk Greek yogurt
Finely grated zest of 1 lemon
Juice of ½ lemon
Fresh cilantro for garnish

Heat the grill to medium. Season the onions with salt and pepper, and drizzle with olive oil. Place the onions cut side down on the grill until lightly charred. Turn with tongs and repeat on the opposite side. Turn the heat off and close the lid. Let the onions cook until they are tender.

In a medium bowl, combine the yogurt, lemon zest, and lemon juice. Season to taste with salt and pepper and stir. Spoon over the onions and garnish with cilantro.

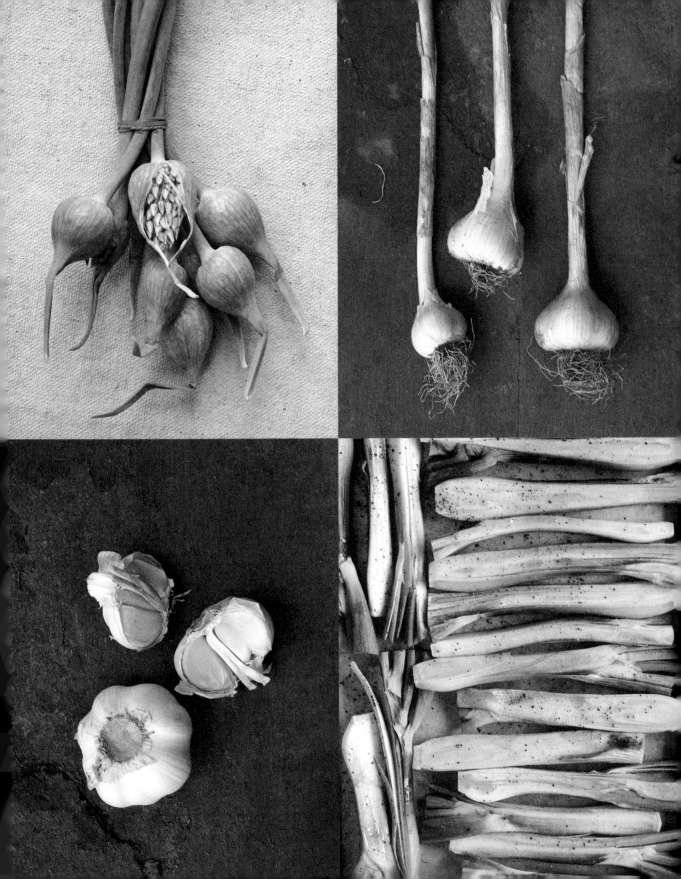

SPRING ONION PIZZA

Pizza is the ideal showcase for the green onions of spring. It cooks quickly, allowing these tender shoots and their bulbs to meld with oozing mozzarella and fresh garden herbs. A pizza stone allows for the ultimate crispy crust, whether you're using your grill or oven. I like to make my own half whole wheat crust, but there are plenty of good premade versions available if you don't feel you have the time to make pizza dough from scratch.

One 12-inch pizza

1 recipe whole wheat Pizza Dough (page 471)
1 spring onion, thinly sliced
1 spring leek, thinly sliced
1 green garlic stalk, thinly sliced (or 1 small garlic clove, finely chopped)
2 scallions, halved lengthwise and cut into 2-inch pieces
4 ounces fresh mozzarella, cut into 8 pieces
½ teaspoon roughly chopped fresh oregano
½ teaspoon roughly chopped fresh marjoram
½ teaspoon roughly chopped fresh thyme leaves
Extra virgin olive oil
Chopped fresh parsley

Place a pizza stone in the oven or on the grill and heat to 500°F.

On a lightly floured surface, roll out the pizza dough to fit the pizza stone. Transfer the dough to a lightly floured cookie sheet or upside-down baking sheet. This will be the vessel to help transfer the pizza to the hot stone. Scatter the onion, leek, garlic, and scallions evenly across the surface of the dough, leaving a 1-inch border. Place the mozzarella pieces randomly across the pizza with space in between them. Sprinkle the oregano, marjoram, and thyme over the pizza. Drizzle the pizza lightly with olive oil.

With a long, wide spatula, transfer the pizza carefully onto the hot stone. If grilling, close the lid to the grill. Let cook 10 to 15 minutes until the dough is fully cooked and crispy on the edges and the toppings are beginning to lightly brown. Cooking time will vary, depending on your grill or oven and the thickness of the crust. If baking in the oven, and the dough is done but the toppings are not, turn on the broiler to finish baking.

When the pizza is ready, remove with a long, wide spatula, and transfer back to the cookie sheet or upside-down baking sheet to cool slightly. Slice the pizza and garnish with fresh parsley.

RADISHES

For many years in a row, several of my closest friends and I would get together for a February escape to Tulum, Mexico, a small beach village with Mayan ruins and eco-resorts. When we had to leave the gorgeous beaches for provisions, we would go into the little town nearby and grab a bite to eat while we shopped. There was a *taquería* that had a particularly wide array of salsas and other condiments, including delicious sliced garden radishes dressed in lime and hot chiles. Though they were designed as a condiment to complement the handmade tacos, I loved the crispness and spice and would eat them as a snack, asking the server to bring extra to the table.

I love radishes in every form: raw, cooked, pickled, it doesn't matter. They add coolness, color, crunch, a burst of juiciness, and subtle heat or spice to just about anything. I even like to eat them whole, like a carrot—though I am well aware that most people find this form too jarring.

SPRING RADISHES: These are quick and easy to grow, reaching full maturity in just twenty-eight days, and they are a good companion plant to most other crops. There are several varieties, in a host of pastel and vibrant colors. D'Avignon, also called French breakfast, is an elegant, thin, tapered radish with dark pink or red coloring on the top and white at the base. White icicle is a very tapered, thin variety that is sweet and crunchy. Easter egg radishes are actually a mix of purple, pink, white, and red; these are planted together and harvested in colorful bundles. The mix includes varieties like cherry belle, pink beauty, and purple plum, and all are small, round, and crisp.

WINTER RADISHES: These are usually harvested in the fall and stored during the winter. They are much larger, are globe shaped, and have a stronger flavor. The watermelon radish, named for its pale green skin and shocking pink interior, is a dense, hard globe. Best served very thinly sliced, it is one of the most beautiful colors on a crudités plate. The black Spanish variety has a dusty charcoal-colored skin with creamy white flesh. This radish seems to me more closely related to a turnip and has a similar starchiness and bite. Daikon radishes, originating in Asia, grow deep into the ground and have an elongated tapered shape and white flesh. They are mild and sweet with a distinctive crunch. Another Asian winter variety is Chinese green luobo radish. It has a slight tapered squat shape with lime green–colored top and a greenish-white base. The center is pale green, and the flesh is starchy with a strong bite.

Radishes are one of the produce items that play better on a team rather than standing alone. One of my favorite ways to eat them as a feature, however, is with butter and salt, especially in the context of a sandwich. The sharp brassica bite of radish can be tempered with any cool and creamy dairy product like feta, yogurt, goat cheese, or ricotta. Radishes are a natural companion to asparagus, and spring is the best time to eat both. They take well to acid or herbs—dress them with lemon and salt, pickle them, or toss them with spring herbs like tarragon, chervil, parsley, and chives. I've learned to appreciate even the leaves, too. They are wonderful with baked eggs, sautéed with garlic and lemon, or chopped and added to a salad if fresh and perky.

In addition to their bracing bite and refreshing crispness, radishes offer great health benefits. They are considered to be a blood purifier, eliminating toxins and waste, and were once prescribed to treat jaundice. They are also a diuretic, and so are beneficial for kidney and urinary tract health.

Look for radishes that are firm and crisp, with healthy leaves that are not too big for their variety. Avoid radishes with woody or very hard roots, softened roots, cracks (which indicate fewer nutrients), or dead greens. Remove the greens immediately, and store separately if you're planning to use them. Keep them covered or wrapped in a damp towel, as the dry air of the refrigerator will wilt both the greens and the roots. Radishes can be placed in ice water to make them extra crisp, but don't store them for more than a few hours this way. They can get waterlogged and lose flavor.

RADISH SANDWICHES WITH BUTTER AND SALT

The French figured out a long time ago that the best way to cut the heat of a raw radish is to dip it into softened butter and sprinkle it with salt. They also take it one step further and put it on a baguette, turning it into a light lunch or a snack with wine. The trick is not to skimp on the radishes or the butter. Think of the radish as the meat and the butter as the mayo. If you're feeling creative, whip the butter with fresh herbs like chives or tarragon. I like to pair this with chilled spring greens soup (page 78) or wrap it in wax paper and take it on a picnic.

6 to 8 small sandwiches or 20 to 24 hors d'oeuvres

1 standard-size baguette
12 tablespoons (1½ sticks) unsalted butter, room temperature
2 teaspoons flaky sea salt
2 bunches radishes, trimmed, washed, and thinly sliced
1 small handful arugula
Pinch fresh garden herbs such as chives or tarragon

Slice the baguette lengthwise and crosswise, creating 4 quarters. Place the bread on a cutting board cut sides up. Spread each quarter with softened butter, and sprinkle with salt. Pile sliced radishes onto each quarter, pressing them firmly into the butter. Lay the arugula and herbs across the bottom quarters, and top with the corresponding tops. Press down on the halves firmly with your palms. Place the sandwiches on a cutting board and cut into small sandwiches or hors d'oeuvres.

FETA SNACK WITH SPRING RADISHES

Though good with any fresh vegetable, this sharp, creamy feta dip, smoothed with a little buttermilk, is exceptional with crisp spring radishes. Much as in the combination above, salt and fat mellow any heat from the raw radishes. Cheesemaker Mary Rigdon of Decimal Place Farm has been brining her goat's milk feta to order for us every week since Miller Union opened. If you have a local farmers' market that sells fresh cheeses, look there first for good-quality feta. I love the little pink, purple, or red garden variety radishes for this dip.

1 cup feta mixture

8 ounces goat's milk feta, preferably in brine
¼ to ½ cup buttermilk
½ teaspoon flaky sea salt
½ teaspoon freshly ground black pepper
Extra virgin olive oil for finishing
Radishes and other vegetables for dipping

In a medium bowl, crumble the feta. With a rigid whisk, smooth out the feta first, then add buttermilk 1 tablespoon at a time until the mixture is smooth and the consistency of a creamy dip. Spoon the mixture into a small serving bowl and top with flaky sea salt, black pepper, and olive oil. Serve with raw radishes or other crudités.

RADISH AND WALNUT SALAD WITH PARMIGIANO-REGGIANO

The two radishes called for in this salad are unlike their petite, familiar spring siblings with delicate tops. Both are so dense and firm that they must be shaved before being eaten. I recommend using a mandoline for many recipes in this book, but for this one, it is essential. I always cut the larger rounds into halves or quarters to make them easier to maneuver with your fork.

Serves 4

¾ cup walnut halves and pieces
2 tablespoons walnut oil
1 medium black radish
1 medium watermelon radish
Juice of ½ lemon
½ teaspoon fine sea salt
Coarse flaky sea salt
1 ounce Parmigiano-Reggiano, swiped on a Swiss peeler

Heat the oven to 300°F. In a small bowl, toss the walnuts with 1 tablespoon of the walnut oil. Spread the nuts on a baking sheet in a single layer and place in the oven. Toast the nuts until fragrant, about 5 minutes, then remove from the oven and let cool. Meanwhile, thinly slice the radishes on a mandoline. Cut any larger rounds into halves or quarters, and mix them together in a medium bowl. Add lemon juice and fine sea salt and mix together.

Divide the radish mixture among 4 salad plates. Sprinkle with the coarse sea salt, toasted nuts, and shaved cheese. Drizzle each plate with the remaining 1 tablespoon walnut oil.

RADISH GREENS AND SPRING GARLIC QUICHE

A lot of folks don't even realize that radish tops are edible. When raw, they sometimes have a prickly fuzz, and can be overly bitter or metallic on the palate. Cooked with creamy eggs and sharp spring garlic, however, they can be transcendent. With the help of a flaky, savory crust and the flexibility to be served warm, chilled, or at room temperature, this quiche is the perfect way to use what would normally be relegated to bunny food or the compost bin. If you don't feel like making the crust from scratch, there are good-quality premade crusts available; just read the ingredients before you buy.

6 to 8 servings

1 recipe Pie Dough (page 470)
2 tablespoons unsalted butter
1 shallot, chopped
1 stalk spring garlic, chopped
1 bunch radish greens, rinsed well and chopped
4 large eggs
1 cup milk
½ cup heavy cream
1 teaspoon kosher salt
4 ounces goat cheese

Prepare and blind-bake the pie crust. In a medium skillet over medium heat, melt the butter. Add the shallot and garlic and cook until translucent, stirring occasionally, about 5 minutes. Add the greens and cook 2 more minutes. Remove from the heat. In a mixing bowl, whisk the eggs. Add the milk, cream, and salt and whisk well. Spread the radish greens mixture evenly over the bottom of the crust. Crumble the goat cheese over the greens. Carefully pour the egg mixture over the filling.

Bake the quiche until the edges are set but the quiche still jiggles a little in the center, 45 to 55 minutes. (If the edges of the crust start to brown, cover with a ring of aluminum foil.) Cool the quiche at least 30 minutes before slicing.

RHUBARB

I have a vision of my grandmother, Ducky, hand-harvesting stalks of wild rhubarb in and around Asheville, North Carolina, and tucking them into her apron to take back to her kitchen. This is my romanticized version of reality, but since the season for rhubarb was usually over by the time we arrived for our annual summer visits, it cannot be disproved. She cooked with rhubarb every spring, and of all the canning jars that lined the shelves of her cellar, her rhubarb-strawberry preserves were my favorite. We slathered them on hot buttered biscuits and used them to make gourmet peanut butter and jelly sandwiches. They were different and special, but not off-putting to my finicky palate.

Pairing rhubarb with strawberries just makes sense. They are in season at the same time, long before most other fruits are ready for harvest, and the natural sweetness of strawberries offsets the puckery tartness of rhubarb. They appear regularly together in pies, crisps, and all manner of preserves.

Though not typically associated with the Southern states, rhubarb does grow well in cooler mountain areas of the region. It is a persistent perennial that reappears in the same spot every year, and needs a hard freeze to regenerate. Rhubarb thrives in cold climates, even in the wilds of Alaska, and begins its growth spurt when ground temperatures peak at around fifty degrees Fahrenheit. The first rhubarb of the season is typically forced, or hothouse grown, so that the plants are shielded from the cold after a few good freezes and held at a steady temperature, which forces the plant to start growing again.

For centuries, rhubarb was highly sought-after for medicinal purposes. It was used for intestinal, liver, and lung ailments and later was introduced as a healthful food into springtime recipes in England in the nineteenth century. During that time, rhubarb became more appealing because it was available at a time of year when pickings were very slim. It could be grown in cellars and greenhouses as well as outdoors, and these options extended its season. Besides being a pungent medicinal herb, the rhubarb plant could also be edible and downright delicious, if combined with a sweeter ingredient like sugar, which was becoming more affordable at the time. As the price of sugar dropped, the quantities of rhubarb produced and sold soared. Rhubarb sales took a nosedive, however, during World War II, when sugar was rationed.

Rhubarb resembles celery but is greenish-pink to ruby red and has large pale green fan-shaped leaves that happen to be poisonous to humans. Its sharp flavor makes it stand out when sweetened in desserts like crisps, turnovers, or pies—from which it gets its second name, "pieplant." But rhubarb also lends a puckery-tart fruitiness to savory dishes, and pairs very nicely with pork and poultry. Rhubarb is high in oxalic acid, the sour taste that is also found in its cousin, sorrel. Rhubarb is also botanically related to buckwheat. When rhubarb is cooked, its fibers begin to melt and it quickly falls apart. When cooked for any length of time, rhubarb gives jams, chutneys, and compotes a jellied consistency. To preserve any color or texture, however, it must be cooked rapidly. Quick heat yields tender but cohesive rhubarb pieces with rich flavor and a natural, glossy sheen.

There are green and red varieties of rhubarb. The green rhubarb has a deeper flavor and gives a higher yield; but consumers are drawn to the more vibrant red-hued selections, which make prettier presentations. Whatever their color, the stalks should be heavy and crisp with taut, shiny skin. Store in the crisper of your refrigerator wrapped in a damp towel. To clean, run under water and wipe the length with a dry towel to remove any sand or dirt.

SAVORY ROASTED RHUBARB

Available for only a brief time, and typically used in sweets or desserts, tangy rhubarb stands out when roasted. Try this layered with Spring Onion Soubise (page 49) and Pickled Ramps (page 48) with the spatchcocked chicken. The clean, sharp taste also works well with other spring vegetables, pork, or lamb.

1 cup

2 stalks rhubarb
2 tablespoons honey
½ teaspoon kosher salt
1 tablespoon extra virgin olive oil

Heat the oven to 350°F. If the rhubarb is wide, slice it lengthwise first before trimming to 1-inch-long pieces. In a medium bowl, combine the rhubarb, honey, salt, and olive oil, and toss well to coat. Spread in a single layer in a shallow roasting pan and bake until fork-tender, 10 to 15 minutes. Stir once after 5 minutes.

SPATCHCOCKED SPRING CHICKEN

Removing the backbone from a bird and flattening it out cuts the cooking time in half and make for an impressive presentation.

2 servings

1 small whole chicken, 2 to 2½ pounds
Kosher salt
Freshly ground black pepper
Fresh thyme, tarragon, or chervil, if desired

Heat the oven to 350°F. Place the chicken on a cutting board breast side up with the neck facing away from you. Insert a long, sharp chef's knife inside the cavity of the chicken with the tip of the knife pointing through the opening in the neck. Align the blade of the knife just to one side of the backbone. With one hand on the base of the knife and another toward the top of the blade, carefully and firmly press down until the blade breaks through the ribs and skin. Then repeat on the other side of the backbone and remove the bone. Flatten out the chicken, breast side up, and forcefully press down on the breastbone until it flattens. At this point, you can roast the chicken whole or, if you prefer individual portions, slice through the middle of the chicken between the two breasts, along the breastbone, to create two equal halves. Season the chicken well on both sides with salt and pepper and place on a roasting rack, skin side up. If desired, place a bed of spring herbs under the chicken. Roast on the middle rack in the oven until the meat is fully cooked and the skin is golden brown, 20 to 25 minutes. If the skin does not brown on its own, use the broiler to finish browning it.

RHUBARB TURNOVERS

I love a fried pie, but a baked turnover achieves a similar crispy crust without the added fat from deep-frying. A quick dab of egg wash and a sprinkling of coarse sugar before baking add sheen and crunch. To avoid using cornstarch, a method for thickening juices released during baking, I macerate the rhubarb first and then, while cooking, reduce the liquid once the rhubarb is removed. Any remaining liquid oozes out of the crust or bubbles through the vents, leaving a trail of jammy streaks wherever it flows.

8 servings

4 cups ½-inch-diced rhubarb (5 to 6 stalks)
Pinch kosher salt
⅛ teaspoon freshly grated nutmeg
1 cup turbinado sugar, plus more for topping
1 double recipe Pie Dough (page 470), substituting 2 ounces cream cheese for
  4 tablespoons of the butter, chilled
1 large egg
Lemon Buttermilk Ice, optional (page 425)

In a wide skillet, combine the rhubarb, salt, and nutmeg. Stir in 1 cup sugar and let rest for 10 minutes. Turn the burner on to medium heat and cook the rhubarb until the juices are released, about 5 minutes. Remove the rhubarb from the pan with a slotted spoon, transfer to a plate, and cool in the refrigerator. Continue to cook the remaining liquid until reduced to a syrupy glaze. Let the glaze cool. Return the strained, cooled rhubarb to the cooled glaze and toss to coat. Return the rhubarb mixture to the refrigerator.

Remove the turnover dough from refrigerator. On a clean, floured surface, roll out the dough to ⅛ inch thick. Using a small plate, bowl, or saucer as a guide, cut out 6-inch circles of dough. Lay each circle on parchment paper, stack the circles, and refrigerate to keep the dough cold.

Heat the oven to 350°F. In a small bowl, whisk the egg with 1 tablespoon water; set aside. Remove the dough circles from the refrigerator and transfer them to a parchment-lined cookie sheet or baking sheet. Spoon ¼ cup of the rhubarb mixture onto one half of each dough circle, leaving ½ inch of space around the edge. Fold the dough over the rhubarb so the edges meet, and crimp the edges with a fork. Brush the top of the turnover with the egg wash and sprinkle with turbinado sugar. Cut thin slits in the top of the dough over the rhubarb with the tip of a paring knife to let steam escape.

Bake on the middle rack of the oven until the dough is crisp and golden brown, 30 to 40 minutes. If desired, serve each turnover with ½ cup Lemon Buttermilk Ice (page 425).

SPRING GREENS

The greens highlighted in the pages that follow are a collection of misfits. They don't necessarily belong together botanically, but they all come up around the same time and have some similar characteristics. If it is not a head lettuce but is sometimes considered a salad green, you might find it here. Most of these can be eaten raw or cooked, and each has its own distinctive qualities.

ARUGULA: This is one of my favorite leaves, and I put it on everything. Arugula was once considered an herb but is now treated more like a lettuce. It is a dark, peppery green from the brassica genus that can be eaten raw or cooked. Wild arugula tends to have more of a kick than the cultivated kind, but in general arugula can range from mild to very spicy, depending on variety and growing conditions.

DANDELION: Although dandelion is often seen growing wild and considered a weed, it is widely revered in many cultures. I have a friend who throws a dandelion dinner party every spring and each dish features the plant in a different way. Dandelion, a relative of the sunflower, has dark green and famously bitter leaves. I love their cleansing, sharp taste, and prefer them raw or barely cooked.

NETTLES: Whether the stinging variety or not, nettles are tasty, herbaceous greens that require cooking. They are very green and have a flavor that is mild and slightly sweet. Nettles are high in iron, potassium, manganese, calcium, and vitamins A and C, and are also a decent source of protein. If you are handling stinging nettles, use gloves. They have tiny hairlike needles that inject histamines, sometimes causing severe reactions in human skin. Once nettles are cooked, the stinging hairs disappear. I like to blanch nettles in salted water briefly and then chop them up and add them to soup, pasta, or pizza.

MÂCHE: Sometimes called lamb's lettuce, mâche is a very delicate, tender green that likes chilly spring weather. It tastes slightly sweet and herbal, and has a cooling quality. Once considered a coarse weed, mâche is now a chic salad green. Before cultivation, mâche was harvested from fields where it grew amid cereal crops like corn, rye, and wheat—hence its old-fashioned name, "corn salat."

MIZUNA: Also called Japanese mustard, mizuna has a sweet chlorophyll flavor mixed with a refreshing bitterness and bite, similar to dandelion. It is part of the brassica genus, which includes mustards, kale, and collards. I tend to use mizuna and dandelion interchangeably in any application.

SORREL: This is nature's sour plant. These green leaves have the same sour-tasting oxalic acid that is found in rhubarb. There are many varieties of sorrel, including the red-veined sorrel prized for its beauty and flavor. Sorrel can add a tart flavor without adding true acidity, and that is the secret of preserving the vivid green in Chilled Watercress, Spring Nettle, and Sorrel Soup on page 78. Lemon or vinegar would make the soup turn a drab olive color.

SPINACH: Spinach thrives in cool, wet weather. This is the most commonly recognized of all these greens, and its best and true season is spring. There are many varieties besides what you see in bags at the grocery store, including red-veined, curly leaf, and flat leaf. Spinach belongs to the chenopod family, which includes beets, chard, and quinoa.

WATERCRESS: This was once a wild green that could be found only in streams and along riverbanks, but it is now cultivated with inventive irrigation or in hydroponic tanks. It has a peppery, green-apple flavor with a strong bite. Watercress is related to the nasturtium and both have a lily pad–shaped leaf and a mellow bitterness. Much cultivated watercress is actually garden cress or upland cress, which grows in the ground and has less bite and crunch than true watercress. Use cress as soon as possible after it's been picked, discarding any yellowed or wilted leaves. Note that the tender stalks are perfectly edible along with the dark green leaves.

CHILLED WATERCRESS, SPRING NETTLE, AND SORREL SOUP

Spring is abundant with greens of all types, both wild and cultivated. You never know what might show up at your market in any given week. It just so happened that I was able to get peppery watercress, wild stinging nettles, and sour sorrel at the same time. I love the idea of a watercress or nettles soup, but it always leaves me wanting acid, which inevitably turns the vibrant green soup to a drab olive. Naturally sour sorrel solves this by adding brightness without acid to balance the flavor. If you have trouble finding nettles, just use more watercress, or substitute arugula, mizuna, or dandelion.

12 servings

2 tablespoons extra virgin olive oil
2 tablespoons unsalted butter
1 spring onion, sliced and washed
2 young leeks, sliced and washed
2 stalks green garlic, sliced and washed (or 1 large garlic clove, chopped)
1 tablespoon kosher salt
4 cups vegetable stock or water
¾ pound watercress (3 to 4 bunches)
¼ pound spring nettles, blanched if stinging variety
1 bunch sorrel leaves (1 to 2 ounces)
Crème fraîche (store-bought, or Crème Fraîche, page 181), extra virgin olive oil, and leek or green garlic tops for garnish

In a large saucepan, warm the olive oil and butter over medium heat until the butter is foamy. Add the onion, leeks, garlic, and salt, and stir to coat. Let cook 10 minutes, then add 4 cups stock or water. Bring to a simmer. Add the watercress and nettles and simmer just until tender. Using a fine-mesh sieve over a bowl, strain the soup, separating the liquid from the solids, but reserve both. Transfer both to the refrigerator and cool 2 hours. Remove the separated cooled soup ingredients from the refrigerator and recombine. Puree the soup in batches in the food processor or in a blender, and add the sorrel leaves a little at a time. The soup will have some texture. When finished processing, taste for seasoning and adjust as needed. Refrigerate until ready to use.

Transfer the soup to chilled bowls and garnish with a spoonful of crème fraîche, a drizzle of olive oil, and a few thin slices of leek tops or green garlic tops.

GUMBO Z'HERBES

I had long been interested in gumbo z'herbes—or "greens gumbo"—which incorporates a multitude of spring greens into a roux-thickened stew and is traditionally served only during Lent in New Orleans and the surrounding Gulf region. I had never tried making it until I was going through chemotherapy, which just happened to be in the spring. I was intent on incorporating as much nutrient-rich produce into my body as possible. I ordered bundles of spring greens from one of my favorite farmers that week. The types of greens can vary but, according to tradition, the number must be odd. I liked it so much that I asked my sous chef, Denver Richardson, to turn my healing home recipe into a featured menu item that we now serve every Lent.

8 servings

½ cup canola oil
1 cup unbleached all-purpose flour
1 cup diced yellow onion
1 cup diced celery
1 cup diced green bell pepper
2 garlic cloves, minced
2 tablespoons gumbo filé
2 tablespoons Hungarian paprika
2 tablespoons kosher salt
½ teaspoon black pepper
½ teaspoon cayenne pepper
½ teaspoon celery seed
½ teaspoon dried thyme leaf
½ teaspoon dried oregano
4 cups chicken, pork, or vegetable stock, heated
11 cups chopped and washed spring greens—ideally 1 cup each of beet tops, turnip tops, chard, mustard greens, mizuna, dandelion, carrot tops, watercress, radish tops, sorrel, and parsley (but any combination will do)
1 recipe Carolina Gold rice (page 442)
4 links smoked andouille sausage, sliced (optional)
Chopped scallions for garnish

In a Dutch oven or large, heavy-bottomed saucepan, start the roux by warming the oil over medium heat. Whisk in the flour and stir continuously until the mixture turns a deep chocolate color, 20 minutes to 1 hour, depending on your level of confidence. If you get any burned flecks in it, throw it out and start over. Immediately add the onion, celery, bell pepper, garlic, gumbo filé, paprika, salt, black pepper, cayenne, celery seed, thyme, and oregano. The mixture will steam and start to thicken. Continue to stir for 5 minutes. Add the heated stock and let simmer for 20 minutes. Stir in the greens and cook for another 20 minutes, until the greens are completely wilted.

Serve with cooked rice and andouille sausage if desired. Garnish with scallions.

VIVA'S ONE-SKILLET GREENS AND EGGS

To photograph the spring chapter of this book, I wanted to find a mountain location near Asheville, where my mother's ancestors lived. I turned to my friend Mike McGirr, an eccentric chef, forager, and organic food advocate who lives nearby and knows every farmer in the region. He arranged a stay for us at a breathtaking working farm set in the mountains just outside Marshall, called Laughing Frog. When we arrived, we realized we were miles from any nearby restaurant. Mike, already settled in, offered to cook dinner for the crew before we started the shoot the next morning. He whipped up this rustic but elegant one-skillet meal that we all devoured. Mike explained that his great-grandmother, Viva Stewart McGirr, used to make it when he visited her in the 1970s on her little organic farm in California. I thought that this was such an inventive use of bitter dandelion that I asked him if I could include it in the book. He generously obliged. Her recipe calls for cider vinegar in the pan, but to preserve the color of the greens, I've opted to drizzle it on just before serving.

Serves 6

8 slices thick-cut bacon, sliced crosswise into ½-inch pieces
1½ to 2 pounds dandelion greens, washed and spun dry
6 large farm-fresh eggs
Kosher salt
Freshly ground black pepper
2 tablespoons apple cider vinegar
2 tablespoons apple cider

Place the bacon in a single layer in a wide cast-iron skillet. Turn the heat on at medium-low and cook the bacon until crispy, stirring occasionally. Divide the dandelion greens into 6 small bundles and add them to the pan, arranging them in a sundial pattern lengthwise from the center of the skillet. Let cook until they begin to wilt, about 1 minute. Turn each bundle over with tongs. Add ½ cup water to keep the greens from browning and to help steam them from the bottom. Make a small crevice between the dandelion bundles. Crack one egg into a small bowl and lower the egg into one of the crevices. Repeat with the remaining crevices until all the eggs are nestled between the dandelion bundles. Season each egg with salt and pepper. Cook until the whites are set but the yolk is still runny, sunny-side-up style. With a spatula, divide each bundle of greens so there is an egg nested in the center and transfer to 6 serving bowls. In a small bowl, whisk together the cider and vinegar, and spoon over each serving.

SPINACH SALAD WITH STRAWBERRIES AND RHUBARB VINAIGRETTE

The idea of tossing strawberries with fresh spinach is not new. But it does make sense, given that they generally grow at about the same time in the season. In fact, the vitamin C found in strawberries helps the body absorb the iron naturally found in raw spinach. My version of this salad incorporates rhubarb into the dressing for added zip and tang.

4 servings

6 cups baby spinach leaves, washed and dried
6 tablespoons Rhubarb Vinaigrette (see recipe)
Kosher salt
1 cup sliced strawberries
4 ounces fresh chèvre, crumbled
¼ cup toasted sunflower seeds
Fennel pollen or shaved fennel bulb (optional)

Place the spinach in a large bowl. Spoon the Rhubarb Vinaigrette onto the sides of the bowl. With your hands, gently lift the spinach up repeatedly, coating the leaves with the dressing from the sides of the bowl. Season to taste with salt. Divide the spinach among 4 salad plates or bowls and garnish with equal amounts of strawberries, chèvre, and sunflower seeds. Though not essential, a sprinkling of fennel pollen or shaved raw fennel can add a sweet and mellow anise finish to this refreshing salad.

RHUBARB VINAIGRETTE

1⅔ cups

1 cup sliced rhubarb
1 scallion, sliced
1 stalk green garlic, sliced (or 1 small garlic clove, sliced)
½ cup Champagne vinegar
2 tablespoons honey
1 teaspoon whole-grain mustard
1 teaspoon minced fresh ginger
2 teaspoons kosher salt
½ cup sunflower oil

Combine the rhubarb, scallion, green garlic, vinegar, honey, mustard, ginger, and salt in a blender pitcher. Puree until smooth. With the motor running, drizzle in the sunflower oil.

SPRING PEAS

Garden peas are unequivocally a sign of springtime. Some are edible, pod and all, while others need a layer or two removed before they can be eaten. They add a touch of bright green sweetness to everything, with very little cooking required. The word "pea" can be a little confusing. In the broadest sense, it covers all legumes that are formed in a pod, which is usually inedible. In this section I am focusing on three peas and one bean I often use in springtime dishes.

ENGLISH PEAS: This inedible pod encases emerald jewels, bursting with sweetness and crunch. Some English peas are so tender and sweet that they can be eaten raw while others have a higher starch content and must be cooked to be enjoyed. These differences are affected by the growing conditions, maturity, and variety of each plant. No one knows exactly where the name "English pea" came from, since this pea variety is known to have originated in regions that span from the Middle East to Central Asia. It is believed to be a term that originated in Colonial America to refer to the English homeland. I make a puree of English peas, green garlic, and mint that I serve with raw vegetables, with crisp crackers, or even as an accompaniment to a perfectly cooked piece of fish. I also love adding peas to a simple pasta dressed in olive oil with some shaved cheese and country ham or prosciutto.

FAVA BEANS: Also called broad beans, fava beans are not technically peas but are often used in similar ways. Fava beans also go by the names horsebeans, English beans, and Windsor beans. They are labor intensive to shell and peel, and therefore can be pricey when offered in restaurants. But their unique, earthy, funky flavor is like no other. The tough outer pod must first be split open, to release the flat beans. Unlike any other legume, each individual fava bean is encased in its own husk and must be peeled again. A simple trick to hasten the extra labor involved in peeling the husks is to boil the fava beans for one minute, then drop them into an ice bath, making them easier to peel. Make a slit in one end of the clinging husk and then gently squeeze until the individual fava pops out.

Favas make a perfect simple salad with good olive oil and a sharp, salty cheese. They become a luxurious meal when sautéed with butter, white wine, lemon, herbs, and shrimp.

SNOW PEAS: The French name for the snow pea is *mange-tout*, meaning "eat it all." This sweet pea pod is entirely edible and is easily served raw or cooked. The snow pea is so thin and flat that you can see the bulge of the immature peas inside. Not long after the snow melts is when these seeds are planted directly into the soil, hence the name. Once the pods form, the plant will actually produce a higher yield if the peas are regularly harvested. Toss them into a salad, add them to a stir-fry, or snack on them alone. I love the little salad of raw, julienned snow peas and herbs that follows in this section (page 88).

SUGAR SNAPS: Sugar snaps are a cross between a snow pea and an English pea and were not developed until the 1970s. They have plump pods with a crisp, snappy texture and do not require shelling. They are entirely edible, pod and all, though often there are tough, fibrous strings that need to be removed first. Both snow peas and snap peas have a sweeter, cooler taste than the garden pea. Sugar snaps might show up under a roast spring lamb, in a sauté with other spring vegetables, or even tossed in the blender with my morning smoothie.

PEA SHOOTS AND TENDRILS: Both the early shoots and the long tendrils of the spring pea plants are edible. Pea shoots can be eaten raw and are often used in salads or as garnishes. The tendrils, which are long and vine-like, can be eaten raw but may need to be cooked if fibrous. Both have a sweet pea flavor, add texture and freshness to any dish, and are very nutritious.

JULIENNED SNOW PEA SALAD WITH SPRING HERBS

In spring 2014, I was a second-time finalist for the James Beard Foundation award of "Best Chef Southeast" and so was my good friend Ashley Christensen of Poole's Diner in Raleigh, North Carolina. The night before the awards, she and some friends threw an amazing dinner party on the roof of the NoMad Hotel. We sat at a long table, shared heartfelt toasts, and vowed that we would be happy no matter who won. One dish that stood out for me that evening was a salad of raw snow peas from the restaurant's kitchen. I don't remember what else was in this salad; it was the slicing technique that impressed me. Ashley and I both remarked on what a smart idea it was. Though it seems like a little detail, this is a perfect example of how the way a vegetable is sliced can completely alter your eating experience. The thin julienne exposes the interior of this sealed pod, creating nooks and crannies that catch bits of dressing and herbs perfectly. While I was finalizing a snow pea dish for this cookbook, the memory of that salad came back to me and I was inspired to create my own version as a salute to Ashley, who took home the award the following night.

6 to 8 servings

1 pound snow peas
2 garlic scapes, blanched or grilled
2 tablespoons Meyer Lemon Sauce (page 429)
2 tablespoons extra virgin olive oil
Flaky sea salt
Freshly ground black pepper
½ cup mixed fresh spring herbs: tarragon, mint, violet, pansy, coriander flower

Thinly slice the snow peas lengthwise and transfer them to a large bowl. Slice the cooked garlic scapes crosswise and add to the bowl. Toss with Meyer Lemon Sauce and olive oil, and season with salt and pepper. Garnish with herbs.

CREAMED RICE WITH ENGLISH PEAS AND COUNTRY HAM

This creamed rice is technically made like risotto, but I prefer Carolina Gold rice, an heirloom long-grain variety from the "lowcountry," instead of the short-grain traditional Arborio from Italy. Stirring the grains with a wooden spoon while they swell with the liquid releases the natural starches, resulting in a savory, comforting porridge. Freshly shelled sweet English peas and finely chopped smoky country ham give it a Southern flair. If you need a break during cooking, you can par-cook the rice up to the step where the wine and water have been absorbed. Just cool it down and refrigerate it until you're ready to pick it up at the next step. I toss the peas in raw toward the end so they pop when you bite into them. You can vary this recipe with asparagus tips, radishes, or a poached egg on top, or apply this technique to other vegetables at any time of the year.

4 servings

1 tablespoon unsalted butter
1 cup dry Carolina Gold rice, or other aromatic long-grain rice such as basmati
¼ cup dry white wine
2 teaspoons kosher salt
2 cups stock, heated (chicken, pork, or vegetable)
2 cups heavy cream, heated
¼ cup finely chopped country ham
1 cup shelled English peas
Parmigiano-Reggiano for garnish

In a wide saucepan or Dutch oven over medium heat, warm the butter until foamy. Add the dry rice and cook, stirring continuously with a wooden spoon, until the grains turn opaque, about 5 minutes. Add the white wine and stir until the rice absorbs the wine. Have 1 cup water ready. Add ¼ cup of the water and continue to stir until the rice absorbs the liquid. Repeat this step until all of the water is absorbed, adding a little at a time.

Slowly add ½ cup of the hot stock and stir until the rice absorbs the liquid. Then add ½ cup of the hot cream and stir until the rice absorbs the liquid. Repeat these steps, alternating another ½ cup each of hot stock and cream, until all the liquid is absorbed. This process should take 35 to 40 minutes, resulting in tender and creamy grains of rice. Stir in the country ham and peas. Taste for seasoning and add salt as needed. Garnish with Parmigiano-Reggiano and serve hot.

ENGLISH PEA HUMMUS

Though the healthful and now mainstream Middle Eastern dip we know as hummus typically includes chickpeas and sesame tahini, this adaptation contains neither. Rather, its similarly smooth texture comes from the natural starch and protein of the English pea. In the summer, I make a variation of this using blanched field peas of any variety, and I substitute thyme for the spring herbs and fresh garlic in place of the early green garlic of spring.

1½ cups

Kosher salt: 1 cup, plus ½ teaspoon or more to taste
2 cups fresh shelled English peas (about 2 pounds unshelled)
1 stalk green garlic, chopped (or 1 small garlic clove, chopped)
2 tablespoons fresh mint leaves
1 tablespoon fresh chervil leaves
2 tablespoons lemon juice
6 tablespoons extra virgin olive oil
¼ teaspoon freshly ground black pepper, plus more to taste

In a large saucepan over high heat, bring 3 quarts water and ½ cup kosher salt to a boil. Prepare an ice bath of 3 quarts water and ice with ½ cup kosher salt stirred in until dissolved. Add the shelled English peas to the boiling water and cook until tender, 2 to 4 minutes. When sweet and tender, immediately remove the peas from the boiling water with a slotted spoon and transfer to the ice bath to stop the cooking. Let sit until the peas are fully cooled, 1 to 2 minutes, then drain.

Combine blanched peas, green garlic, mint, chervil, lemon, olive oil, ½ teaspoon salt, and the pepper in a food processor and puree until smooth. Taste for seasoning and adjust as needed. Serve with crudités or Crackers (page 472; use the buckwheat-walnut version).

SUGAR SNAPS IN PRESERVED LEMON BROTH WITH ROAST LAMB

Sweet, crisp sugar snaps do not need much done to them. They can be delicious raw, but when cooked, they turn even sweeter. I like to simmer them in a light broth made from the bone of a roast spring lamb. This is an impressive dish to serve for Easter or Mother's Day. The clean fresh taste of garden peas and mint lightens the rich garlicky lamb.

4 servings

2 cups Roasted Lamb Bone Broth (see recipe)
¼ cup Preserved Lemon rind, diced (page 427)
1 pound sugar snap peas, strings removed
About 1 pound sliced Roast Spring Lamb (see recipe)
Chopped fresh mint leaves for garnish
A drizzle of Meyer Lemon Sauce (page 429)

In a wide saucepan, bring the broth and the preserved lemon rind to a simmer. Add the sugar snaps and simmer until crisp-tender, 4 to 5 minutes. Remove the peas with a slotted spoon and divide among 4 dinner plates. Spoon some of the liquid over the peas and layer with sliced lamb, freshly chopped mint, and Meyer Lemon Sauce.

ROAST SPRING LAMB

On dairy farms—sheep, cow, or goat—only a certain number of the males can stick around. They don't produce milk, and you can't have too many males in a herd. This means that in springtime a number of these males will be sacrificed to preserve the herd, and a fine feast is often the result. It can help us understand where the notion of spring lamb came from, at a time when we had a stronger connection to agrarian life. Ask your butcher to remove the bone from a fresh lamb leg and tie the leg for easy roasting. Save the bone to make a flavorsome broth that can be used to cook the spring peas above.

12 servings

One 6- to 8-pound leg of lamb, bone removed and meat tied
Kosher salt
Freshly ground black pepper
2 stalks green garlic, chopped, tops reserved (or 3 garlic cloves, finely chopped)
4 sprigs rosemary, leaves removed and chopped, branches reserved
1 bottle fruity white wine

Heat the oven to 375°F. Season the meat liberally with salt and pepper. Rub with garlic and rosemary and let sit for a minimum of 30 minutes or up to 2 hours at room temperature. Place the seasoned lamb on a roasting rack that fits into a roasting pan. Pour the bottle of white wine into the bottom of the pan. This will be your basting liquid and will prevent the fat that drips into the bottom of the pan from burning and smoking up your kitchen. Roast the lamb, basting every 20 minutes with the white wine and pan juices. After 1 hour, insert a meat thermometer into the thickest part of the roast to check for doneness. Pull the roast from the oven when it registers between 140° and 145° F for a pink center, about 2 hours. Let rest 20 minutes before slicing.

ROASTED LAMB BONE BROTH

Reserved bones from leg of lamb
2 spring leeks, roughly chopped
2 small carrots, roughly chopped
4 ribs celery, roughly chopped
Reserved garlic tops
Reserved rosemary branches
2 bay leaves
1 sprig fresh thyme
12 whole black peppercorns

While the leg of lamb is roasting, roast the bone alongside it in the oven for 30 minutes.

Meanwhile, in a large stockpot, combine the leeks, carrots, celery, garlic tops, rosemary branches, bay leaves, thyme, and peppercorns. Add water to cover by 2 to 3 inches, about 6 cups, and bring to a lively simmer over medium-high heat. When the bone comes out of the oven, immediately add it to the pot and continue to simmer for 1½ to 2 hours. Remove the bone from the stock, strain the stock, and discard the solids. Cool the stock and store it covered and refrigerated for up to 1 week, or frozen for up to 6 months.

SHRIMP AND FAVA BEANS

Fresh fava beans have been a mainstay of Middle Eastern and Mediterranean diets for centuries, and lately they have been enjoying popularity in the United States. Bright green and firm-fleshed with a sweet and mildly nutty flavor, they resemble lima beans but are really more like an overgrown split pea. Fava beans are a bit time-consuming, as they require double peeling: first the outer pod, and then the hull that protects this little spring gem. Once you're done, you will have more debris than edible beans, but it's worth it, as this recipe will demonstrate. The gentle butter poaching method for the shrimp yields tender, succulent meat that contrasts beautifully with the spring fava bean.

4 servings

1 cup kosher salt, plus more for seasoning
3 pounds whole fava pods, about 1½ cups beans after shelling
4 tablespoons (½ stick) unsalted butter, cut into small pieces
1½ pounds medium shrimp, peeled and deveined
Freshly ground black pepper
Juice of 1 lemon
½ cup fruity white wine
1 or 2 radishes, thinly sliced
Flat-leaf parsley leaves for garnish

Set a large pot on the stove. Put in 1 gallon water and 1 cup kosher salt. Bring to a boil. Ready a large bowl of ice water.

Tear open the fava pods and remove the beans, discarding the outer pods. Place the beans in the boiling water for 1 to 2 minutes, then remove with a slotted spoon and transfer to a bowl of ice water to stop the cooking. When cooled, remove the outer hull of each bean and place the shelled beans in a bowl, discarding the hulls. Set aside.

Place the butter and the shrimp in a wide skillet and set on the stove. Turn the heat to the lowest setting and stir as the butter melts and the shrimp begin to cook. Season with salt and pepper and add lemon juice and white wine. As the temperature rises, keep a close eye on the shrimp, stirring frequently. Remove with a slotted spoon when the shrimp are pink and slightly curled. Set aside.

Add the peeled favas to the pan and increase the heat to medium-high. Cook until the favas are heated all the way through, then taste for seasoning and adjust. Be sure to taste both the beans and the liquid. Add the radishes to the pan and turn off the heat. Return the shrimp to the pan and toss to combine. Divide the shrimp and fava mixture with the juice among 4 bowls, and garnish with parsley. Serve immediately.

STRAWBERRIES

One Sunday afternoon in May, my friend Maria and I took a leisurely drive to Riverview Farms, two hundred acres of rich certified organic farmland in the foothills of the Appalachians about an hour north of Atlanta. Wes and Charlotte Swancy, who tend the farm with their large extended family, were up to their ankles in strawberries and, with a newborn in the house, were too tired to pick anymore. So Charlotte handed us buckets and told us to help ourselves. "They are growing so fast that by the time I've picked through all the rows, there are newly ripened ones on the first!" Maria and I entered the field with gusto, and soon realized what Charlotte meant. It was peak season and it did seem that they were practically ripening before our eyes. I tasted, for the first time, a strawberry right off the plant. It was still warm from the sun, and so juicy and intensely flavored I have never forgotten it.

As with all fruits, the original version was found in the wild. Wild strawberries, when eaten by birds, are distributed near and far. The tiny seeds of the strawberry pass through the birds' digestive system intact, and since the seeds germinate in response to light rather than moisture, they need no covering of soil to sprout. But most of us are more familiar with the farmed strawberry, which happens to be the most cultivated berry in the United States. Strawberries can be grown in containers as well as raised beds, and can tolerate cold far better than most fruits. Although they have become increasingly available year-round, they are at the peak of their season from April through July. Most of the strawberries sold at the supermarket come from California or Florida. But because the commercial ones have been bred to have tougher skins to withstand long-distance travel, even the best of those can't compete with the fragile, ephemeral, heart-shaped fruits picked close to home—especially if you're lucky enough to get to pop one into your mouth straight from the patch. There are hundreds of varieties developed for different conditions and locales, ranging in size from large to small, and in flavor from racy acid to mellow sweetness. Where I live, the window of opportunity is mid-spring. They are one of the first local fruits of the year, and they last until they can no longer withstand the heat.

Botanically, strawberries are related to roses, apples, pears, raspberries, and stone fruits. They are technically not berries as their seeds are on the outside of the fruit. Part of enjoying a ripe strawberry is crunching on those sandy-textured seeds while the juices burst in your mouth.

With strawberries, I tend to stick to simple, classic pairings: fresh cream, tart rhubarb, tender spinach leaves, goat cheese, honey. But I also love them with less conventional companions such as rose water, black pepper, pistachios, fresh fennel, green garlic, scallions, or ginger.

Most strawberries are very thin skinned and therefore tend to absorb moisture easily. Wash strawberries only right before using and do not let them sit in water. Transfer them to a colander to drip dry, then place them on paper towels to air-dry in the refrigerator.

When removing the hull, don't chop off the entire top, which has plenty of edible fruit. Pinch the leaves together to form a crown and, with a small paring knife, carve out the green from the hard core on top of the berry. If your berries are slightly tart, you can macerate them by sprinkling a little sugar on them and letting them sit. Not only does this add sweetness, but it creates a delicious fresh strawberry syrup that can be drizzled over your favorite dessert. Strawberries are also easy to muddle—a term that means crushing them in the bottom of a glass or tin with a wooden baton, called a muddler. Use this method to make fresh strawberry lemonade or an à la minute strawberry cocktail.

To freeze strawberries whole, remove the cap and stem. Arrange them in a single layer on a baking pan or cookie sheet and place them in the freezer. Once the berries are frozen, transfer them to a freezer bag and return them to the freezer, where they will keep for up to a year.

STRAWBERRIES AND CREAM WITH ROSE WATER AND PISTACHIOS

Strawberries and cream are a classic combination that can easily be thrown together and quickly devoured.

6 servings

1 quart fresh strawberries (about 1 pound)
½ cup sugar
Pinch salt
1 teaspoon rose water
2 cups heavy cream
1 cup toasted, coarsely chopped pistachios

Wash the strawberries, trim off the greens, and slice into quarters lengthwise. Transfer the sliced berries to a medium bowl and mix with ¼ cup of the sugar, the salt, and the rose water. Set aside to macerate the fruit. Meanwhile, in an electric mixer or in a metal bowl with a whisk, whip the cream with the remaining ¼ cup sugar until soft peaks form. Pour the juices from the berries over the whipped cream, and lightly whisk until the cream is fluffy again. Layer the cream with the berries and pistachios and serve with Shortbread (page 473; use the pistachio–black pepper version.).

FRESH STRAWBERRY DAIQUIRI

The first daiquiri was concocted in Cuba by sprinkling a little sugar over ice, mixing in some fresh lime juice, topping it off with rum, and stirring. Somewhere along the way it morphed into the insipidly sweet, artificially flavored, slushy abominations bearing no resemblance to the wonderfully simple quaff that purists recognize as the real thing. Made in the spirit of the original recipe, this strawberry version will hopefully help restore its once classy reputation.

1 cocktail

2 ounces light rum
¾ ounce freshly squeezed lime juice
¾ ounce strawberry puree (see recipe)

In a cocktail shaker, combine the rum, lime juice, and strawberry puree. Shake with ice and strain into a glass.

STRAWBERRY PUREE

⅔ cup

1 cup strawberries
1 tablespoon sugar
Pinch kosher salt

Combine the strawberries, sugar, and salt in a blender or food processor. Puree.

THE PIMM'S PATCH

Often associated with the Napoleon House in New Orleans, the Pimm's cup was actually invented by an oyster bar owner in London named James Pimm in the 1850s. Each spring at Miller Union, we shake his original formula with muddled strawberries and a touch of gin for a fun seasonal twist on this classic cocktail.

1 cocktail

2 or 3 strawberries
1 ounce Pimm's liqueur
½ ounce gin
¾ ounce lime juice
½ ounce simple syrup (see Note)
Cucumber for garnish

In a cocktail shaker, muddle the strawberries. Add the Pimm's, gin, lime juice, and simple syrup. Shake with ice and strain over ice or serve "up."

Note: To make simple syrup, in a small saucepan over medium heat, stir together 1 cup sugar and 1 cup water until the sugar is dissolved. Cool to room temperature.

STRAWBERRY PRESERVES

When life gives you strawberries, make strawberry preserves!

1 pint preserves

5 cups washed, stemmed, and quartered strawberries (24 ounces)
1½ cups sugar
Juice of ½ large lemon
Pinch salt

Place the strawberries, sugar, lemon, and salt in a large bowl and stir gently to combine. Let sit for 15 minutes. Transfer the strawberry mixture to a wide skillet and bring to a boil over high heat. While the berries are cooking, skim away any foam that may rise and observe the liquid as it cooks down. The bubbles will become larger and the liquid will begin to clarify. Observe the berries. They will darken and become almost translucent. At this point, remove the pan from the heat. Transfer the berries to sterilized jars and process according to standard canning procedures for shelf-stable storage, or cool and then refrigerate.

Variations: Add ½ to 1 teaspoon minced fresh lavender or lemon thyme. Or add ½ teaspoon freshly ground black pepper with 2 tablespoons balsamic vinegar.

NEXT SPREAD
SPRING VEGETABLE FEAST (clockwise from top left), Braised Fennel with Olives and Orange; Creamed Rice with English Peas and Country Ham; The Pimm's Patch; Strawberry Preserves; green garlic Popovers; Grilled Torpedo Onions with Greek Yogurt; Roasted Asparagus with Green Garlic and Radishes; Julienned Snow Pea Salad with Spring Herbs; Sorghum-Glazed Baby Carrots

SUMMER

The days are long and hot, interrupted by refreshing afternoon
thunderstorms. Everything is alive and lush, teeming with energy.
Brightly colored berries, summer squashes, juicy tomatoes, crisp beans,
and fresh okra fill the tables at the farmers' markets.

BERRIES

Blackberries and raspberries are in the same botanical family and have clusters of fruit that make up the berry shape. The blueberry, however, has a spherical shape and smooth skin with almost undetectable seeds. Though these sweet summer jewels have their differences, they all come into season around the same time and can be somewhat interchangeable.

BLUEBERRIES are common where I grew up. We used to visit a "U-pick-em" blueberry farm in rural Georgia. We made quite a family portrait. Mom outfitted us with wide-brimmed hats to shield us from the sun. My three siblings and I raced to fill our baskets as fast as possible, knowing that once they were full, we could escape the heat in the air-conditioned station wagon with all the blueberries we could eat on the way home. To this day, the kid in me can't resist those simple nostalgic dishes where any summer berries are traditionally seen: crisps, pancakes, muffins, coffee cake. But my adult palate also craves more sophisticated berry treatments, like savory jams, a semifreddo, or a cocktail.

Blueberries are indigenous to North America and were available only in the wild until the twentieth century. Prior to their first successful cultivation in 1916 by a cranberry farmer's daughter, blueberries could be enjoyed only if foraged. An important food source for Native Americans, this nutritious fruit helped colonists, settlers, and wildlife survive when food was scarce. The blueberry, related to the cranberry and bilberry, is a perennial flowering plant with leaves that can be either deciduous or evergreen, depending on the variety. Today dozens of varieties of blueberries are grown in thirty-eight states. The three main types are highbush, lowbush, and a hybrid of the two. Many seed varieties echo the fruit's namesake color, such as beckyblue, bluebell, briteblue, and powder blue.

Blueberries should be dusty blue in color, uniform in size, and firm, plump, and dry. They soften and become more fragrant after harvest.

They are notorious pest magnets and, as a result, highly sprayed with pesticides and fungicides. Look for organic whenever possible. Store them loosely covered in the refrigerator for several days. Do not wash until ready to use. Freeze in a single layer on a flat surface, then transfer to an airtight container or freezer bag, for up to six months.

BLACKBERRIES AND RASPBERRIES belong to the family Rosaceae, which includes stone fruits, roses, almonds, apples, and pears. More specifically, they are considered caneberries, composed of clusters of pinhead-size fruits called drupelets. Each drupelet contains a single seed and is held together by tiny hairlike structures that form around the core, or the "rasp." You might think that the best way to distinguish between the two is to look at the color, but this could be deceiving. For instance, there are red and black raspberries, and an unripe blackberry on the bush starts out as red before it ripens to dark indigo. There is a key to deciphering this code, however. When a raspberry is picked, the berry slips off the rasp, leaving it attached to the prickly vine with a hollow berry remaining. The blackberry, however, comes clean from the stem and the rasp remains inside the berry as a soft, white edible core.

Seedy varieties are best for syrups or sauces where the fruit is crushed and the solids are removed. Acidic berries might need the help of sugar or honey to balance the fruit flavor. Choose blackberries or raspberries that are plump for their size, without hulls, possessing a deep, rich color. They do not ripen after picking, but they will spoil quickly. Check the bottom of their storage container for visible signs of moisture or mold. Do not submerge in water. Instead, place berries in the center of a clean towel and mist them with a spray bottle. Store on a dry cotton napkin or paper towel and refrigerate, loosely covered. Freeze in a single layer on a flat surface, then transfer to an airtight container or freezer bag, for up to six months.

BLACKBERRY SHRUB

Drinking vinegar may not sound palatable, but in the form of a shrub, it has quite a history. This fruit-infused vinegar syrup was popular in England in the seventeenth century, when there was a need for acidity but no access to citrus. American colonists later used the shrub technique to preserve fragile summer fruits without refrigeration. Original historic recipes call for letting the fruit sit in the vinegar for over a week and then removing the solids and cooking only the fruit-infused vinegar. I've greatly simplified the original, speeding up the process. Make a refreshing soda by mixing 1 part shrub to 4 parts sparkling water and serve over ice. Or try Miller Union's boozy Black Jack Cocktail below.

THE SHRUB

About 1 quart concentrate

4 cups fresh blackberries, about 1 pound
2 cups apple cider vinegar
2 cups sugar
Pinch kosher salt

Place the blackberries in a nonmetal bowl or pitcher; add the vinegar, sugar, and salt. Stir well to combine and cover with plastic wrap or a lid; refrigerate for 1 to 2 days. Transfer the berry mixture into a nonreactive saucepan and place over medium heat. When the mixture comes to a simmer, let cook for about 10 minutes, skimming any foam that may rise to the surface. Strain the cooked berry mixture into a fine-mesh sieve over a heatproof storage container. Press the blackberries against the sieve to extract all liquid. Discard the solids. Store the shrub, covered and refrigerated, for up to 6 weeks.

THE BLACK JACK COCKTAIL

1 serving

1½ ounces Laird's apple brandy (you can use whiskey, bourbon, or cognac if
    Laird's is not available)
½ ounce freshly squeezed lemon juice
½ ounce freshly squeezed orange juice
1 ounce blackberry shrub
Crushed ice
Fresh mint for garnish

Combine the brandy, lemon juice, orange juice, and blackberry shrub in a cock-tail shaker with ice and shake well until cold and combined. Strain over cocktail glasses filled with crushed ice. Garnish with fresh mint.

RASPBERRY VERRINE

A verrine is a recent invention from French cuisine that showcases ingredients with contrasting texture, flavor, temperature, and color. The word literally means "protective glass," referring to the vessel used to contain its artful layers. It is much like a glorified parfait, and can be sweet or savory. In this example, jewel-like raspberries are nestled between layers of pastry cream thinned with buttermilk, raspberry jam, and crunchy gingersnap crumbs. Once you master this technique, you can have fun experimenting with other fruits or vegetables and complementary ingredients in any season.

4 servings

1 cup whole milk
2 tablespoons cornstarch
¼ cup sugar
⅛ teaspoon kosher salt
1 large egg
¼ teaspoon vanilla extract
2 tablespoons unsalted butter
½ cup buttermilk
½ cup Raspberry and Lemon Balm Fresh Jam (page 118)
1 pint fresh raspberries
1 cup gingersnap cookie crumbs

In a medium heavy-bottomed saucepan, bring the milk to a low boil over medium heat. Meanwhile, in a medium bowl, whisk together the cornstarch, sugar, salt, and egg until smooth. When the milk comes to a boil, remove it from the heat. Temper the egg mixture by slowly adding one-third of the hot milk to the bowl and whisking to combine. Return the tempered egg mixture to the pot with the hot milk, and whisk to combine.

Return the pot to the stove, and over medium-low heat, cook the mixture until thickened, whisking continuously. When the mixture begins to bubble, remove it from the heat and add vanilla and butter. Whisk until the butter is melted and incorporated. If the custard has lumps, press it through a sieve. Transfer to a container and cover the surface with wax paper or plastic wrap. Refrigerate until chilled. Whisk the chilled custard with the buttermilk until smooth. Set aside.

Into each of 4 footed glasses, spoon ¼ cup buttermilk custard. Add 1 tablespoon jam, followed by ¼ cup fresh raspberries. Then spoon 2 tablespoons of the gingersnap cookie crumbs across the raspberries. Repeat each layer. Serve immediately.

COLD BRINE–PICKLED
BLACKBERRIES

One summer when we had a bumper crop of blackberries, my former chef de cuisine, Justin Burdett, suggested pickling some to extend the harvest. He made a pickling brine but then cooled it before pouring it over the blackberries, to protect their shape and texture. I loved the outcome so much that this recipe makes a comeback every summer in various forms. We might scatter the blackberries over a piece of fatty pork (see below), or toss them with green beans or other summer vegetables to add a surprising pop of flavor. The leftover vinegar can be used as the base of a vinaigrette or as a glaze over roasted quail or duck.

1 quart

4 cups blackberries, picked over
6 juniper berries, or a shot of London dry-style gin if juniper berries are not available
8 black peppercorns
1 small bay leaf
½-inch piece fresh ginger, sliced
3 allspice berries
2 cups red wine vinegar
6 tablespoons sugar
3 tablespoons kosher salt
1 sprig fresh thyme
1 shallot, quartered

Fill a clean 1-quart jar with blackberries and place in the refrigerator. With a mortar and pestle, lightly crush the juniper berries, peppercorns, bay leaf, ginger, and allspice. In a medium saucepan over high heat, combine the vinegar, sugar, salt, and 2 cups water and stir to dissolve the sugar. Add the crushed spices, thyme, and shallot. When the mixture comes to a boil, reduce the heat and simmer for 10 minutes. Remove from the heat and cool to room temperature. Strain out the solids and discard. Chill the liquid for 1 hour. Pour the cooled brine over the berries. Cover and refrigerate for up to 4 weeks.

How to grill a pork chop: Heat the grill. If using gas, set to medium-high. If cooking over wood or charcoal, allow the flames to die down until the embers are glowing. Season ¾- to 1-inch-thick bone-in pork chops on both sides liberally with salt and pepper, and brush with olive oil. Place them directly on the grill grate and let cook, undisturbed, for 4 to 5 minutes. Extinguish any flare-ups with a little water from a spray or squeeze bottle. Turn the pork chops 90 degrees but do not flip. Let cook for 4 to 5 minutes. Then flip and repeat the steps above. I like to serve my pork medium (140° to 145°F internal temperature), so that it is still slightly pink in the center. Let rest a few minutes before serving.

RASPBERRY AND LEMON BALM FRESH JAM

I learned how to make this no-cook fresh jam with raspberries or blackberries while working brunches at Watershed restaurant in Decatur, Georgia. Natural yeasts on the fruit's surface and in the air feed on the sugars and thicken the mixture. My revised version incorporates lemon balm, a member of the mint family, which adds a lovely herbal note to this crimson condiment. Use this when making Raspberry Verrine (page 113), spoon it onto hot biscuits or English muffins, or serve it with cheese.

1 quart jar

2 pints fresh raspberries
1 cup sugar
1 cup loosely packed fresh lemon balm leaves
Pinch kosher salt

In a flat-bottomed container, crush the berries with a potato masher. Add the sugar and continue to mash until dissolved. Place the lemon balm leaves in the base of a blender pitcher. Add 1 cup of the raspberry mixture and blend until smooth. Add the lemon balm–raspberry mixture to the mashed raspberries and mix well to combine. Transfer to a wide-mouthed jar, cover with cheesecloth, and fasten the cloth securely with tape or twine. This will keep unwanted particles or pests away but will still allow the mixture to breathe. Let sit on the countertop at room temperature until the fruit puree rises above the juices and fills with bubbles, 2 to 3 days. A dry skin may form, but this is normal. Just stir to combine, and refrigerate. The jam will be the consistency of a thick sauce.

BLUEBERRY COFFEE CAKE WITH STREUSEL

There's barely enough batter to coat the fruit in this recipe, but don't worry—that's how it's supposed to be. The resulting light, tender cake underneath the crunchy streusel topping bursts with berries. Enjoy on a warm summer morning, with an iced coffee or espresso.

12 servings

Streusel topping

½ cup rolled oats (not instant)
6 tablespoons all-purpose flour
¼ cup packed light brown sugar
Pinch kosher salt
Pinch freshly grated nutmeg
4 tablespoons (½ stick) unsalted butter

Cake

5 tablespoons unsalted butter: 1 tablespoon for greasing pan; plus 4 tablespoons
    (½ stick), melted, for the cake
4 cups blueberries
2 cups unbleached all-purpose flour
1 teaspoon baking powder
½ teaspoon baking soda
½ teaspoon kosher salt
½ cup whole milk
½ cup crème fraîche (store-bought, or see Crème Fraîche, page 181), or sour cream
½ cup granulated sugar
2 large eggs, room temperature

Prepare the streusel topping: In a small bowl, combine the oats, flour, brown sugar, salt, and nutmeg. Add the butter in pieces and, with your fingers, gently rub the dry ingredients into the butter until they are incorporated and crumbly. Refrigerate until ready to use.

Preheat the oven to 350°F. Grease a 9-inch square glass baking dish with 1 tablespoon butter. Wash and drain the blueberries; spread them out on paper towels to dry, removing any bits of leaf or stem.

Prepare the cake: In a large mixing bowl, combine the 2 cups flour, baking powder, baking soda, and ½ teaspoon salt. Stir until well mixed. In a medium bowl, whisk together the milk, crème fraîche, sugar, eggs, and 4 tablespoons melted butter. Add the wet ingredients to the flour mixture, stirring to blend well. Gently fold in the blueberries.

Spread the batter in the prepared dish. Sprinkle evenly with the streusel topping. Bake until a wooden pick inserted in the center of the cake comes out clean, 45 to 50 minutes. Cool on a wire rack at least 20 minutes before serving.

BLUEBERRY MOSTARDA

Emily Hansford, chef de cuisine at Miller Union, developed this winning idea for finishing crispy duck breast. Her goal was to retain the integrity of whole berries while still allowing the natural pectins to thicken the sauce. Half of the blueberries are cooked down to a syrupy consistency, and the remaining berries are stirred in at the end, while the sauce is still hot. The mostarda is also delicious with crispy skin-on chicken thighs or sautéed quail, or on a cheese plate.

2 cups

½ cup Champagne vinegar
¼ cup sugar
1 shallot, minced
1 teaspoon mustard seeds
½ teaspoon minced fresh ginger
1 bay leaf
1 sprig fresh thyme
Pinch kosher salt
1 pint blueberries, washed

In a small saucepan, combine the Champagne vinegar, sugar, shallot, mustard seeds, ginger, bay leaf, thyme, and salt, and bring to a boil. Lower the heat and simmer until the mixture is reduced by half, then add half of the blueberries. Cook until the sauce starts to thicken and the blueberries have burst, then add the remaining berries and immediately turn off the heat. Let cool to room temperature. Store covered and refrigerated for up to 2 weeks.

How to sauté duck breast: Good-quality duck breast is one of the easiest and most delicious things you can prepare at home, and guests will always be wowed. Trim off any silverskin that may be present on the flesh side of the breast. Score the fat side by inserting the tip of a sharp slicing knife into the fat, being careful not to puncture the meat below, and draw parallel lines that are ⅛ inch apart. Rotate the breast 90 degrees and repeat, making a crisscross pattern in the fat. The quill pattern on the fat is a good visual guide. Season both sides of the breast liberally with salt and then, on the flesh side only, season lightly with pepper. Place the breast fat side down in a cold nonstick or cast-iron skillet. Turn the heat to medium-low and allow the fat to render until the breast is crisp and golden brown, 12 to 14 minutes. Turn the breast over and cook in the rendered fat for another 1 to 2 minutes, then remove from the pan and transfer to a cutting board. Allow the meat to rest 5 minutes. Cut one slice of duck to check for doneness. The flesh should be rosy and medium-rare. If you prefer it more done, return it to the skillet. Reserve the rendered duck fat by straining it through a cheesecloth or wire mesh strainer, and refrigerate it for a later use.

CORN

Corn and its by-products are all around us. Corn satisfies us at summer picnics, fuels our cars, starches our shirts, cooks up as grits, gets us liquored up, entertains us at the movies, and sweetens everything from store-bought cookies to spaghetti sauce. In fact, it can be a challenge to find a box, bottle, or can that doesn't have high-fructose corn syrup listed as an ingredient.

Corn—or maize—is a human invention that does not grow naturally in the wild. Aztec and Mayan Indians living in what is now Mexico developed it from a large wild grass known as teosinte some seven thousand years ago. It is related to grasses such as wheat, oats, barley, sorghum, and rice. Eventually it became the dietary mainstay throughout North and South America.

Before Columbus made his famous voyage, corn was unknown in Europe. Sweet corn wasn't developed until the 1700s, and most of the bland early corn—what we now know as field corn—was fried in cakes, baked in puddings, fed to livestock, or dried and ground into meal or flour. Many battles over cornfields were fought between the early settlers and the Native Americans, for their survival depended on corn. There is a long-held theory that growing cereals enabled the spread of human culture and the growth of cities.

Today, corn is the third-largest human food crop in the world, after wheat and rice. Nearly every part of the corn plant has a use. The kernels can be dried and fed to livestock, or ground into grits, meal, and flour. The husks are dried for wrapping tamales, the cobs can be boiled into a stock for vegetarian soups, and even the silk can be simmered for a fragrant tea. There are two main categories of corn: sweet corn and drying corn.

SWEET CORN: is grown for eating freshly picked at its "milk" stage and is divided into three types: "Standard" corn is "old-fashioned," like the kind your grandfather used to grow, and includes heirloom varieties that are not hybridized or genetically modified. The downside of these is that they lose their sweetness very quickly as the natural sugars convert to starch the minute they are plucked from the stalk. Sugar-enhanced corn is a hybridized variety that has been bred to hold its sugar content for several days after harvesting, making it more appealing to the grower or purchaser as a reliable source of sweetness with less risk of turning to starch. Supersweet corn is a hybridized variety that produces the sweetest flavor, but it requires soil sixty-five degrees or warmer, which means that the grower will often need to cover the ground in black plastic to insulate the soil and raise the temperature.

DRYING CORN: "Flint" corn, when dried, forms a hard outer shell around the kernel. Specific flint varieties include red and blue corn, Indian corn, and also popcorn—a superflint that has such a hard endosperm that moisture is trapped inside, causing the kernel to explode when heated. "Dent" corn is slightly softer when dried and has a slight dent in the kernel. This is also known as field corn and is commonly fed to livestock. Both flint and dent can be used for making cornmeal, grits, and polenta.

When selecting sweet corn, choose ears with deep brown silk tips and bright green, moist husks that cling snugly to the corn. Peel back the husk and check to be sure that the top rows of kernels are plump and dense, and exude a milky juice when pierced with a fingernail. The easiest way to remove corn silk is to rub the ears with a damp paper or terry cloth towel. The silk tends to wipe right off with a little agitation. Corn can easily be sliced off the cob and frozen, and the kernels will retain much of their flavor. Once frozen, however, they will become mushier when thawed and are best suited for soups or stews where texture isn't an issue. Organic dried corn products like grits, polenta, and cornmeal are easy to find at farmers' markets and vary, depending on what is being grown in your area.

SUMMER SUCCOTASH

There are countless interpretations of succotash throughout the South and beyond, but corn and butter beans or field peas are the common denominators. Squash, okra, peppers, and tomatoes might appear, but I rely on a little minced country ham and sweet Vidalia onion to deepen the flavor. A sprinkling of fresh herbs adds a light, modern touch to this classic side dish.

6 servings

4 tablespoons (½ stick) unsalted butter
3 tablespoons finely diced Vidalia onion
2 cups blanched butter beans or field peas or a mix (page 193)
2 cups sweet corn kernels, cut off the cob
1 tablespoon minced country ham
¼ cup heavy cream
¼ cup Sweet Corncob Broth (see recipe)
1 teaspoon chopped fresh tarragon
1 teaspoon chopped fresh parsley
Salt and pepper to taste

In a skillet, heat the butter until foamy and add the Vidalia onion. Cook until the onion is translucent, but do not brown. Add the beans, corn, ham, cream, and broth. Cook until the cream and stock have reduced and are slightly thickened, and the vegetables are well coated. Season with salt and pepper to taste and garnish with fresh herbs.

JOHNNYCAKES

Johnnycakes, griddle cakes, hoecakes: they all mean the same thing, but I prefer the more whimsical nickname derived from the term "journey cake." During colonial times, these crisp, dense cornmeal pancakes that were sometimes cooked on a hot garden hoe were sturdy enough to withstand a long trip and still offer sustenance. I use these as a vessel for many flavors, including braised pork, grilled shrimp, and roasted vegetables. Note that there is no leavening and no need to grease the pan.

4 cups batter, about 32 small cakes

½ cup whole milk
8 tablespoons (1 stick) butter
2 cups fine cornmeal (white, blue, or yellow)
1 tablespoon kosher salt

In a small saucepan over medium heat, warm the milk and butter together until the butter is melted. Set aside. In a large bowl, whisk together the cornmeal and salt. Whisk in 1½ cups boiling water first, then add the hot milk and butter mixture. Stir to combine. Warm an ungreased cast-iron skillet or griddle over medium-high heat. Drop spoonfuls of the batter onto the hot surface. Cook until lightly browned and crisp, then turn and finish cooking on the other side. Serve hot.

SKILLET CORNBREAD

Most old-school methods for making Southern cornbread start with a skillet that is sizzling with hot pork fat. I prefer a cold pan and cold batter to go into a hot oven. This minimizes the chance of burning the bottom. However, like any true Southerner, I am adamant about using straight cornmeal and no sugar. To avoid orange flecks, I use just enough baking soda to give it a little lift, relying on the eggs to do the rest.

One 9-inch, 1½-inch-high cake

5 tablespoons unsalted butter: 1 tablespoon for greasing; plus 4 tablespoons
  (½ stick), melted, for the batter
2 cups fine cornmeal
1½ teaspoons kosher salt
½ teaspoon baking soda
2 large eggs
2 cups buttermilk

Heat the oven to 425°F. Grease a cast-iron skillet with 1 tablespoon butter. In a large bowl, whisk together the cornmeal, salt, and baking soda. In a small bowl, whisk the eggs until lightly beaten and then whisk in the buttermilk. Add the wet ingredients to the dry. Whisk in the 4 tablespoons melted butter. Pour the batter into the skillet and bake until set, 15 to 20 minutes. Let cool at least 15 minutes before removing from the pan.

SWEET CORNCOB BROTH

When I make dishes involving fresh corn, I like to use the leftover cobs to make a light, summery vegetarian broth that can be used in myriad ways. I cook with it in place of water to intensify the corn flavor of grits or polenta, as the base of a soup, or in a vegetable sauté. Don't worry about measuring or peeling anything; if you are already prepping vegetables, just add them and allow the flavors to develop while you do other things in the kitchen.

About 2 quarts

1 onion, skin on, quartered
2 to 3 shallots, skin on, halved
A few garlic cloves
A few ribs celery, including leaves, roughly chopped
Mushroom stems from cleaning mushrooms
6 corncobs, kernels removed for other use
Herb stems such as parsley, tarragon, and thyme
12 black peppercorns, slightly crushed
1 tablespoon kosher salt

Put all the ingredients into a large pot and cover with 10 cups of water. Bring just to a boil over high heat, then reduce to a simmer. Cook until the broth is flavorful, at least 1 hour. Pour through a fine-mesh sieve, then chill or freeze for later use.

CORN PUDDING

This 1800s corn pudding recipe has stood the test of time with a strong emphasis on purity of ingredients and little technique. In *A Love Affair with Southern Cooking*, Jean Anderson traces its origins to the James River area of Virginia. The only adaptation I've made is roughly chopping the corn to further distribute its sweet summer flavor throughout the savory baked custard. I like to divide the batter into individual ramekins, but if you wish to feed eight people easily, double the recipe and bake in a buttered 8-inch square pan.

4 individual servings

2 tablespoons unsalted butter, plus more to prepare pans
Kernels from 2 ears corn, enough to yield 1 cup processed
1 large egg
2 tablespoons unbleached all-purpose flour
1 cup whole milk, warmed
½ teaspoon kosher salt
Pinch freshly ground black pepper
Pinch freshly grated nutmeg

Heat the oven to 325°F. Lightly butter four 5-ounce ramekins. Pulse the corn kernels in a food processor until coarse and wet, but not completely pulverized, and measure out 1 cup. Set aside. Whisk the egg in a medium bowl, and set aside.

In a medium saucepan, melt the 2 tablespoons butter over medium heat. Add the flour, whisk until smooth, and cook for 1 minute. Slowly add the warm milk, whisking constantly, and cook until thickened, about 5 minutes. Reduce the heat to medium-low. Slowly add about one-third of the hot milk mixture to the beaten egg, whisking constantly to temper. Then slowly transfer the tempered egg and milk mixture back into the saucepan, whisking all the while. With a wooden spoon or rubber spatula, stir constantly over low heat until the mixture thickens; do not allow it to boil. Remove from the heat and add the 1 cup corn, salt, pepper, and nutmeg. Divide among the ramekins.

Bring a kettle of water to a boil. Place the ramekins in a roasting pan large enough to hold them and deeper than they are. Pour hot water into the pan around the ramekins to come halfway up the sides of the cups. Bake until the pudding is set like custard—set on the sides but still creamy and slightly jiggly in the center—about 30 minutes. Serve warm.

LIGHTLY CREAMED CORN WITH SUMMER MUSHROOMS

Creamed corn is a Southern summer icon. I love it the simple, old-fashioned way, but it can sometimes be a bit heavy. Rather than encumber it with a thick, buttery roux, I prefer to lighten it with a mixture of my corncob broth, to offset the milk and cream. A hint of tarragon and some chanterelles—or whatever summer mushrooms you can gather—make this version more sophisticated.

6 to 8 servings

1 tablespoons extra virgin olive oil
1 cup loosely packed torn chanterelles, oyster mushrooms, or a mix
1 tablespoon unsalted butter
1 small shallot, minced
2 garlic cloves, minced
Kosher salt
Freshly ground black pepper
3 cups fresh corn kernels
2 tablespoons whole milk
2 tablespoons heavy cream
2 to 3 tablespoons Sweet Corncob Broth (page 131)
1 teaspoon thinly sliced fresh chives

In a medium skillet, heat the oil over high heat. Add the mushrooms and sauté them until lightly browned. Add the butter, shallot, and garlic, and season lightly with salt and pepper. Add the corn and sauté 1 minute more. Add the milk, cream, and broth, and cook until the sauce reduces by half. Taste for seasoning and add the chives just before serving.

CREAMY STONE-GROUND GRITS OR POLENTA

These days there's not a lot of difference between grits and polenta. Both are coarsely ground dried corn slow-cooked with liquid into a creamy porridge. Historically, the real difference is the type of corn. Southerners used dent corn for their milling, while Italians used flint corn, which holds its texture better. Over time the line between the two has blurred and essentially they are interchangeable. This multipurpose recipe works well with either.

6 to 8 servings

2 cups heavy cream
1 cup stone-ground grits or polenta
2 to 3 teaspoons kosher salt
4 tablespoons (½ stick) unsalted butter

In a medium saucepan over medium heat, combine 2 cups water and the cream. Add the grits or polenta and 2 teaspoons of the salt. Stir frequently with a whisk or wooden spoon, taking care that the grain does not stick to the bottom of the pan. Cook until thickened, about 30 minutes. Stir in the butter. Taste for seasoning and adjust salt if needed. If the mixture is too thick, add a little water or cream to thin. Cover and keep warm on the stove until ready to use.

CUCUMBERS

The year-round presence of cucumbers in supermarkets makes it easy for us to forget that they are a summer crop. Not only are cucumbers more flavorful when they are locally grown and in season, but our bodies tend to crave them more the hotter it is outside. The expression "cool as a cucumber" is literally accurate. Even without refrigeration, this relative of the squash and the melon maintains a temperature that can be up to twenty degrees cooler than the outside air temperature. Chinese traditional medicine prescribes eating cucumber for its cooling properties to remove heat and toxins from the body. And in our culture, chilled cucumber slices are a signature home spa treatment for tired eyes.

I take advantage of this cooling characteristic in the kitchen all summer long. Cucumbers are extremely versatile and pair well with many other summer fruits and vegetables. Besides being eaten raw and pickled, they can even be enjoyed hot. I like tossing thin slices off the mandoline into Lemon Vinaigrette (page 221) with fresh mint and serving them with grilled chicken or summer squash. These lightly pickled cucumbers are excellent with fish, or turn them into an inventive vegetable salad with squash blossoms and Cold Brine–Pickled Blackberries (page 117). Juicing cucumbers is fruitful, with a large, rewarding yield. Add other summer fruits or vegetables to the mix while your juicer is set up, and cool down quickly and healthily.

Cucumbers love warm sun while growing. They also love water. An under-irrigated cucumber plant produces an unpleasant bitter taste in the fruit. Georgia just happens to be the top cucumber-producing state. Cucumbers are originally from India, however, with a history that predates biblical times. For centuries they were prized by Roman and British aristocrats, although from the sixteenth to nineteenth centuries the cucumber's tough, bitter skin became associated with indigestion, and many Britishers came to believe it was fit only for cattle, nicknaming it "cow cumber."

It wasn't so long ago that the ubiquitous thick-skinned, dark green slicing cucumber, heavily waxed for long journeys and extended shelf life, was all you could find. Now even supermarkets devote a section to the long, thin-skinned burpless or "hothouse" cucumbers and small, unwaxed pickling cucumbers. In the summertime at farmers' markets, the options are much more varied. Cucumbers may be light green or dark green, yellow or white, or even orange. English and Armenian cucumbers have thin skins that do not need to be peeled and soft, tiny seeds that do not need to be removed. They are best eaten raw, and are not good choices for pickling. Persian cucumbers are similar to English but come in a variety of sizes. Suyo cucumbers look like long tangly melons with spiny ridges. Kirby cucumbers, also known as pickling cucumbers, are short with bumpy skins and crunchy flesh. If they are harvested young, their seeds are small and easily digested. The "salt and pepper" or yellow pickling cucumber is very similar to the Kirby but is smaller with light green flesh. Lemon cucumbers are the size and shape of tennis balls, with sweet flesh and a mottled yellow skin. They are good raw or pickled, but if grown too large develop thick skins and woody seeds. All of them are mildly sweet and refreshing, but I think the Kirby cucumbers are my favorite, as I find them to be most adaptable to any recipe.

Look for firm, unblemished cucumbers without soft spots. Unwaxed cucumbers can get slimy and turn rotten quickly. They are also susceptible to cold and will shrivel if held below forty degrees Fahrenheit. Wrap them loosely in plastic or in a dish towel and store in the vegetable bin for up to a week. Cucumbers don't freeze well at all. If you want to preserve them before they turn, it's easy to make a quick pickle that will last in the refrigerator for weeks. Because some cucumbers can be bitter if not watered regularly, be sure to taste a piece from each before moving forward with any recipe. The bitterness can be so strong that it can ruin a dish, but if detected during prep, it can be completely avoided.

HILDA'S ICEBOX PICKLES

My grandmother Hilda Duckworth always kept a big jar of these crisp, tart pickles in the refrigerator. Everyone loved them. They were so refreshing after a long road trip in the back of a hot station wagon. My cousins would head straight to the refrigerator and start shoving them into their mouths the minute they walked in the door. There is not much to them, but in this case, the sum is greater than the parts—always crisp, with bits of sweet onion. This no-cook method requires neither pickling spices nor processing. The magic happens in the refrigerator, where the pickles sit for a few days soaking up the flavorful brine. At Miller Union, we serve these at lunch every day alongside our hot and cold sandwiches.

Fills a 1-gallon jar

¼ cup kosher salt
2 teaspoons coarsely ground black pepper
4 cups distilled white vinegar
3 pounds pickling cucumbers, washed and quartered lengthwise
1 yellow onion, peeled, halved, and cut into crescents
4 garlic cloves, peeled and quartered

In a 1-gallon glass jar, combine the salt, the pepper, 4 cups water, and the vinegar, and stir briskly to dissolve the salt. Add the cucumbers, onion, and garlic. Cover and refrigerate for a minimum of 2 days. These are best enjoyed within 1 week.

SAUTÉED CUCUMBERS WITH DILL

When cooked, cucumbers turn from crisp to tender, like summer squash, but juicier and bursting with flavor in every bite. Usually I find dill overwhelming and noisy on the palate. But used judiciously, it harmonizes perfectly with the warm cucumber. These cukes are excellent with seafood and with fried squash blossoms, or spooned over creamy white beans or simmered field peas.

4 servings

2 tablespoons extra virgin olive oil
½ small Vidalia onion, cut into crescents
Kosher salt
Freshly ground black pepper
4 pickling cucumbers, peeled, halved lengthwise, and cut crosswise into ⅓-inch half-moons
Juice of ½ lemon
1 tablespoon unsalted butter
1 teaspoon finely snipped fresh dill

Put the olive oil and onion in a skillet over medium heat. Season with salt and pepper and cook until the onion is tender, about 5 minutes. Add the cucumbers; season with salt and pepper. Cook until the cucumber slices are tender-crisp, about 2 minutes. Add the lemon juice and butter. Adjust the seasoning if needed. Garnish with dill.

CUCUMBER, TOMATO, AND ONION SALAD

A traditional "summer salad" of marinated cucumber, tomato, and onion has variations throughout the South. The dressing is straight vinegar, which is typically seasoned with salt and a little granulated sugar, but I prefer the softer tone of honey instead. This salad is a refreshing and acidic counterpoint to fried chicken or catfish, but it also plays well with a team of other summer vegetables. You can regulate the sharpness of the salad by keeping track of how long it sits and tasting periodically. The longer it sits, the tangier it gets.

4 servings

1 cup apple cider vinegar
2 tablespoons honey
1 tablespoon kosher salt
½ teaspoon freshly ground black pepper
2 to 3 medium pickling cucumbers, sliced lengthwise and cut into ¼-inch crosswise pieces
1 large Vidalia onion, sliced into crescents
2 large or 3 small ripe tomatoes, cut into ½-inch dice
Fresh basil, torn into small pieces

In a nonreactive mixing bowl, whisk together the vinegar, honey, salt, and pepper. Add the cucumbers, onion, and tomatoes. Chill for 1 to 2 hours to allow the flavors to develop, stirring occasionally by turning from the bottom to the top to ensure that the vegetables are evenly "pickled." With a slotted spoon, remove the salad from the liquid and transfer to a serving dish. Toss in the torn basil.

CUCUMBER AND CRAB SALAD

Deliciously simple, fresh crab and cool crisp cucumber make an impromptu canapé that is as quick to make as it is fun to eat.

About 3 cups salad or about 40 canapés

1 pound fresh lump crabmeat
1 small cucumber, peeled, seeded, and diced to ⅛-inch thickness; plus more cucumbers, cut into round slices for serving
2 pieces Preserved Lemon (page 427), blanched and minced
Juice and zest of 1 lemon
Kosher salt
Freshly ground black pepper
1 to 2 tablespoons Homemade Mayonnaise (see page 37)
A few fresh basil leaves, sliced into small pieces

Place the crabmeat in a wide shallow container and carefully pick through to check for pieces of shell. Add the diced cucumber, preserved lemon, lemon zest, and lemon juice and season with salt and pepper. Stir in mayonnaise to the desired consistency and taste for seasoning. Adjust as needed, then chill for 30 minutes. Serve on cucumber slices and garnish with the basil.

EGGPLANT

One summer I had the good fortune of collaborating with my friends Joe Reynolds and Judith Winfrey from Love Is Love Farm and the traveling farm-centric dinner party, Outstanding in the Field. All of the produce to feed the 150 guests was selected from the farm, and since the eggplant harvest was in full swing, I decided to feature it on the menu. I had intended to grill it directly over hot coals, but since the grill was already packed with pork loins and peppers, I had to think on my feet. Resorting to sautéing it separately, I refused to serve it until the chalky, rubbery texture had dissipated. When at last it reached its proper tenderness, dinner was served and the guests were very happy with the results.

Summer vegetables usually don't need much cooking: a flash on the grill, a quick sauté, or nothing at all. Eggplant is not one of those vegetables. In its raw, or even undercooked, state, it's virtually inedible. Aside from having a texture like foam rubber, unripe eggplant can make your mouth itch, or just make you sick. When it is cooked, the tiny air pockets between its cells collapse, turning it creamy and tender and allowing its absorbent flesh to adapt to the characteristics of whatever it mingles with. Eggplant is so malleable that it takes well to just about any form of cooking: grilling, roasting, sautéing, pureeing, stewing, and frying. It mixes seductively with any full-flavored oil; pairs well with walnuts, almonds, or peanuts; and mingles effortlessly with tomato, peppers, garlic, onion, squash, and summer herbs.

Eggplant was cultivated in China at least as far back as the sixth century B.C. When eggplants were first identified, they were described as small and white, like eggs drooping from the vine, hence the origin of the name. In Europe, they were used mostly as garden ornaments until less bitter varieties were developed in the eighteenth century. Eggplant once had the nickname "apple of madness." It was long believed—like other nightshades—to contain toxins that would cause fever, epilepsy, or even insanity. Its flavor and texture are so off-putting when it is eaten raw that it could have been avoided for this reason alone. Though no longer regarded as poisonous, it does have the highest concentration of nicotine of any food, which is no surprise, since tobacco is also part of the night-shade family. The two main types of eggplant that are cultivated today come from two parts of the world.

ITALIAN EGGPLANTS: These are all globe-shaped varieties. They include the ubiquitous shiny purple-skinned ones, but they also come in an array of striking colors—pure white, white streaked with pink or purple, pink with purple and brown stripes, or pure black. The fatter, rounder varieties yield more creamy flesh when cooked and are excellent for roasting, baking, or frying.

ASIAN EGGPLANTS: The Asian eggplants include the long, thin Japanese varieties with vivid electric-purple hues; and the small, round Thai eggplants that may be speckled green or lavender, with purple and dark green variegation. Asian eggplants have a smaller flesh-to-skin ratio than the globe varieties. They tend to be a little sweeter, and cook more quickly as well. These are best suited for sautéing, grilling, or roasting.

A perfectly ripe eggplant should spring back when pressed with your thumb. It should be heavy for its size, with shiny, unblemished skin and a bright green top. Store eggplant unpeeled and unwashed either at room temperature temporarily, or in a plastic bag in the refrigerator. Because eggplants are accustomed to hot-weather growing conditions, over-chilling can cause the interior and the exterior to brown and off flavors to develop. Do not cut an eggplant until right before you plan to use it, as it deteriorates and discolors quickly once it's been cut. To reduce bit-terness, salt eggplant lightly after it has been sliced or diced, and allow the bitter juices to drain off before using.

EGGPLANT CAPONATA

Originally from Sicily, this complexly flavored side dish varies widely from region to region but always contains eggplant, vinegar, and some form of sweet. It's my favorite way to showcase eggplant's tender yet meaty texture and chameleon-like flavor. And I also love that it can be served at any temperature: cold as a relish, at room temperature, or warm as a side dish. Because it incorporates each of the five basic tastes on the tongue—bitter, sweet, salty, sour, and umami—this dish is best served with a simply prepared protein or as part of a vegetable plate.

6 to 8 servings

6 cups ¾-inch-diced eggplant (about 1 large or 3 small globe eggplants), skin on
3 teaspoons kosher salt
¼ cup plus 2 tablespoons extra virgin olive oil
1 cup ¼-inch-diced yellow onion (about 1 medium)
4 garlic cloves, peeled and thinly sliced
¼ teaspoon fresh thyme leaves
¼ teaspoon crushed red pepper flakes
2 cups ½-inch-diced ripe tomatoes (about 2 medium), juices and seeds included
¼ cup golden raisins or currants
2 tablespoons sherry vinegar
2 teaspoons honey
¼ teaspoon freshly ground black pepper
Chiffonade of fresh parsley and mint leaves for garnish

Heat the oven to 350°F. Place the eggplant in a bowl and toss with 2 teaspoons kosher salt. Transfer the eggplant to a wire rack over a pan or onto a layer of paper towels. After 30 minutes, transfer the drained eggplant back to the bowl and toss with ¼ cup olive oil. Spread the eggplant in a shallow roasting pan and cook until slightly caramelized but still intact, with a creamy, almost sticky texture on the inside, 30 to 45 minutes. (Since some pieces will cook faster than others, try a random sampling across the pan.)

Heat the remaining 2 tablespoons olive oil in a skillet over medium-low heat. Sauté the onion, garlic, thyme, and red pepper flakes with ½ teaspoon salt until tender, 8 to 10 minutes. Add the chopped tomatoes and the remaining ½ teaspoon salt and cook for 3 to 4 minutes, stirring frequently. Add the raisins, vinegar, honey, and black pepper, and stir to combine. Return to a simmer and cook 5 more minutes. Pour the sauce over the eggplant and stir to combine. Taste for seasoning and adjust salt as needed. Allow the caponata to cool and rest about 1 hour. Serve at room temperature, chilled, or reheated. Top with fresh parsley and mint.

EGGPLANT AND PEANUT BABA GHANOUSH

A lot of people say they do not like eggplant, yet they love baba ghanoush. The Middle Eastern dish of roasted charred eggplant, garlic, lemon, and sesame tahini capitalizes on eggplant's ability to take on whatever flavors it is paired with. Because it is cooked until creamy, the spongy texture that eggplant haters find so off-putting is no longer an issue. My take on baba ghanoush has a decidedly Southern accent, using peanuts instead of sesame. I brighten the flavor with sweet onion, fresh tomato, and herbs.

2½ cups

1 medium globe eggplant
1 medium tomato
2 tablespoons olive oil, plus more for serving
1 small Vidalia or other sweet onion, diced
1 garlic clove, chopped
1 teaspoon sea salt, or more to taste
½ teaspoon fresh thyme leaves
½ cup shelled roasted peanuts
Juice of 1 lemon
¼ teaspoon crushed red pepper flakes or 1 dried hot chile, chopped
1½ teaspoons fresh parsley for garnish
1½ teaspoons fresh mint for garnish
Chopped toasted peanuts for garnish

Heat the oven to 350°F. Over an open flame, under the broiler, or on a hot grill, char the outside of the eggplant and tomato evenly on all sides. Place the charred eggplant on a parchment-lined roasting pan and bake in the oven until very tender (it will collapse slightly), 30 to 40 minutes. Meanwhile, peel the skin off and roughly chop the cooled, charred tomato. Remove the roasted eggplant from the oven and let cool. Peel the charred skin off the eggplant and discard. Save the eggplant flesh, including any liquid that may come off after cooking.

In a wide skillet over medium heat, warm 2 tablespoons olive oil. Sauté the onion and garlic together with ½ teaspoon sea salt. Add the chopped tomato and thyme leaves and sauté a few minutes more. Set aside.

In a food processor, chop the peanuts. Add the eggplant and reserved liquid, tomato-onion mixture, lemon juice, red pepper flakes, and remaining salt. Puree until smooth. Taste for seasoning and adjust as necessary. Transfer to a wide serving bowl, and drizzle with more olive oil. Garnish with the parsley, mint, and chopped peanuts. Serve with warm pita, sliced cucumbers, goat's milk feta, or Roasted Tomatoes (page 238).

FIGS

Fig trees flourish in my part of the world as they do in other warm climates, and during their brief season, Southerners often feverishly pick and consume the figs as soon as they fall off the tree, or cook them in batches of preserves. My dad used to tell us about visiting his great-aunt's dairy farm in Alabama in the summertime; it had several fig trees, and he stuffed his face with so many figs that he would have a stomach-ache for the rest of the night. And then the next day he would go back for more. But my mom never had a taste for them. They appeared in our house only in the form of Fig Newtons. My first real exposure to fresh figs came during my formative restaurant years, and I have been slightly obsessed with them ever since.

Fig trees are in the genus *Ficus* and are related to mulberries, jack-fruit, and breadfruit. Their fruit has been a gourmet treat for some five thousand years. Ancient Romans regarded them as sacred. Greeks considered them a symbol of fertility and deemed it unlawful to export the highest-quality figs, reserving the best for their own personal consumption. The fig tree can live as long as a hundred years and, if untouched, can grow a hundred feet tall. Domestic trees are kept pruned to a height of about sixteen feet for ease of harvesting the fruit. Some trees have a quick, shorter season in early summer, and others a longer season in late summer and early fall. Some of this depends on variety but in some cases it's the location and exposure to direct sunlight. If you happen to have access to a fig tree, pick daily during peak season, which usually lasts a couple of weeks. Figs are ripe when they soften and begin to sag on the limb.

On one recent trip to Greece, while meandering through the open-air markets, I was captivated by the many varieties of figs available at every stall: fresh plump green ones, deep purples, small ambers, and even strings of golden figs dried in the sun. Back home we are more limited in our choices, and I always try to make the most of each. Figs come in fast, ripen all at once, and then the next thing you know, they're gone.

Here's a summary of the figs that turn up most often in this country. Jammy and deeply flavored Black Mission figs have a dark purple skin and pink flesh, and grow primarily in California, where they were originally planted by Spanish missionaries. Kadotas have a green skin and purplish flesh. Floral and slightly vegetal Brown Turkey and Celeste both have amber skin with purple tinges and are the main varieties that we tend to find in the South. Calimyrnas have greenish-yellow skin and amber flesh with honey and butterscotch tones. Adriatic figs, with their light green skin and tan flesh, are most often used for making fig bars. Though all of these types have different sizes and properties, they are essentially interchangeable.

Because they are so delicate, and don't travel well, figs are often dried either in the sun or industrially, with sulfur dioxide gas and sulfites used during the drying process to extend their life and preserve the color.

Choose figs that are richly colored, free of bruises and of milky liquid around the stem, but already soft—not mushy or moldy—as they don't ripen after picking. They should have a mildly sweet fragrance—if they smell sour they very well may be. A slightly bent stem indicates that the fig is heavy with sweet juices. Being a little wrinkled and even partially split is OK, so long as the figs are not oozing or shriveled. Figs deteriorate quickly, so plan to use them as soon as possible after picking or purchasing. If you aren't eating them right away, refrigerate uncovered, allowing them to breathe. For best flavor, let them come to room temperature before eating. Darker figs tend to last longer than the lighter-skinned varieties. Juicy and honey-sweet, fresh figs can be added to just about anything with little fuss and make a big impression. Embellish a cheese platter, a summer fruit salad, or a pizza with ham and arugula. Or make simple hors d'oeuvres with nuts, cheese, honey, and herbs.

FRESH FIG JAM WITH LEMON AND CINNAMON

In this delightfully unusual preserve, lemon, black pepper, and cinnamon marry well with fresh figs, without upstaging the fig's delicate flavor.

2 half-pint jars

1 cup sugar
1 quart fresh whole figs, the smaller figs halved and the larger figs quartered
½ teaspoon fine sea salt
Juice of 2 lemons
Zest of 1 lemon, swiped into wide strips with a vegetable peeler
1 cinammon stick
12 whole black peppercorns

In a medium saucepan over medium heat, combine sugar and 1 cup water and bring to a simmer. Add the figs, salt, and lemon juice. Simmer until the figs just begin to show signs of translucence, 15 to 20 minutes. Remove the figs from the hot syrup and set aside. Add the lemon zest, cinnamon stick, and peppercorns to the simmering syrup and reduce until it is the thickness of warm honey. Return the figs to the pan to reheat, then spoon the preserves into jars. Store covered and refrigerated for up to 6 weeks.

FIG, COUNTRY HAM, AND GOAT CHEESE SANDWICH

Inspired by Italian flavors, this open-face, knife-and-fork sandwich combines salty ham with sweet figs, creamy goat cheese, and the peppery bite of arugula. This is a lunch that is quick and easy but feels fancy.

1 serving

2 ounces soft goat cheese
1 large slice pain au levain or European sourdough, toasted
2 or 3 ripe figs
Coarse sea salt
Freshly ground black pepper
2 or 3 thin slices country ham or prosciutto
1 teaspoon freshly squeezed lemon juice
2 teaspoons extra virgin olive oil
Handful arugula

Spread the cheese onto the bread. Slice the figs into halves or quarters and then place on the cheese, pushing them in slightly to stay in place. Season the figs with salt and pepper. Place the ham on top of the figs. In a small bowl, whisk together the lemon juice, olive oil, and a pinch of salt. Add the arugula and toss to coat. Top the sandwich with the dressed arugula and serve.

MELONS

Related to cucumbers, squashes, and gourds, melons include bright yellow casabas, football-shaped canary melons, waxy multihued crenshaws, the mottled-skinned Santa Claus variety, and round orange-skinned pepinos with purple stripes. To keep it simple, I'm focusing on the three varieties that we see the most. If I do anything to melons other than slice and serve them, I like to offset their refreshing sweetness with counterpoints like salt, acid, fat, or spicy heat: a crumble of salty feta with sweet watermelon; a shaving of prosciutto or country ham with cantaloupe; a squeeze of lime and a sprinkle of cayenne with honeydew.

WATERMELON: When I was a kid, watermelon was the only melon I would eat. It was the star of our neighborhood Fourth of July parties, which typically involved a seafood boil, lots of fireworks, and a watermelon seed-spitting contest. Watermelons are believed to have originated in the Kalahari Desert of Africa. The first recorded watermelon harvest can be traced back to Egypt some five thousand years ago. From there watermelons spread to China, and by the thirteenth century they had reached Europe. The first watermelons in the United States arrived on slave ships. They are now the most popular melon in America and have become a symbol of our food culture. Watermelons are sorted into three sizes: personal (less than six pounds), icebox (six to fifteen pounds), and picnic (over fifteen pounds). Their flesh can range from vivid red to reddish pink to orange or yellow.

Some people swear that thumping a watermelon and listening for a deep thud is the best way to judge ripeness, but this is a skill that takes practice. Select a melon that is symmetrical, heavy for its size, with no dents. It is sign of ripeness for the skin of a watermelon to be slightly waxy and dull. Inspect the bottom of the melon to check its ground spot, where the melon rested while ripening. If that spot is creamy yellow, it is ripe and ready to eat. If that spot is white or light green, it is not fully ripe and should be avoided since watermelons do not ripen after they are picked from the vine. Store whole watermelons refrigerated for up to a week; store cut melon refrigerated and tightly wrapped for up to three days.

CANTALOUPE is a muskmelon with origins in Persia. It is by far the most nutritious of the melons, owing its creamsicle color to high beta-carotene levels. You can tell that cantaloupes are ripe if the color under the netted pattern of the skin has turned from green to yellowish and the blossom end has a sweet, fruity aroma. This is easier to detect if the melon is at room temperature. Cantaloupe does continue to ripen after picking, so if it needs more time, just leave it out at room temperature. Be sure to refrigerate ripe cantaloupe so it does not deteriorate too quickly.

The intricate veining pattern on the skin of cantaloupe can trap bacteria. The blade of your knife could potentially drag these bacteria from the netted skin through the fruit, causing contact contamination. To avoid this, scrub cantaloupe with warm, soapy water and a natural bristle brush, then rinse and pat dry before slicing with a clean knife on a clean surface. Discard all of the rind and refrigerate the fruit if not serving immediately. Store ripe cantaloupe in the crisper of your refrigerator for three to four days. Do not wash it until right before you plan to cut it, as the skin will absorb some of the moisture, decreasing the shelf life.

HONEYDEW is the American name for the white Antibes, a melon that was cultivated in France and Algeria centuries ago. Related more closely to the cantaloupe, honeydews are part of the muskmelon cultivar group, which includes crenshaw, casaba, Persian melon, and Armenian cucumbers. As with watermelon, look for honeydew melons that have a waxy, pale rind and feel heavy for their size. When honeydew is ripe, the aroma should be apparent when holding the whole melon up to your nose at the blossom end. As with the cantaloupe, if it's not quite ripe, let the melon sit out at room temperature until it is fragrant. Refrigerate ripe honeydew melon and store cut melon, wrapped in plastic, for up to three days.

CANTALOUPE WITH COUNTRY HAM AND MINT

Prosciutto and melon are a classic Italian combination that is simple and refreshing. Country ham stands in for the prosciutto in this Southern American rendition.

4 to 6 servings

½ cantaloupe
A few slices country ham, cut into bite-size pieces
2 tablespoons torn fresh mint leaves, basil leaves, or both
Coursely ground black pepper
Extra virgin olive oil

Scrub the outside of the cantaloupe with warm soapy water and rinse well. Cut the melon in half, stem end to blossom end. Scoop out the seeds in each half and then cover one half with plastic wrap and refrigerate for later use.

Cut the remaining half into 2-inch-wide sections radially, about 6 slices total. Then, using the tip of your knife, and following the natural curve, remove the rind and the white flesh just below it. Discard the rinds. Cut the slices of fruit in half. Arrange on a platter and lay the country ham pieces across the top. Then scatter the herbs over the platter. Season with coarsely ground black pepper and drizzle with olive oil.

HONEYDEW, SEA SALT, CAYENNE, AND LIME

In the past I avoided honeydew melons, as I found them to be cloyingly sweet. Then Laura Ramirez, a chef from Acapulco I worked with, showed me this simple trick of adding hints of salt, heat, and acid to a freshly cut honeydew, and I realized just how good it could be.

6 to 8 servings

1 honeydew melon
Coarse sea salt
Cayenne pepper
½ lime

Scrub the outside of the honeydew with warm soapy water and rinse well. Cut the melon in half, stem end to blossom end. Scoop out the seeds in each half and then cover one half with plastic wrap and refrigerate for later use.

Cut the remaining half into wedges and remove the rind. Slice the wedges into 1-inch pieces and arrange on a serving platter. Squeeze lime juice over the melon pieces and sprinkle with coarse sea salt and a tiny pinch or two of cayenne pepper.

WATERMELON SALAD WITH FETA AND GREEN TOMATO

Yearning for fresh ideas, American chefs increasingly turn to other cultures for inspiration. Watermelon and feta, a generations-old duo common in Greece and Israel, is one example of a flavor profile that has made its way into U.S. kitchens, coast to coast, and stuck. For my take, I have added ingredients close to home: green tomatoes, Vidalia onions, and sweet and hot peppers. In the heat of summer, this salad satisfies and refreshes like no other.

8 to 12 servings

2 tablespoons Vidalia onion, minced
1 small hot pepper such as serrano, seeded and minced
1 small sweet bell pepper, seeded and minced
2 tablespoons sherry vinegar
1 teaspoon local honey
¼ cup extra virgin olive oil
Sea salt
Freshly ground black pepper
1 small watermelon, flesh cut into ½-inch cubes, seeds removed
1 pint green (unripe) cherry tomatoes, halved, or 1 full-size green tomato cut into bite-size pieces
½ cup torn fresh mint leaves
1 large handful arugula
6 ounces goat's milk feta cheese

In a large bowl, combine the onion, hot and sweet peppers, vinegar, and honey. Whisk in the olive oil, and season with salt and pepper. Add the watermelon and green tomatoes to the dressing and gently toss to combine. Remove the watermelon mixture from the dressing with a slotted spoon and place on a serving platter. Add the mint and arugula to the bowl with the dressing and toss lightly to coat, then scatter the greens over the serving plate. Top with crumbled feta and a few more grindings of pepper.

PICKLED WATERMELON RIND

The pale barrier that separates the outer skin of the watermelon from the sweet red flesh inside is not the most appetizing part of the fruit. But it is indeed edible, and in fact quite delicious when cooked in a spiced syrup.

Watermelon pickles of yesteryear were loaded with sugar to compensate for the lack of sweetness in this part of the melon. In my refrigerator pickle version, I've dialed down the sweetness and cranked up the acid while retaining the traditional spice profile. Remove the tough green skin first, before cooking, but if a little of the pink flesh remains, there is no need to trim it away.

About 3 cups

2½ pounds firm watermelon rind (tough outer peel removed with a Swiss peeler), cut into 2-inch squares
1 cup freshly squeezed lime juice
¼ cup kosher salt
1 cup sugar
3 cups apple cider vinegar or Champagne vinegar
12 whole cloves
12 whole allspice berries
3 cinnamon sticks

Combine the watermelon rind, lime juice, and salt in a large nonreactive saucepan. Have 2 cups water ready, and add enough just to cover. Bring to a simmer over medium-high heat, then reduce the heat to low, maintaining the liquid just below the bubbling point. Cook, uncovered, until the rind is crisp-tender, about 1 hour. Strain and set aside to let cool.

Combine the sugar, vinegar, cloves, allspice, and cinnamon sticks in a nonreactive saucepan over medium-high heat and bring to a boil, then reduce to a simmer and cook for 10 minutes.

Remove the mixture from the heat and pour it over the cooled watermelon rind; let cool again to room temperature. Cover and refrigerate until ready to serve. The rind will keep for several weeks.

WATERMELON MARGARITA

Tequila and limes go hand in hand. Fresh watermelon juice also fits into this taste combination—especially in a glass with a salted rim. And when you consider how much juice you can get out of a watermelon, it can be a refreshingly economical way to enliven a summer party. Offer the nonalcoholic version (agua de sandia) to kids and nondrinkers. A juicer is ideal for making clear, concentrated juice, but if you don't have one, you can puree the fruit in a blender and strain it through a fine-mesh strainer. Be sure to remove as many seeds as possible before blending, to avoid a bitter taste.

1 cocktail

Ice
2 ounces tequila blanco, 100 percent agave
2½ ounces watermelon juice, about ⅓ cup
½ to 1 ounce fresh lime juice, depending on your taste
Kosher salt for the glass rim

In a cocktail shaker, combine the ice, tequila, watermelon juice, and lime juice. Shake until well chilled. Strain and pour into an ice-filled cocktail glass with a salted rim.

BIG BATCH RECIPE

12 servings

One 750-ml bottle tequila blanco, 100 percent agave
4 cups watermelon juice
½ cup freshfy squeezed lime juice, or more to taste
Kosher salt for the glass rims

Combine the tequila, watermelon juice, and lime juice in a large container and chill until ready to serve. Pour into ice-filled cocktail glasses with salted rims.

OKRA

I remember rediscovering okra as a young chef. One of the farmers who delivered our summer produce invited us to his farm for a visit. I had never seen okra growing in the field before, and was mesmerized by the sight: verdant rows of lanky stalks with broad leaves and gorgeous, hibiscus-like flowers blooming alongside ridged, finger-like pods pointing toward the sun. He clipped off a young tender pod and bit right into it, next offering me one. It was sweet and crunchy, and warm from the afternoon heat. I had only ever tried okra cooked and was stunned at how good it was raw, straight from the plant.

Until then, I had never thought much about okra beyond the traditional fried and stewed versions, which can both be either amazing or horrible depending on how they are prepared. Now it's one of my favorite summer vegetables to work with. It is incredibly versatile: crisp and sweet when raw, sumptuous and meaty when roasted or sautéed, addictive when dipped in cornmeal and deep-fried. It builds layers of flavor and texture when stewed in soups and gumbos.

A relative of cotton and hibiscus, okra is a member of the mallow family and thrives in tropical, warm, and temperate climates. Other cousins include rose of Sharon, hollyhock, and cocoa. Okra arrived on our shores from Africa on slave ships three centuries ago, and took well to the soil and sunny climate of the South. It quickly became a regional staple, prized for the natural thickening agent released from the seeds and finding its way into gumbos, stews, soups, and many other dishes. We cannot talk about okra without addressing its mucilaginous qualities. Some may call it slimy, but I prefer the term "well lubricated." In fact, my version of fried okra relies on this property as the binder for the cornmeal coating. This is what makes the outside crispy by forming a seal around the tender pod, preserving its integrity even after a dip in the hot oil.

The pods are best picked every couple of days while they are young and tender, about two to three inches long. Harvesters use pruning shears for clean cuts, and wear long sleeves and gloves; the ridged surfaces of the pods have short hairs notorious for scratching and irritating human skin.

When buying fresh okra, look for young, brightly colored pods free of bruises and dark spots. They should be tender but not soft, and no more than four inches long. There are several varieties, but the ones seen the most at farmers' markets are dark green, light green, or scarlet. There are heirloom varieties that have long elegant shapes and shorter ones with a wider girth. The scarlet or burgundy varieties tend to have more sharp angles in their cross section and are often more slender and delicate.

Raw okra may be refrigerated either in a paper bag or wrapped in a paper towel in a perforated plastic bag, for two to three days. Avoid storing okra in an airtight container; it holds up best in a "breathable" situation. It will dry or wilt if left in open-air refrigeration.

Wash okra in cool water and pat dry before using. Okra picked the same day may have the irritating prickly hairs still clinging to it, so handle with care. Avoid cooking okra in an iron, copper, or brass pot or pan, which can turn it a harmless but unappetizing-looking shade of gray. Use nonreactive stainless steel, enamel, or glass bakeware instead.

To freeze, blanch whole for one minute in boiling water, then plunge into ice-cold water. Spread out on a kitchen towel and pat dry. Then transfer to a small cookie sheet and lay flat in the freezer. When frozen solid, transfer to a freezer bag and freeze for up to nine months.

ROASTED OKRA AND SUMMER VEGETABLES

Turning on the oven and tossing in a garden variety of summer vegetables is about the easiest dinner you could possibly make. Once you have washed and chopped your way through, you're practically done. I've tried countless vegetable mixtures, but this one that features okra resonates especially with me, because it highlights okra's natural sweetness and tender texture. Serve alongside fish or chicken, or as a hearty breakfast or lunch with hot cornbread and an egg cooked sunny side up.

8 servings

1 pound okra pods, washed, capped, and halved lengthwise
1 small Vidalia (or other sweet) onion, ends trimmed and sliced into crescents
3 cups total of a variety of these items:
  Trimmed snap beans or pole beans
  Sliced summer squash
  Sweet corn kernels, cut off the cob
  Blanched field peas or butter beans
  Chopped fresh tomatoes
Kosher salt
Freshly ground black pepper
Extra virgin olive oil
Fresh basil, chopped
Fresh mint, chopped

Preheat the oven to 400°F. Combine the okra, onion, and other vegetables in a bowl. Season with salt and pepper, drizzle with olive oil, and toss well to coat. Transfer the vegetable mixture to a roasting pan or a rimmed baking sheet and spread out into a single layer. Roast until the vegetables are just tender, about 10 minutes. Toss with the herbs.

CRISPY CORNMEAL-FRIED OKRA

Fried okra is served all over the South, but not all of it is good. Often it is over-coated in breading, too soggy, salty, greasy, or even dry. Fresh-tasting, perfectly crisped fried okra relies on several things: the cornmeal grind, the way it is sliced, and a simple technique involving water and a little agitation. Rather than relying on an egg wash to make the coating adhere, I utilize the natural mucilaginous agent that the seeds expel. The hot oil crisps the cornmeal to a satisfying crunch, sealing in juiciness and flavor.

6 to 8 servings

2 pounds fresh okra, smallest size preferred, washed
½ teaspoon kosher salt
3 quarts frying oil (canola oil or peanut oil is best)
2 cups extra-fine cornmeal
5 tablespoons cornstarch
1 teaspoon fine sea salt, plus more to taste

Trim the tops off the okra and slice the okra in half lengthwise. Place the trimmed okra in a shallow dish and pour 1 cup water over it, then sprinkle with ½ teaspoon kosher salt. Lightly agitate the okra in the water and let it sit 10 to 15 minutes. While the okra is soaking, using a frying thermometer, slowly heat the oil in a Dutch oven or wide saucepan to 350°F.

In a medium bowl, whisk together the cornmeal, cornstarch, and sea salt. Pull a handful of okra from the dish and allow it to drain in your fingers a few seconds, then drop the okra slices, a few at a time, into the cornmeal mixture. Toss evenly to coat well and, using a wire-mesh strainer, remove the okra from the dredge and sift the excess dredge away, being careful not to knock off too much coating. Repeat the dredging process until all the okra is coated and ready to fry. Working in batches, carefully drop the coated okra into the hot oil and fry until crisp and golden, about 5 minutes. Do not overcrowd the pot—the hot oil could potentially spill over. Transfer the hot okra to paper towels to drain, and sprinkle with more fine sea salt. Serve immediately.

GRILLED OKRA
WITH CHILE OIL
AND CILANTRO

Southerners often combine okra with onion and tomato, but rarely this way. If you've never tasted it, grilled okra is a true revelation. The warm heat of chile oil and the smoke from wood or charcoal take this Southern icon into new territory. If the grates on your grill are widely spaced, use a vegetable grilling screen to prevent the vegetables from falling into the coals.

I especially like to serve this with Confit New Potatoes (page 220) reheated on the grill and my Pepper and Peanut Romesco (page 211).

4 servings

1 pound small okra pods, washed
1 Vidalia or other sweet onion, peeled and sliced into rings
1 pint cherry tomatoes
2 tablespoons chile oil (see below)
Kosher salt
1 small bunch cilantro, washed and stemmed

Heat the grill. Spread the okra, onion, and cherry tomatoes in a single layer on a baking sheet. Drizzle with chile oil and season with some of the salt. Place the seasoned vegetables on the hot grill. Use a vegetable grilling screen if needed. Using tongs, roll the okra and tomatoes until slightly charred and tender, and remove. Lightly char the onions on one side; then, with a spatula, turn and lightly char the other side. Season with more salt, garnish with cilantro leaves, and serve.

CHILE OIL

1 cup

1 tablespoon crushed red pepper flakes
1 cup canola oil

In a saucepan, combine the red pepper flakes and canola oil, and place on medium heat. When the pepper flakes begin to sizzle and bubble, immediately remove the pan from the heat. Cool, transfer to an airtight container, and refrigerate for at least 24 hours to maximize flavor. Strain out the chile flakes before using. Chile oil keeps for several months refrigerated.

PEACHES AND PLUMS

Stone fruits, the succulent tree fruits in the rose family, have some common traits: thin skin, juicy flesh, and an inedible pit in the center. Apricots, cherries, nectarines, peaches, plums, and pluots all fall into this category, but because my focus is regional cuisine, I work mostly with the peaches and plums that are available in my area. Peaches were first introduced to Georgia in the 1700s and took well to the sand and clay soil and warm climate. Plums are predominantly a West Coast fruit, but we have several varieties that thrive in the Southeast. The plums that grow here are relatively small, ripen quickly, and have a wonderful tartness.

PEACHES: Of all the stone fruits, the peach is the most prevalent in Georgia. When the first local peaches start appearing in farmers' markets, it's a cause for celebration. My local community market has a "peach jam festival" in July, with a cobbler contest and lots of peach-themed fun. Georgia earned its designation "Peach State" shortly after Raphael Moses, from Columbus, Georgia, began shipping peaches outside the state in Champagne baskets in the 1850s. The peach is thought to have originated in China and then passed through Persia to Europe before Spanish explorers brought it to America in the sixteenth century. By the mid-1700s the Cherokee were cultivating them, and in the 1920s production reached an all-time high of eight million bushels.

Most peaches are in one of two categories: clingstone, in which the fruit is attached to the pit; and freestone, in which the fruit separates easily from the pit. Clingstones are soft-textured and tend to be sweeter and juicier than freestones, the preferred fruit for canning and preserving. Freestones tend to be larger, firmer, and less juicy.

Peaches are available in the hottest months of the year. Buy organic, unsprayed peaches if possible, as the commercial crops are heavily sprayed against pests. If peaches are bruised on the outside, simply cut away the bruised areas and salvage the rest. The center of the pit is considered poisonous.

Underripe peaches can be cooked or pickled—whole or sliced. But if you want to ripen them, store them in a single layer at room temperature, stem side down, until ripened. To speed the ripening, wrap them in a paper bag and check once a day. The gases that build up can make them ripen quickly. When you are prepping ripe peaches, they will quickly turn brown from exposure to air. You can slow down this process by acidulating them—that is, by coating them with an acidic solution. I prefer lemon juice or lightly flavored white wine vinegar, mixed with water, as either is light enough to still let the flavor of the peach shine through.

PLUMS: Like all members of the genus *Prunus*, plums are considered drupes, which have a hard stone pit surrounding their seeds. Dried plums are called prunes. Mature plum fruit often has a dusty-white coating that gives it a glaucous appearance. This is known as "wax bloom." The most common plums are the prune types, purplish-blue ovals with meaty flesh. Plum-apricot hybrids, known as pluots, are generally sweeter than plums and more complex in aroma. There are also the minor plums, which include the English damson, a clingstone prized for preserves; and the sloe, an astringent fruit that is steeped in gin to make sloe gin.

Plums are classified into six general categories—Japanese, American, damson, ornamental, wild, and European/garden—whose size, shape, and colors vary. Although usually round, plums can also be oval or heart-shaped. The skins of plums can be red, purple, blue-black, green, yellow, or amber, while their flesh comes in hues such as yellow, green, pink, and orange. Plums are best enjoyed firm-ripe and not soft. Plums that are not yet ripe can be left at room temperature, but they ripen quickly and should be transferred to the refrigerator when fully ripe. Avoid buying plums that are excessively hard, as they will be immature and will probably not develop a good taste and texture profile. Plums soften and become more aromatic as they ripen.

WHISKEYED PEACH SHORTCAKES

Firm peach slices will hold their shape even when they are doused in sugar and whiskey and put to a flame. They're delicious on their own, over ice cream, or in this case with sweetened crème fraîche spooned over homemade shortcakes. If you plan to make your own crème fraîche, you'll need to start it a day or two in advance.

8 to 12 servings

2 tablespoons unsalted butter
4 firm-ripe (slightly hard) peaches, peeled and cut into 1-inch pieces
Juice of 1 lemon
½ cup whiskey or bourbon
½ cup sugar
½ teaspoon kosher salt
1 vanilla bean, split, or ½ teaspoon vanilla extract
1 recipe Whipped Sweetened Crème Fraîche (see recipe)
1 recipe Shortcakes (see recipe)

Make the whiskeyed peaches: In a large skillet over high heat, melt the butter until foamy. Add the peaches, lemon juice, whiskey, sugar, salt, and vanilla and sauté, stirring to prevent burning, until the peaches are tender, 5 to 10 minutes, depending on their initial firmness. Remove from the heat and let cool. (You should have about 3 cups.) Make the sweetened crème fraîche.

To assemble: Split the shortcakes in half and place the bottoms, cut side up, on each plate. Spoon a large dollop of the sweetened crème fraîche onto each half, then layer a scant ⅓ cup peach mixture and some of the syrup onto each half. Layer with more sweetened crème fraîche and then set the other halves on top.

SHORTCAKES

8 to 12 shortcakes

2½ cups unbleached all-purpose flour
1 tablespoon baking powder
⅓ cup granulated sugar
1 teaspoon fine sea salt
¾ cup (1½ sticks) cold unsalted butter, cut into 1-inch pieces
¾ cup half-and-half, plus more as needed
2 egg yolks
1 whole egg plus 1 tablespoon water, whisked together to make an egg wash
¼ cup turbinado sugar

Heat the oven to 475°F. In a mixing bowl, combine the flour, baking powder, granulated sugar, and salt. Add the butter to the dry ingredients and work the mixture between your thumbs and fingers to stretch the butter into flat pieces. Leave a few larger chunks of cold butter in the flour mixture. Start by adding ¾ cup half-and-half, and stir it into the flour mixture with a large spoon. If the mixture is too dry, add a little more half-and-half until it holds together. Do not overmix.

Turn the dough out onto a lightly floured surface, and gently knead—just two to three turns—and form into a ball. Pat the dough ball down to create a flat surface. With a lightly floured rolling pin, roll the dough out to 1 inch thick. With the tines of a fork dipped in dry flour, pierce the dough about every inch, making sure to pierce through to the bottom of the dough, to create holes for steam to escape. Using a pastry brush, lightly coat the surface of the rolled-out dough with the egg wash, then sprinkle the turbinado sugar across the top evenly. Using a 3-inch biscuit cutter, cut out the shortcakes with a deliberate vertical push and then gently remove from the cutter. Place shortcakes side by side on a parchment-lined baking sheet, with edges touching. Use scraps of dough to fill in any large gaps between shortcakes; this helps the cakes hold their shape.

Bake until the cakes are golden brown and spring back when lightly touched, 10 to 12 minutes. Let cool 5 minutes, then transfer to a wire rack to cool completely.

WHIPPED SWEETENED CRÈME FRAÎCHE

About 2 cups

¼ cup heavy cream, plus more if needed
3 tablespoons granulated sugar
1 cup Crème Fraîche (see recipe)

Whisk the heavy cream and sugar to combine. Add the crème fraîche and whisk rapidly until it tightens up to whipped cream consistency with soft peaks, 1 to 2 minutes. If the mixture gets overwhipped, fold in a little more cream to thin it out.

CRÈME FRAÎCHE

Crème fraîche is easy. Don't be afraid to leave this dairy mixture out at room temperature overnight. The buttermilk cultures the cream with good bacteria until it thickens and that's all there is to it.

2 cups

2 cups heavy cream
2 tablespoons buttermilk

Combine the cream and buttermilk in a shallow container that holds the liquid at a depth of 1 to 2 inches. Cover the container with a lid or plastic wrap and let sit at room temperature overnight. Refrigerate when thickened.

Variation: When we made this dessert for the photo shoot, recipe tester Deborah Geering layered the extra shortcake halves, peaches and their juices, and whipped crème fraîche in a casserole dish like a summer pudding.

CHAI-SPICED PEACH AND BUTTERMILK LASSI

I often like to start my day with a smoothie, using the summer fruits that I've frozen when they are at their peak. Here, I have drawn inspiration from the classic Indian drink, substituting peaches for mangoes and buttermilk for yogurt. Rather than pulling out the usual chai spices—cardamom, cinnamon, clove, ginger, and pepper—I simply add a spoonful of dried chai tea, which includes all of those spices plus black tea leaves, adding an elusive hint of tannin.

2 servings

2 cups frozen sliced peaches (from about 3 peaches)
2 cups chilled buttermilk
¼ teaspoon fine sea salt
1 tablespoon honey
1 tablespoon chai-spiced tea leaves (about 1 tea bag)

Combine everything in a blender and blend until smooth.

GRILLED PEACH SALSA

More often than not, peaches that aren't eaten out of hand wind up in a dessert or another sweet application. Here's what happens when this fruit meets fire. The smoke from the grill and heat from the chiles add layers of flavor that make an especially nice match for grilled pork or fish tacos.

3½ cups

4 firm-ripe freestone peaches
Olive oil
Salt and pepper
1 small sweet yellow onion, diced small
1 hot serrano or jalapeño chile, minced (seeds removed if desired to tame the heat)
Juice of 1 lime
2 tablespoons chopped fresh cilantro or 1 tablespoon each cilantro and basil, chopped

Preheat the grill. Peel the peaches and then cut into halves, removing the pit. Coat lightly with olive oil, salt, and pepper, and place on the hot grill, cut side down. Turn over once and allow to warm through on both sides. Remove from the heat and allow to cool. Cut the peaches into rough dice and then place in a bowl and combine with the onion, chile, lime, and herbs. Season to taste with additional salt.

PICKLED PLUMS

This recipe is made in the style of pickled peaches, but without the sweet, syrupy brine that most traditional Southern pickled peaches fall into. I've taken some liberties with the spices for this variation with plums. Because the skin of the plum is thin and smooth, there's no need to peel. To keep the fruit from turning mushy, I never process these in a water bath. Instead I just pour the hot brine over the top for a refrigerator pickle. I serve these to counterbalance the richness of fatty items like confit duck leg or a double cream cheese.

1 quart

5 to 6 firm-ripe plums, about 1 pound
1 cup Champagne vinegar
¼ cup sugar
1 tablespoon kosher salt
1 teaspoon each coriander seed, juniper berries, allspice berries, and black
   peppercorns
4 green cardamom pods
4 whole cloves
1 star anise pod

Cut the plums into quarters, removing and discarding each pit and any pit fragments that may cling to the fruit. In a small saucepan over high heat, bring to a boil 1 cup of water and the vinegar, sugar, and salt. In a 1-quart jar, combine the plums, coriander, juniper, allspice, peppercorns, cardamom, cloves, and star anise. Pour the hot vinegar brine into the jar to cover the plums. Refrigerate for a minimum of 1 day before serving. Store, covered and refrigerated, for up to 4 weeks.

PLUM CLAFOUTIS

The joy of this simple dessert is that it is even better at room temperature, so you can make it in advance with ease. Be sure to pull it from the oven when the egg mixture is just set, so that the luscious cooked plum texture can meld perfectly with the batter. Think of it as a thick fruit pancake cooked effortlessly in the oven while you do other things.

6 servings

1 tablespoon unsalted butter
6 to 8 medium plums
⅔ cup granulated sugar
4 eggs
½ cup unbleached all-purpose flour
¼ teaspoon fine sea salt
1½ cups whole milk
1 tablespoon vanilla extract
Confectioners' sugar

Heat the oven to 350°F. Butter a cast-iron skillet and set aside. Trim the plums into wedges that are ¼ inch wide on the skin side of the cut. Toss the plums with ⅓ cup of the granulated sugar, and arrange them evenly in the skillet and set aside. In a medium bowl, whisk the eggs with the remaining ⅓ cup sugar, flour, and salt. Whisk in the milk and vanilla. Pour the batter into the skillet, and place on the center rack in the oven. Bake just until set, about 1 hour. When cooled, remove from the skillet and slice into wedges. Dust with confectioners' sugar before serving.

PEAS AND BEANS

Field peas and green beans—or snap beans—are essential to the Southern table. Both are legumes, but all are distant relatives of a bean that originated in Peru. Migrating Native tribes spread them throughout South and Central America, and Spanish explorers of the sixteenth century consequently discovered them on voyages to the New World and took them back to Europe.

FIELD PEAS: Not so very long ago, field peas had to be shelled by hand. Shelling was incredibly time-consuming, but Southerners often looked upon it as more of a ritual than a chore. On visits to my grandmother's house when I was a child, we would sit on her front porch in the afternoon, splitting open pods and dumping their contents into a bowl while swapping family stories.

"Field peas" is a colloquial term for fresh-shelled peas or beans with an inedible pod. No vegetable illustrates the terroir or the history of the South more than field peas. These varieties are the result of highly local seed saving, long before the practice came into vogue. They go by folksy names like zippers, lady peas, crowders, blackeyes, pink-eyes, rattlesnakes, Red Rippers, Dixie Lees, Old Timers, whippoorwills, butter beans, and butter peas, to name a few. Field peas have always been a staple of the Southern diet, surpassed only by corn, but before the Civil War they were considered poor folks' food only. The Union general Sherman changed that attitude when he and his troops charged through the region, slaughtering livestock and burning down storehouses. They didn't bother the field peas, though, assuming those were feed for livestock and slaves. Aristocratic Southerners who had once looked down upon them now ate them to keep from starving, and in time came to revere them.

Field peas are similar in taste and texture, though each has its own distinction. Brown and white speckled butter beans have a starchy, creamy texture and an earthy, nutty flavor. Crowders—so named because they are crowded so close together in the pod that they square off as they grow—are prized for their hearty flavor and rich, dark pot likker. Pink-eyed peas have a colorful purple hull and a cleaner taste than their blackeyed cousins. "Butter beans"—the colloquial name for baby green lima beans—have a high starch content and take on a buttery texture when cooked. Lady peas, the most elegant and petite of the cream peas, are sweeter than other field peas and produce a light, clear pot likker.

All field peas and beans freeze well. Just blanch the washed peas in salted boiling water until tender, drain, and cool immediately in salted ice water. Drain well and then transfer to a container with a lid or resealable plastic freezer bags, removing as much air as possible. Seal, and freeze for up to six months.

SNAP BEANS: Often called green beans, these have edible pods and may also come in shades of yellow, purple, and red. Common varieties include wax beans, pole beans, and filet beans. Wax beans are milder and waxier-textured versions of green beans with round pods. Pole beans such as Romanos have flat pods and grow long vines that must be supported by trellises. The filet bean, also called haricot vert, which means "green bean" in French, is a tiny variety that is sought-after for its sweetness and tenderness.

Many varieties contain strings that run up the seam of the bean, sometimes on both sides, and must be removed before cooking. Snap off the stem end and pull it to one side. Since pole beans tend to be stringier, I break them into one-inch pieces, checking for strings at each tear.

Choose beans that are smooth and slender, with a bright color, firm texture, and no bulging seeds, which can indicate that they were harvested too late. They'll keep at least several days in a plastic bag in the refrigerator. Make sure the skin is taut and crisp looking. Old beans have leathery loose skin, and they are sometimes limp. If you break a bean in half and hear the signature snap, the bean is fresh.

FIELD PEA, SNAP BEAN, AND TOMATO SALAD

Essentially, this is a modern version of a three-bean salad. Nutty field peas, creamy butter beans, and grassy snap beans are tossed in a tangy vinaigrette punctuated with sweet cherry tomatoes and herbs.

4 to 6 servings

1 cup field peas, blanched (page 193)
1 cup butter beans, blanched (page 193)
1 cup snap beans cut into 1-inch pieces, blanched (page 193)
1 cup halved cherry tomatoes
2 tablespoons Sherry Vinaigrette (see recipe)
1 tablespoon chopped fresh mint and basil combined
Kosher salt

In a serving bowl, combine the blanched field peas, butter beans, and snap beans, and the tomatoes. Drizzle with the vinaigrette, sprinkle with the herbs, and toss to lightly coat. Season to taste with salt.

SHERRY VINAIGRETTE

About 1 cup

6 tablespoons sherry vinegar
2 tablespoons amontillado sherry
4 garlic cloves, halved
1½ teaspoons kosher salt
2 teaspoons Dijon mustard
Black pepper, 10 turns from a pepper mill
¾ cup extra virgin olive oil

In a medium bowl, combine the sherry vinegar, sherry, and garlic and marinate for 20 minutes. With a slotted spoon, remove and discard the garlic, then whisk in the salt, mustard, and pepper. Slowly drizzle in the olive oil while whisking, and continue to whisk until emulsified. Store covered and refrigerated for up to 2 weeks.

SLOW-SIMMERED FIELD PEAS

This is how most Southerners cook field peas, and for good reason. The flavor develops slowly in the pot to create a rich broth that we call pot likker. There is so much deep flavor in these broths that they are often sopped up with cornbread and never drained or discarded. I add fennel bulb, celery, and fresh thyme to my field peas to increase the produce content and add complexity to this one-pot wonder.

6 to 8 servings

4 cups fresh shelled field peas (lady peas, pinkeyed peas, blackeyed peas, crowder peas, zipper peas, or a mix)
3 tablespoons extra virgin olive oil
½ cup finely diced (⅛-inch) yellow onion
½ cup finely diced celery
½ cup finely diced fennel bulb
Kosher salt
Freshly ground black pepper
1 thick slice country ham or 1 small piece of smoked ham hock
1 sprig fresh thyme

Place the peas in a large pot, cover with water, and agitate them gently. Pull them out in small handfuls and check for blemishes or debris. Set the washed peas aside.

In a large saucepan, heat the oil over medium heat. Add the onion, celery, and fennel; season with a little salt and pepper; and sauté until translucent, about 5 minutes. Add the ham, peas, and thyme, and then add water to cover by 1 inch. Simmer on low heat until the peas are tender, skimming all the while, 45 to 60 minutes.

GREEN BEANS, ROASTED PEPPER, AND POTATO SALAD

Vibrant, blanched green beans need little embellishment, but when I want to dress them up, I might turn to the flavors of a niçoise salad for inspiration. This vegetable ensemble is both hearty and light. A scattering of green picholine olives or some sliced good-quality tuna is welcome in the mix.

6 servings

½ pound new potatoes
½ cup apple cider vinegar
¼ cup kosher salt
1 anchovy fillet
Juice and zest of 1 lemon
Juice and zest of 1 orange
1 small shallot, minced
¼ cup parsley leaves, roughly chopped
3 tablespoons extra virgin olive oil
2 roasted red or yellow bell peppers, cleaned and seeded, reserving any juice from roasting (page 206)
2 cups blanched green beans, filet beans, wax beans, or a mix (page 193)

Place the potatoes in a small saucepan and cover with cold water by 2 inches. Add the vinegar and salt to the water and place over medium-high heat. Cook until the potatoes are just tender, about 20 minutes, then drain well in a colander and set aside. In a small bowl, mash the anchovy fillet with the back of a fork. Make the dressing by adding the citrus juices and zest, shallot, chopped parsley, and olive oil to the bowl and whisk to combine. Slice the potatoes into quarters while still warm and toss with the dressing. Slice the roasted peppers into thin strips, about the same size as the green beans. Toss the green beans and peppers together, including any juice from roasting the peppers, then add to the potato mixture and toss to combine. Taste for seasoning and adjust as needed. Serve at room temperature.

POLE BEANS IN EGGPLANT-PEPPER BROTH

When I was growing up, the only way I had ever eaten pole beans was the way my grandmother made them, simmered with onions and fatback. Much later, I toyed with the idea of cooking these summertime beans in a heady mix of roasted eggplant, peppers, and tomato. This complexly flavored backdrop became my new favorite way to show off the meaty broad bean's best attributes. If you like, add some cooked farro or wheat berries to make it a more filling entrée.

8 servings

1 large or 2 small globe eggplants
1 red bell pepper
1 ripe beefsteak tomato

2 tablespoons extra virgin olive oil, plus additional for garnish
1 tablespoon bacon fat (or more olive oil)
1 small onion, roughly chopped
1 shallot, chopped
2 garlic cloves, sliced
1 small hot chile, seeded and roughly chopped
1 teaspoon fresh thyme leaves
½ teaspoon smoked paprika
Salt and pepper
1 quart chicken or vegetable stock, warmed
2 pounds pole beans, stringed and snapped in half
Chopped parsley, basil, and mint for garnish

Heat the oven to 375°F. Prick the eggplant with the tip of a knife and place on a baking pan. Roast until partially collapsed, 30 to 40 minutes. Place the pepper and tomato in a separate baking dish, brush lightly with some of the 2 tablespoons olive oil, and roast until the skin splits on the tomato and lightly browns on the pepper, 15 to 20 minutes. Remove the vegetables from the oven and allow to cool until they can be handled.

Hold the tomato over a strainer set in a bowl to catch the juice, and peel off the skin. Cut the peeled tomato into a few large pieces, removing the core, and set aside. Hold the pepper over the strainer, remove the skin and seeds, and roughly chop the cleaned pepper. Peel the skin from the cooked eggplant and combine all, including the reserved juices from the tomato and pepper.

In a medium saucepan or soup pot, heat the remainder of the 2 tablespons olive oil and the bacon fat over medium heat. Add the onion, shallot, garlic, chile, thyme, and paprika, and sprinkle with a little salt and pepper. Sauté until the onion is soft, about 5 minutes. Add the eggplant, pepper, and tomato mixture. Cook 2 to 3 minutes, then add enough warmed stock to cover the vegetables. Bring to a simmer; taste for seasoning.

Puree the sauce in a blender, in batches if needed, covering the lid with a towel to prevent splatters. Return to the pot, bring to a simmer, and taste for seasoning. Add the trimmed pole beans and simmer until they are tender, 15 to 25 minutes depending on the variety. Divide among bowls and garnish each serving with a sprinkling of chopped parsley, basil, and mint, and a drizzle of additional olive oil. Serve with warm crusty bread.

PEPPERS

There was what seemed to be a never-ending trend of roasted red pepper dishes in the 1980s and 1990s. So much so that, to distinguish themselves, many accomplished chefs avoided featuring peppers on their menus. Now it appears that the pepper is in full swing again. With the diversity and range of varieties that are available now, peppers are being explored in a way that feels more respectful of their worth.

Sweet peppers and hot chile peppers are all members of the genus *Capsicum*. Though available year-round and shipped in from other regions to supermarkets, they flourish locally in late summer and early fall. As different as they are from three other members of the nightshade family—potatoes, tomatoes, and eggplant—they are highly compatible with each of these.

SWEET PEPPERS: These range from large to miniature and from squat to long and thin; can be tapered: and can be green, red, orange, purple, or yellow. Bell peppers are the most commonly used and the largest of the peppers, with a round shape that is good for stuffing, roasting, or slicing raw. Green bell peppers are merely underripe and have a grassy, slightly bitter taste. I find that they are better for cooking than eating raw. If left on the vine, they will fully mature and change color. To roast sweet peppers, coat them with olive oil and place in a hot oven. Cook until they are slightly deflated and the skins are lightly browned. Place them in a bowl and cover them to steam and finish cooking. When cool, peel away the skin and separate the flesh from the seeds. I always do this over a bowl to catch any flavorful juices and then use the juices along with the roasted peppers. Some people have a problem eating raw peppers, but it is usually the undigestible skin that causes this problem, The skin can be easily removed after cooking if desired.

HOT PEPPERS: Capsaicin is the naturally occurring chemical that gives hot peppers their heat. The plant produces it according to its genetic design but is also affected by external conditions. Look at desert-climate peppers, for instance. The temperature variance can be up to forty degrees, with hot days and cool nights. This type of change causes stress in the plant as it tries to stabilize with the changes. The plant produces capsaicin, which is stored in the fruit, or the pepper. The largest concentration of this agent is in the ribs and seeds. There are general guidelines for hot peppers' heat, but you cannot really tell how hot a pepper will be until you try it. A trick that I use is to slice off the top and touch the tip of my finger to the exposed seeds and ribs. Then I touch my finger to my lip to test for heat. This can help you determine how much or little to use, or if you prefer to remove the seeds or not. Working with hot peppers can be painful if you're not careful. If you have latex gloves, it's best to wear them when slicing hot peppers. If you don't, try to avoid touching the seeds or inner flesh and do not touch your face, eyes, or other sensitive body parts. After cutting, wash your hands, cutting board, and knife.

Cayenne pepper is prevalent in the South and is often dried and ground to be used as a spice. It is light green when underripe and a dark, glossy red when ripe. The dark green jalapeño pepper is common in Mexico and North America, and ranges from mild to extra hot. Serrano peppers are small, smooth, and light green with a compact seed pocket, and they pack a punch. Poblano, cubanelle, and banana peppers are all generally mild but with some heat, and have a long tapered shape. Some of the hottest known to man are the ghost pepper, Thai chiles, the Scotch bonnet, and the habanero. Padron peppers are a mild, small green chile, but one in every ten is a shocker, as it may be hot without warning.

Choose peppers with firm, glossy skin, free of wrinkles and blemishes. Peppers are nonporous, so they do not need to be covered, but they should be refrigerated to keep them firm, and should be used within a week.

HOT SAUCE

Most people purchase bottled hot sauce, but in fact it is incredibly easy to make at home and does not take too much time. My favorite peppers for this particular recipe are Nardello (a sweet Italian frying pepper named for the family who saved it from disappearing) and cayenne. If you use these, you'll end up with a sauce that looks and tastes almost identical to sriracha, but you can use any combination of sweet and hot. If you can't stand the heat, there's no need to get out of the kitchen; just use more sweet peppers than hot.

3 cups

½ pound fresh whole cayenne peppers
½ pound fresh whole Nardello, pimiento, or other sweet peppers
1 small onion, roughly chopped
2 garlic cloves, sliced
1 to 1½ cups apple cider vinegar
1 tablespoon kosher salt
1 tablespoon sugar

Wearing vinyl or latex gloves, roughly slice the cayenne peppers, removing the stems but including the seeds. Roughly slice the Nardello peppers, removing the stems and as many hard seeds as possible. Place the peppers in a saucepan with the onion and garlic. Add enough cider vinegar to just come to the top of the peppers. Add the salt and sugar. Bring the mixture to a simmer and cook until the peppers are tender, 15 to 20 minutes. If you want a smooth sauce, puree the mixture, in small batches, in a blender. If you prefer a sauce with a little texture, pulse the mixture in batches in a food processor. Store in the refrigerator. covered, for up to 3 months.

HOT PEPPER VINEGAR

This condiment is a staple in the South. In older eating places, you may find it just sitting out on the table. Folks put it on everything: greens, cornbread, field peas, fried fish. It gets full-flavored with age and can be stored at room temperature or refrigerated. This recipe is a sketch, as it can be made in any size batch.

Wash and pick over hot peppers; an assortment is best. Place the peppers in a clean jar. Meanwhile, heat enough vinegar to just cover them, and add some salt to your taste. Distilled vinegar and apple cider vinegar are traditional, but you can use any kind of light-flavored vinegar. When the seasoned vinegar comes to a boil, remove it from the heat and pour it into the jar of peppers. To seal and put up for later use, be sure to leave ¼ inch of headspace at the top of the jar, wipe the edges of the lip of the jar, and place a clean lid on top. Screw on the ring to hold the lid in place and turn the jar upside down for 5 minutes, then turn right side up again. Store in a cool dry place until ready to use.

PEPPER AND PEANUT ROMESCO

In Spain, romesco—a zesty pepper sauce—is usually made with almonds, pine nuts, or hazelnuts. To adapt it to my region, I incorporate fresh peanuts into a blend of their seasonal counterparts: sweet and hot peppers and ripe tomatoes, the riper the better. The bread can be omitted for a gluten-free version, but the sauce will be thinner as a result. Serve this with Grilled Okra with Chile Oil and Cilantro (page 174) or Confit New Potatoes (page 220).

2 cups

1 cup raw blanched peanuts (see instructions for blanching field peas, page 193)
1 large slice stale bread, toasted and cut into cubes, about ½ cup
1 medium tomato, roughly chopped
2 medium sweet peppers, seeded and roughly chopped
½ medium red onion, roughly chopped
2 garlic cloves, halved
1 small hot pepper, halved and seeded
1 tablespoon olive oil
½ teaspoon kosher salt
⅛ teaspoon freshly ground black pepper
1 to 2 tablespoons sherry vinegar

Heat the oven to 400°F. Spread the peanuts in a single layer on a rimmed baking sheet. Bake until golden and aromatic, about 10 minutes. Remove and transfer to a bowl to cool. In a mixing bowl, toss the bread cubes, tomato, sweet peppers, onion, garlic, and hot pepper with the olive oil, salt, and black pepper. Spread on the baking sheet. Roast until the vegetables are soft, about 10 minutes. Put the roasted peanuts and bread mixture, including any pan juices, into a blender. Add the sherry vinegar and process to combine. If you prefer a more rustic consistency, blend it a little less or use a food processor instead. Taste and adjust seasonings.

ROASTED STUFFED PEPPERS

The bitter grassy flavor of unripe green bell peppers is perfect in the Cajun or Creole mirepoix called "holy trinity," which also includes onion and celery. For the main ingredient, however, I lean toward ripe sweet peppers. If you can get a variety of colors, it makes for a beautiful presentation. I've replaced the traditional ground beef filling with whole grains, feta, and cherry tomatoes. Because these are halved and cooked open-face, it's important to keep them covered and baste a few times so that the filling does not dry out.

8 servings

3 cups cooked grain (farro, quinoa, or bulgur wheat)
1 cup halved cherry tomatoes
¼ cup extra virgin olive oil, plus more for drizzling
1 quart vegetable stock
4 large evenly shaped ripe bell peppers, cut in half lengthwise, stem on, membrane
  and seeds removed
¼ cup goat's milk feta
1 tablespoon each chopped fresh parsley and basil

Preheat the oven to 400°F. In a large bowl, combine the cooked grain, tomatoes, and olive oil. Add enough vegetable stock to make a very moist mixture. Fill the pepper halves and place in a baking dish large enough to hold them snugly. Drizzle with olive oil. Pour about ¼ inch of vegetable stock into the dish. Cover with parchment paper and tightly seal with aluminum foil. Bake until the peppers are tender, about 1 hour. Every 15 minutes during baking, remove the covering, baste the peppers with the pan juices, and re-cover.

When the peppers are tender, remove the cover. Sprinkle each pepper with a little crumbled feta and another drizzle of olive oil. Return to the oven to lightly brown the feta, 5 to 10 minutes. To serve, baste the peppers a final time with the cooking liquid. Transfer to plates and garnish with the chopped herbs.

POTATOES

First cultivated in the Andes, potatoes went on to take root in all inhabited continents, and have since become the most widely consumed of all vegetables. They are the fifth most important crop on the globe, after wheat, corn, rice, and sugarcane. Though there are thousands of varieties, in the United States the potato market is dominated by a few predictable or genetically modified species that are generally consumed in the form of salty fried chips or french fries, giving this underground dweller a junky reputation. In its unadulterated state, the potato is actually quite nutritious, providing a good source of vitamin C and an abundance of potassium. Some heirloom potatoes with deeply colored pink, blue, purple, or red flesh have even higher levels of nutrients than their pale-colored cousins. These heirlooms had nearly disappeared, but today we are seeing a resurgence of them as chefs and consumers alike seek out interesting new flavors and varieties in the vegetable kingdom.

When I realized this nightshade was a summer shoulder-season crop, I have to admit, I was perplexed. I had always thought of potatoes as rib-sticking cold weather food. Yes, potatoes are abundant year-round and we may crave them in the wintertime, but fully mature potatoes are harvested in the milder summer months and are then dried or cured for long-term storage, much like onions, garlic, or sweet potatoes.

After a lot of research, I realized that attempting to categorize all the types of potatoes would be more than a little confusing. There are no clear definitions, nor is there a directory, to simply sum up this vegetable. Potatoes are categorized not only by size, shape, and even age, but also by texture. I find texture to be the best approach.

WAXY potatoes are generally new potatoes, which are not a variety at all but simply a baby version of any potato that is harvested early to make room for the rest of the crop to mature. These thin-skinned potatoes are usually sweeter, lighter in texture, and more flavorful than their older siblings, because their sugars have not fully developed into starch.

Consequently, in the kitchen they require different treatment from the high-starch potatoes that tend to fall apart after cooking. Because these young potatoes stay firm and hold their shape, they are ideal choices for serving cooked in salads, roasted or presented in any way that displays their natural form.

STARCHY potatoes, which include the Idaho and russet varieties, are the type that we are most familiar with. These are the potatoes that we see year-round, and they have many applications, but they are not the focus here.

ALL-PURPOSE potatoes fall into a "somewhere in between" category: part waxy and part starchy. Yukon Gold is a classic example of an all-purpose potato. This extremely versatile hybrid, developed in the mid-1960s, straddles the line between sweet, firm new potatoes and creamy, dense russets, so it is ideal for just about any application. The fingerling potato, which grows to a small, elongated shape like a finger, also fits into this category. Though similar to new potatoes in size, fingerlings have a flavor and texture closer to a mature potato, with a higher density and starch content.

Regardless of their texture, size, or age, choose potatoes that have a smooth skin, with no green patches or blemishes and few eyes. Discolored spots can taste bitter or be a sign of disease or decay and should be removed. Potatoes are remarkable at reproducing themselves and partner especially well with sweet corn, sunflowers, or trellised tomatoes in the field. As temperatures rise, the tall crops nearby provide cooling shade for the potatoes; this is a planting practice that has been observed in South America for thousands of years.

The first photograph in this section shows a full-size russet potato alongside freshly dug farmers' market new potatoes and fingerlings to give a sense of scale and context.

CONFIT NEW POTATOES

This decadent method for cooking new potatoes, submerged in richly flavored olive oil, yields forkfuls of tender, creamy, satisfying starch. They are delicious straight out of the pan, but can be even better crisped in a hot skillet or caramelized on a charcoal grill after cooking. The large amount of olive oil called for is drained off after cooking and can be reused several times thereafter.

4 servings

1½ pounds new potatoes, rinsed, dried, and halved if large
Kosher salt and freshly ground black pepper
4 garlic cloves, peeled and halved lengthwise
1 shallot, sliced
2 sprigs fresh marjoram
2 sprigs fresh oregano
3 to 4 cups extra virgin olive oil

In a shallow 9 x 9-inch baking dish, arrange the potatoes snugly in a single layer. Season liberally with salt and pepper. Spread the garlic, shallot, and herbs across the potatoes and gently pat them into the crevices. Cover the potatoes completely with olive oil. Place the dish in a cold oven, then turn it on to 250°F. Cook until the potatoes are tender (test with the tip of a knife), 1 to 1½ hours. Let cool, then remove the potatoes from the fat. Strain the excess fat into a container and refrigerate, covered, for future use. The potatoes can be cooked a day in advance, covered, and refrigerated until you are ready to use them. To serve, reheat the potatoes in a hot cast-iron skillet or on a hot grill.

BUTTERMILK WHIPPED POTATOES WITH HERBS

These herb-spiked potatoes are light and tangy. Made with newly harvested Yukon Golds, they feel particularly special in a summer vegetable spread or alongside a simple grilled steak.

6 to 8 servings

2 pounds Yukon Gold potatoes, rinsed (peel if desired)
4 tablespoons (½ stick) unsalted butter, room temperature
2 cups buttermilk, room temperature
Salt and pepper
2 teaspoons each freshly chopped chives, marjoram, and parsley

Cut the potatoes into uniform-size pieces, 3 to 4 inches thick, and place them in a large pot. Cover with 3 to 4 quarts cold water. Bring to a boil and then reduce to a lively simmer. Cook until tender in the center (use the tip of a knife to test them). Allow the potatoes to drain in a colander for 5 minutes. Place the butter in the bowl of a stand mixer and then add the potatoes to the bowl. Using the whip attachment, mix on low to break up the potatoes and incorporate the butter. With the mixer running on medium, slowly pour in the buttermilk. Season to taste with salt (start with 2 teaspoons) and a little pepper. Fold in the herbs. Taste for seasoning and adjust.

FINGERLINGS IN VINAIGRETTE

A fingerling potato, named for its peewee size and elongated shape, can come in shades of purple, rose, and gold, which carry more nutrients than a regular potato. Fingerlings have a deep, sweet, earthy flavor that contrasts nicely with their milder cousins. My favorite way to serve them is to simmer them in seasoned water, and toss them in lemony vinaigrette while they are still warm.

4 to 6 servings

2 pounds fingerling potatoes
⅓ cup apple cider vinegar
⅓ cup kosher salt, plus more for seasoning
Freshly ground black pepper
About ½ cup Lemon Vinaigrette (see recipe)
2 teaspoons chopped fresh cilantro, marjoram, or basil, or a mix

In a large pot, combine the potatoes, 1 gallon water, the vinegar, and ⅓ cup salt. Place on medium-high heat until the water just begins to boil; reduce the heat to medium-low and simmer until the potatoes are tender to the center. Check with the tip of a knife for doneness. When the potatoes are tender, pour them into a colander and let drain for 10 minutes. Cut the potatoes into uniformly sized pieces while still warm and place in a shallow wide dish. Season lightly with salt and pepper and then dress with enough of the vinaigrette to fully moisten and coat them, about ½ cup. Let sit a few minutes to absorb the dressing, and then taste for seasoning. Adjust as needed. Sprinkle with the chopped herb or herbs.

LEMON VINAIGRETTE

1½ cups

Zest of 1 lemon
½ cup freshly squeezed lemon juice (from approximately 2 large lemons)
1 garlic clove
1 tablespoon Dijon mustard
1 teaspoon Champagne vinegar
2 teaspoons kosher salt
½ teaspoon finely ground black pepper
1 cup extra virgin olive oil

In a blender, combine the lemon zest, lemon juice, garlic, mustard, vinegar, salt, and pepper. Cover and blend at medium speed until the ingredients are smooth. With the motor running, slowly add the olive oil in a steady stream until the dressing emulsifies—it will be lemony yellow and a little creamy. Taste for seasoning.

SUMMER SQUASH

For many a gardener, the thrill of the first summer squash wears off quickly. In the heat of summer, these sun-loving plants fruit so fast, sometimes within five to six days of flowering, that the squashes must be harvested daily. Turn your back for more than a day, and you'll end up with a garden full of baseball bats and doorstops. By the time August arrives, most home gardeners and farmers will unload their bounty on just about anyone who will take it off their hands. Did you know August 8 was national "Sneak Zucchini onto Your Neighbor's Porch Day"? That's a real thing.

Luckily, I don't have the burden of harvesting. My only challenge is deciding how to prepare squash in different ways to keep summer meals interesting, and to me that's the fun part. There is no end to the possibilities for incorporating summer squashes into side dishes, salads, main courses, and even breads or desserts. Summer squashes are mostly water and therefore not as nutrient-rich as other vegetables. But they can add meaty substance to a dish without the calories and fat, and they readily absorb whatever flavors they are cooked with. One easy preparation is to cut a mixture of various squashes into thick wedges; toss them with olive oil, salt, and pepper; and sear them on a hot grill. Mix the grilled squash with herbs like marjoram, oregano, or basil and throw in some halved cherry tomatoes. You can serve it hot or room temperature.

Summer squashes belong to the cucurbit family that also includes cucumbers, melons, fall squash, and gourds. Female flowers produce the fruit; the delicate, orange male flowers do not contain fruit, but rather provide pollen for bees to fertilize the female flower. These blossoms are picked early and are often stuffed and fried or torn up and put into salads or pastas.

Summer squashes are descendants of a wild squash from South America with bitter, inedible flesh that was cultivated for its seeds. The modern version spread throughout the Americas and was brought back to Europe by Christopher Columbus. Summer squashes come in many shapes, colors, and sizes, and are largely categorized as squash or zucchini.

SQUASH: The flying saucer–shaped pattypan has a thicker skin and is firmer than the other squashes. It's great for grilling and roasting, but I prefer not to serve it raw. Yellow crookneck, which comes smooth or pebbled; the yellow straightneck; and the zephyr, a straightneck variety that is pale yellow at the top and a cool green at the bottom, are all delicate and mild. These are excellent lightly cooked, baked into a squash casserole, or shaved raw into a salad.

ZUCCHINI: This comes in standard straightneck green, golden, or tiger-striped and is slightly meatier and denser than yellow squash. I love zucchini for roasting or panfrying but they are also delicious raw. The less common varieties, like the round eight ball or the golden ball and the pale green "limelight," are even denser and are really best cooked.

Choose squashes that are heavy for their size, with bright, unblemished skins that aren't too hard. Ideally, elongated varieties should be picked at six to eight inches, when the skin, seeds, and flesh are all tender and edible.

Larger squashes can be bitter or woody, but they can work fine in recipes where lots of flavor will be added. Just cut them into smaller, uniformly shaped pieces before proceeding. If they are completely overgrown, don't throw them into the compost pile just yet. Remove the thick seeds and tough skin and grate the flesh for fritters, pancakes, or baked goods. Store a whole squash unwashed and covered in the refrigerator for three to five days. Grated zucchini and squash can be frozen if you are not ready to use them immediately.

PATTYPAN SQUASH WITH TOMATO SAUCE

The alien spaceship of summer squashes, pattypan might catch your eye in a basket at a farmers' market, but you may be intimidated if you don't know where to start. Trust your instincts; it is a little different from other summer squashes. Pattypans have tougher skin and firmer flesh, and their scalloped edges pose geometric challenges when you are approaching with a knife. Consider this recipe a good primer for getting to know this underused but surprisingly rewarding vegetable. Serve it on its own as a side, or turn it into a main dish over pasta or quinoa.

4 servings

2 large or 4 small pattypan squash
2 tablespoons unsalted butter
1 tablespoon extra virgin olive oil
1 large onion, diced
2 garlic cloves, minced
Kosher salt
1 quart home-canned tomatoes (or fresh tomatoes, peeled), roughly chopped, including juice
½ teaspoon chopped fresh oregano leaves
2 to 3 tablespoons freshly grated Parmigiano-Reggiano or thin slices Gouda for garnish, optional

Cut each pattypan squash in half from stem end to blossom end. Place the cut end down on your work surface. Working from the outside of the squash toward the center of the cut edge radially, cut into ¼-inch-wide wedges.

In a deep skillet over medium heat, melt the butter with the olive oil. Add the onion and garlic with a sprinkling of salt; cook until the onion is translucent, about 5 minutes. Add the sliced squash and season again with salt and pepper; cook for 5 minutes more. Add the tomatoes and juice with a sprinkling of salt and cook an additional 10 to 12 minutes until the squash is tender. Add the fresh oregano and gently stir to combine. Taste for seasoning. Transfer to individual plates or a serving platter and garnish with the cheese.

SQUASH BLOSSOM FRITTATA

Many flowers are edible, but few are as versatile as the ethereal squash blossom. Often harvested to keep the squash abundance at bay, this by-product of pruning has long been revered by chefs as the perfect vessel for stuffing. Deep-fried, cheese-filled squash blossoms have become menu staples. I also like to tear squash blossoms and toss them into an herb salad, fill them with crabmeat to serve hot or chilled, or in this case, add them to eggs for a creamy main dish. To save time and prevent drying out, note that the eggs are warmed through prior to being placed in the oven, and that the frittata is pulled out before the center is fully cooked. The residual heat in the pan will continue to cook the frittata out of the oven.

4 to 6 servings

8 large eggs
2 tablespoons unsalted butter
1 teaspoon kosher salt
⅛ teaspoon freshly ground black pepper
6 ounces fresh chèvre
¼ cup finely sliced fresh chives
4 large or 6 to 8 small squash blossoms, cut lengthwise in half, brushed clean

Preheat the oven to 400°F. In a medium mixing bowl, whisk the eggs until thoroughly blended. In an oven-safe skillet over medium-low heat, melt the butter. Add the whisked eggs, salt, and pepper. Crumble in the chèvre and, using a rubber spatula, stir frequently. Cook for about 5 minutes, stirring all the while, until the mixture is warmed through but not cooked. Remove from the heat and stir in half of the chives. Arrange the cleaned blossoms on top and gently push them under the eggs.

Place the skillet in the oven. Cook until the eggs are just set on the edges and a little jiggly in the middle, 20 to 25 minutes. Remove from the oven and let rest for 10 minutes; the frittata will continue to cook. Cut into slices and top each serving with the reserved chives.

ZUCCHINI WITH GARLIC, RED PEPPER, AND MINT

Of all the summer squashes, zucchini may be the most underrated and misunderstood. It's full of water and can be quite bland. The trick is to salt it first, and then replace the excess water with fat and flavor. In this preparation, I sear the salted and drained zucchini wedges in olive oil infused with garlic and crushed red pepper flakes, and finish with the high top notes of lemon, Champagne vinegar, and lots of fresh mint. A little honey brings out the natural sweetness of the squash. Although I typically gravitate toward young, tender squashes, this recipe can work just fine with more mature sizes, picked a little too late.

4 servings

8 small or 4 medium to large zucchini (green or yellow varieties), washed
Kosher salt
1 tablespoon Champagne vinegar
1 tablespoon freshly squeezed lemon juice
1 teaspoon honey, local if possible
⅓ cup plus ¼ cup extra virgin olive oil
½ teaspoon crushed red pepper flakes
3 to 4 cloves garlic, peeled and thinly sliced
1 large handful fresh mint leaves, roughly chopped

Cut the zucchini lengthwise into ½-inch-wide spears, then trim them to approximately 3 inches in length. Place the zucchini spears on a platter in a single layer and season well with kosher salt on all sides. Transfer to a wire rack or a paper towel–lined surface to drain. Allow to sit for 1 hour. In a small nonreactive bowl, whisk together the vinegar, lemon juice, honey, and ⅓ cup olive oil to make the vinaigrette; salt to taste.

Warm a wide cast-iron skillet over low heat. Pat the zucchini dry. In a small skillet over low heat, warm the remaining ¼ cup olive oil with the red pepper flakes and garlic until the garlic is lightly browned. Strain the oil into the warmed skillet and reserve the solids. Increase the heat to medium and sear the zucchini in the flavored oil until lightly browned on all sides. Turn the heat off and transfer the cooked zucchini to a plate. Add the reserved garlic and red pepper mixture to the dressing. When the squash has cooled, spoon the vinaigrette over it and top with fresh mint. Serve at room temperature.

SHAVED RAW SQUASH
AND FENNEL SALAD

Crisp anise-scented fennel slices and thin ribbons of mild summer squash are an unlikely match, but sweet cherry tomatoes and a lemony vinaigrette can string these two ingredients together beautifully. This is a creative alternative to a summer slaw or a solid pairing with any fish. A mandoline is my preferred tool and is especially handy for making thin, uniform slices. If you do not have one, a sharp knife and some extra patience will do the job.

6 servings

1 large or 2 small fennel bulbs
2 medium or 3 small yellow squashes and/or zucchini, washed
1 cup cherry or grape tomatoes, halved
Kosher salt
Freshly ground black pepper
2 to 3 tablespoons Lemon Vinaigrette (page 221) or more as needed
1 tablespoon chopped fresh basil
1 tablespoon chopped fresh parsley

Halve the fennel bulb lengthwise and cut away the hard core at the base. Using a mandoline, slice the fennel crosswise into very thin boomerang-shaped strips. Slice the squashes lengthwise on the mandoline into thin ribbons.

Place the squash and fennel in a nonreactive bowl and gently toss to combine. Add the cherry tomatoes and season all with salt and pepper. Drizzle in 2 to 3 tablespoons of the vinaigrette and toss lightly to dress. Add the basil and parsley, and taste for seasoning. If the salad seems dry, add more dressing as needed.

TOMATOES

I have Bill Yoder to thank for some of the best-tasting tomatoes we serve at Miller Union. He is not a farmer—just an extremely enthusiastic backyard tomato grower who often shows up at the restaurant in the middle of summer with a box of thirty or forty gorgeous heirlooms and specialized breeds for us to play with in the kitchen. On his single acre, Bill has about three hundred different varieties and twice that many plants. He creates new breeds and flavors every season with grafting and cross-pollination, and will take out his iPhone and show me photos of his tomato plants growing, as if they were his kids. Whenever he stops by, we get lost in geeky tomato talk until I realize that I need to get back to work.

Americans cannot get enough tomatoes. Each year the United States produces some 2 billion pounds of tomatoes and imports 700 million pounds or so from Mexico. They are a year-round fruit for people who can't imagine a salad without them, even if they're as tough and tasteless as tennis balls. But not for me, and not for legions of others who believe passionately that, for all the technological advancements in producing a year-round tomato, there is still no comparison to a flavorful tomato kissed by the summer sun. Most of the tomatoes you see in supermarkets are newer hybrids bred for uniform shape and color, tougher skins able to withstand mechanical harvesting and shipping, and slower ripening so that they can be picked green and then gassed with ethylene to produce the acceptable shade of red. I'd wager that nothing brings out the farmers' market shoppers in droves like the season's first vine-ripened tomatoes.

Tomatoes are thought to have been first cultivated in Peru in the eighth century by Aztecs and Incas. Spanish explorers brought them to Europe around the sixteenth century. Italians were the first Europeans to eat them, followed by the Spanish and the French.

Their nickname, "love apples," comes from a belief that they might be the forbidden fruit of Eden. Tomatoes are part of the infamous nightshade family, which keeps cropping up in summer and includes potatoes, peppers, and eggplants. While tomatoes are botanically a fruit, they are technically a berry and legally a vegetable. In 1893, the U.S. Supreme Court classified them as vegetables because they were most frequently used in savory preparations in the kitchen, as they are today. Whatever their classification, they are rich in vitamins A and C, potassium, and niacin. Some medical studies indicate that people with diets rich in tomatoes, which contain an antioxidant compound called lycopene, may have less risk of some cancers, including stomach, lung, and prostate cancer.

There are hundreds of tomato varieties to choose from these days, and they can be categorized in a variety of ways as well. We group tomatoes by use (slicers and roma tomatoes), by size (grape to beefsteaks), by breeding method (open-pollinated heirlooms and hybrids), and by growth type (indeterminate vines, which produce fruit until frost; and determinate "bush" plants, which produce a single crop of fruit), all of which can be a little overwhelming. No matter how you slice them, you'll want to follow a few simple rules in selecting and storing them. Choose plump, fragrant, unblemished fruits. Tomatoes continue to ripen after harvest, so if you want to use them a few days after purchase, choose fruit that is still firm. To speed ripening, place tomatoes with a ripe apple in a paper bag punched with a few holes, or place in indirect sunlight, between sixty and seventy-five degrees. Avoid refrigerating tomatoes unless it's necessary. There are a few reasons to chill them, though: if you've cut into one and did not use it all; if they are ripening but you are not ready to use them. If you are preserving the rest of a beautiful cut tomato, cover the cut side with plastic wrap and use within a day. If a tomato is ripe and you can't use it for a day or two, refrigerate it; then pull it out an hour or so before you plan to serve so that it can come to room temperature. This method works especially well for expensive heirloom tomatoes or ripe cherry tomatoes, which both have a high water content and do not become mealy if chilled briefly. Beefsteaks and romas do not fare as well in the cooler and are best left at room temperature.

HEIRLOOM TOMATO PANZANELLA

Panzanella is a classic Italian peasant dish that is the best way I know of to use stale bread and ripe tomatoes. Heirloom tomatoes tend to have a higher water content than beefsteaks, making them a better fit for this salad. I have tried a lot of panzanella salads that I did not like because the bread became too soggy for my taste. To get around that, my version starts with a crispy crouton made from stale bread tossed with garlicky olive oil. The tomato juice that is released when the tomatoes are marinated with the other vegetables becomes part of the dressing. Right before I serve it, I toss all of the ingredients with the crispy croutons so that the juices just begin to absorb into the bread.

6 to 8 servings

2 garlic cloves, minced
Kosher salt
½ cup extra virgin olive oil
5 cups cubed sourdough bread, preferably slightly stale
1 small Vidalia onion, cut into crescents
3 tablespoons sherry vinegar
4 medium heirloom tomatoes, chopped
2 small cucumbers, peeled, quartered lengthwise, and chopped
2 ribs celery, sliced crosswise
2 tablespoons chopped fresh basil

Heat the oven to 300°F. In a medium bowl, combine the garlic, ½ teaspoon salt, and the olive oil; stir until the salt dissolves. Place the cubed bread in a mixing bowl, drizzle the bread with the garlic oil mixture, and toss well to evenly distribute the oil. Spread the bread on a baking sheet and bake until crisped but not dark, 10 to 12 minutes. Remove from the oven and cool.

Place the onion in a medium bowl, sprinkle with a little salt, and pour the sherry vinegar over it. Let rest 10 minutes. Add the tomatoes, cucumbers, celery, and 2 teaspoons salt. Toss with the bread cubes and basil. Taste for seasoning. Keep in mind that the longer this sits, the soggier the bread will become.

THE "BAT" SANDWICH

This is my citified take on the summer classic. I use crusty sourdough in place of white bread and peppery arugula instead of plain old lettuce, and I add a kick of fresh garlic to my mayonnaise. But dead-ripe tomatoes and good, crisp bacon are still the stars.

1 sandwich

1 medium tomato
Coarse sea salt and freshly ground black pepper
4 teaspoons Homemade Mayonnaise (page 37)
1 small garlic clove, shaved on a microplane
1 teaspoon freshly squeezed lemon juice
2 slices sourdough bread, toasted
3 slices crispy bacon
1 handful arugula

Starting at the base of the tomato, thinly slice off the bottom, and then cut ½-inch-thick slices. Season the tomato slices liberally with salt and pepper on both sides. In a small bowl, whisk the mayonnaise with the garlic and lemon juice. Spread 2 teaspoons garlic mayo onto each slice of bread. Layer tomato and then bacon on one slice. Add arugula. Top with the remaining slice of bread, mayo side down, and press on the sandwich gently so that it will hold together when you pick it up. Cut in half and serve.

ROASTED TOMATOES FOR FREEZING

This is an easy way to preserve tomatoes for a quick pasta sauce or a cozy cold-weather soup long after the tomato season has ended. But the heady aroma that fills your kitchen when you roast the tomatoes is so enticing that you may decide to serve some at once.

About 4 cups

2 pounds roma tomatoes
2 large sprigs thyme
2 large sprigs oregano
¼ cup extra virgin olive oil
1 tablespoon kosher salt
½ teaspoon finely ground black pepper

Heat the oven to 375°F. Slice the tomatoes in half lengthwise and arrange cut side up in a baking dish just large enough to hold them. Roughly chop the herbs into slightly smaller pieces and scatter across the surface. Drizzle with the olive oil and season with salt and pepper. Roast until the skins split and the tomatoes deflate, about 15 minutes. Remove from oven and cool. Slip the skins off and place the tomatoes in resealable freezer bags on a flat surface to maximize storage potential. Store in the freezer for up to 2 months.

SMOKY TOMATO
RATATOUILLE

The secret of a successful ratatouille, according to Julia Child, is layering the flavors. It might be a temptation to just throw the vegetables into a pot and cook them all at once, but I take Julia's more intentional approach, adding the vegetables one at a time and seasoning as I go. I purposely omit eggplant, which requires longer cooking, and instead focus on harmonizing tomatoes and other stars of summer with smoky flavors. If you have a backyard smoker going, consider adding a layer of real smoke. Place some halved fresh tomatoes on the smoker rack, cut side up so as not to lose any of the juices. If you're not ready to make this dish right away, smoked tomatoes will keep in the refrigerator a few days.

4 servings

1 tablespoon unsalted butter
1 tablespoon bacon fat
1 medium onion, cut into ½-inch dice
Kosher salt
Freshly ground black pepper
1 red bell pepper, seeded and cut into ½-inch dice
1 yellow squash or zucchini, cut into ½-inch dice
2 large, juicy beefsteak tomatoes (smoked if desired), peeled and cut into ½-inch
  cubes, juice reserved
1 to 2 cups chicken or vegetable stock
½ teaspoon fresh thyme leaves
¼ teaspoon smoked paprika
Basil Pistou (see recipe) for garnish

In a Dutch oven or deep skillet over medium-high heat, melt the butter with the bacon fat. Add the onion and season with salt and pepper. Cook until the onion is softened, about 4 minutes. Add the bell pepper; season with salt and black pepper. Cook for 2 minutes. Add the squash; season with salt and pepper. Cook for 2 or 3 minutes, then add the tomato and the reserved juices; season with salt and pepper. Add enough stock to moisten the vegetables. Stir in the thyme and smoked paprika. Sauté until all the vegetables are tender, about 5 more minutes. Adjust the seasoning. Top with a drizzle of Basil Pistou.

BASIL PISTOU

1 garlic clove
Zest of 1 lemon
1 large handful fresh basil leaves
⅛ teaspoon fine sea salt
¼ cup of extra virgin olive oil, plus more as needed

In a blender, combine the garlic, lemon zest, basil, and salt. With the motor running, drizzle in the oil.

NEXT SPREAD

SUMMER VEGETABLE FEAST (clockwise from top left): Slow-Simmered Field Peas; sliced tomatoes; Skillet Cornbread; Crispy Cornmeal-Fried Okra; Blackberry Shrub; Eggplant Caponata; blanched green beans

FALL

As the color palette of autumn leaves deepens, so does the flavor of fall produce. The chill in the air reminds us that pumpkin patches, apple harvests, new-crop pecans, and wild grapes are on the way.

APPLES AND PEARS

Early each autumn, our apple delivery guy from Mercier Orchards, Brandon Smith, brings samples of the season's first pickings to the restaurant and gives our kitchen staff a quick tutorial. We taste informally, comparing the varieties side by side, and discuss the flavor and textural nuances of each type. This helps us develop our new fall dishes involving apples.

There are so many varieties out there, in addition to the five or six that you typically see, and for every region, the selection varies. The same is true of pears. Peak season for both is October, with different types ripening at different times from August to November. These two edible members of the rose family share some characteristics that allow us to use them interchangeably in many recipes. They can be baked, broiled, grilled, poached, sliced raw, grated, juiced, and more. The seeds, stem, and core are usually removed before eating. Many household kitchens are equipped with a corer, used to carve out the middle of an apple or a pear, but I am not a fan. It is just as easy to quarter the fruit and then section off the seeds and core with your knife. After the fruit is cut, if you are serving it raw, drop the pieces into acidulated water—that is, water with a splash of lemon or vinegar to slow down the browning process. When making a salad, I let the fruit rest in the acid of the dressing while I do other things, then remove it and whisk the dressing together.

Cutting apples or pears crosswise reveals creamy-white flesh with seeds that form a unique star pattern in the center. If planted, these seeds may grow into trees. However, there is no guarantee what variety will appear once a tree fruits. A tree planted from the seed of a sweet apple could very well produce fruit that is sour and bitter. Apple and pear trees are almost always grafted with cuttings to produce the fruit that the grower wants to achieve.

APPLES: Apples are harvested from small deciduous trees, ten to thirty feet tall, with tender white and pink blossoms in spring, followed by late summer and autumn fruits with up to fifteen seeds. There are hundreds of apple varieties—some unidentified from natural seed mutations and others inedible and astringent, used only for making cider. Those with a mealy texture are better for cooking (Stayman, Winesap, Rome, Empire, McIntosh). Others are best for eating out of hand or raw in a salad (Cameo, Fuji, Honeycrisp, Mutsu, Gala, Pink Lady), owing to their crisp texture and sweet or tart flavors. Apples do not ripen after picking, but they can deteriorate if not refrigerated. Keep them cold in the crisper of your refrigerator and do not store next to other fruits unless you are trying to ripen them faster. Apples give off ethylene gas, which speeds up the ripening of just about any fruit around it.

PEARS: Most pears have an elegant, tapered stem end. The Asian pear, sometimes called apple pear, is an exception and is round like an apple. Unlike apples, pears ripen after they are picked. There are just as many pear varieties as there are apples: yellow-green and speckled Bartletts, dusty brown-skinned Bosc, red or green and plump Comice, compact and sweet Anjou, and the tiny, sugary Seckel, to name just a few.

Since pears are very perishable once ripe, the pears you find when shopping will generally be unripe and will require a few days of maturing. Look for pears that are firm, but not too hard. They should have smooth skin, free of bruises or mold. Good-quality pears may be russeted, with brown-speckled patches on the skin; this is an acceptable and expected characteristic of pears, and often indicates a more developed flavor. Avoid pears that are punctured or have dark soft spots. To check a pear for ripeness, place your thumb or index finger on the flesh at the very top, just next to the stem. If it is tender there, the pear is ripe and ready to use. Once pears get soft on the outside, they are considered overripe by connoisseurs, but can still be cooked into a jam or preserve.

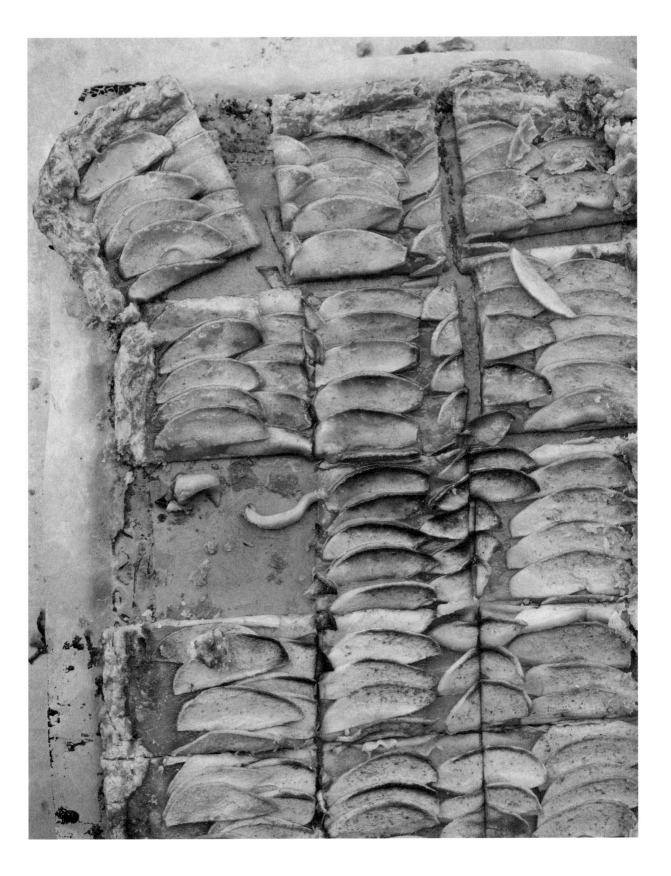

RUSTIC APPLE TART

When I eat desserts, I gravitate toward the ones that incorporate seasonal fruit. I even prefer a fruit dessert over chocolate. I like the idea that apples may add some nutrition to otherwise empty calories. This free-form tart is almost like a fruit pizza. Though it feels rustic, be picky about how the apples are sliced and arranged over the dough.

12 servings

1 double recipe Pie Dough (page 470)
4 to 5 medium tart-sweet apples
½ cup maple syrup or Apple Jelly (page 251)
2 tablespoons unsalted butter
2 tablespoons lemon juice
⅛ teaspoon fine sea salt
Fresh whole nutmeg for grating

Make Pie Dough recipe and allow time to chill.

Heat the oven to 375°F. Cover a cookie sheet with a piece of parchment. Place the dough on the parchment and roll it out to the edges. Refrigerate the rolled-out dough while preparing the apples and the glaze. If necessary, the dough can be rolled up in the parchment if it won't fit on the refrigerator shelf otherwise.

Peel all the apples and then slice each vertically into 4 equal quarters. Place each quarter cut side down, with the seeds facing your knife. With the blade at a 45-degree angle, slice away the seeds and core from each quarter. Be sure to save the seeds and peels if you plan to make another batch of apple jelly later.

Cut each apple quarter lengthwise, with the core side facing down, into ¼-inch-thick wedges, your blade following the natural curve of the apple surface. Place all of the apple wedges in a large mixing bowl. In a small saucepan, bring the maple syrup or apple jelly to a simmer with the butter, lemon juice, and salt. When the butter is melted, remove from the heat and add just enough of the glaze mixture to coat the apples.

Pull the tart dough from the refrigerator and place on a baking sheet. Arrange glaze-coated apples on the pastry surface in rows facing the same direction and overlapping slightly. Leave a 2-inch gap on all sides between the fruit and the edge of the dough. Fold the dough inward to meet the edge of the apples, and then firmly crimp the folded dough with the tines of a fork. Brush the remaining glaze on the edges of the dough and on top of the apples, and then grate the nutmeg over the top. Immediately place the tart in the center rack of the oven. Bake until the crust is lightly browned, 25 to 35 minutes. Cut into squares and serve hot or at room temperature. Excellent with vanilla ice cream or crème anglaise.

APPLE JELLY

Though not traditional, my technique for jelly is very economical and nearly fool-proof. Pectin, the naturally occurring substance in fruits that enables jellies to set, is most abundant in the seeds and peel of apples. Instead of discarding these scraps, save them anytime you prep apples and store them in the freezer until you are ready to start. Toss them into a pot along with some cranberries for tartness and color, and you are halfway to jelly. By heating, cooling, and then reheating, you reduce the risk of caramelizing the sugar, which ruins the fresh fruit taste. This recipe works just as well with pears.

Four 8-ounce jelly jars

8 cups apple scraps (chopped whole apples can be used to meet this yield)
4 cups sugar
1 cup cranberries
4 cups fresh-pressed apple cider
1 cup apple cider vinegar
½ teaspoon fine sea salt
2 lemons, quartered

In a large pot, combine the apple scraps, sugar, cranberries, cider, vinegar, and salt with 4 cups water. Squeeze the lemons into the pot and then drop in the lemon rinds. Cook on low heat until the ingredients are very soft, about 45 minutes. Strain the solids through a fine-mesh sieve, being careful not to press on them. This will make a clearer jelly. Drain 30 minutes. Discard the solids, and put the strained liquid back into a medium saucepan. Cook over medium-low heat and skim any foam that collects on the surface. Let cook until large bubbles form, skimming all the while until the jelly is clarified and thickened, about 25 minutes. Remove from the heat and refrigerate until cooled. Return the cooled liquid to a saucepan and, over medium heat, cook one more time until large bubbles form again.

The longer you cook the jelly at this stage, the thicker the result. I prefer to bring it just to the large-bubble stage, so that the jelly is slightly runny when cooled, about the consistency of chilled maple syrup. Refrigerate for up to 3 months.

APPLE CIDER–BRAISED CABBAGE

Apple cider is a by-product of the apple harvest. All varieties of the "seconds," or ugly, bruised apples that cannot be sold at market, are combined and pressed into juice. This naturally sweet and tart unfiltered beverage can add an autumnal note to many dishes. I like it for deepening the flavor of a braise, but it can also be used as part of the liquid in a muffin, reduced by half for a sharp sauce paired with pork, or as the base of a seasonal cocktail. What I especially love about this cabbage dish is that it is very forgiving. You can cook it on the stove, in a slow cooker, or in the oven. I prefer the oven, as it frees up the stove-top burners. A little undercooked or overcooked, this side dish will still taste great. The sweet and sour, brightly colored cabbage goes exceptionally well with a mild sausage, such as bratwurst, and a healthy dollop of whole-grain mustard.

6 servings

½ cup packed light brown sugar
2 tablespoons kosher salt
1 cup apple cider vinegar
1 cup fresh-pressed apple cider
½ red onion, cut into crescents
1 head red cabbage, quartered, cored, and cut lengthwise into ½-inch-thick strips

Heat the oven to 350°F. Place the brown sugar and salt in a 9 x 13-inch baking dish. Pour the vinegar and apple cider over the sugar and salt, and stir to dissolve. Add the onion and the cabbage, and gently stir and turn to coat with the liquid. Cover the pan with a sheet of parchment paper, and then cover and seal with aluminum foil. Cook for 1 hour; the cabbage should be tender. If using a slow cooker or stove-top method, cover and cook on medium-low heat for a minimum of 1 hour.

How to cook a fresh sausage: Most grocery stores and specialty markets carry fresh sausage, but I prefer to make my own, or buy it from an artisanal sausage producer that sources pork from local farms. Plan to have one link per person for a light meal or two links for a fuller meal.

In a wide skillet, warm 1 tablespoon olive oil over medium-high heat. While the pan is heating, add the sausages to the skillet one by one, all curving in the same direction, so that they fit nicely into the pan. Brown on one side, then, using tongs, carefully turn each over, in the same direction. When the other side is browned, make an incision with the tip of a knife to check the center for doneness. The juices should run clear, but the center can still be slightly pink.

APPLE, BOK CHOY, AND
RADISH SLAW

My friend Marie Nygren, cofounder of the sustainable planned community and resort Serenbe, about an hour outside Atlanta, often hosts cooking classes with chefs to benefit nonprofits. On the cool fall day that I was slated to teach, I was so rushed I didn't have time to eat and I arrived famished. She kindly brought me, from her farmhouse kitchen, a plate consisting of her family's famous fried chicken, mac and cheese, blackeyed peas, and an innovative slaw with raw collard greens, apples, and radishes. Everything was delicious, but what stood out to me the most was this sharp, lively slaw that contrasted so well with the traditional Southern plate. I re-created a version of this, substituting young, tender bok choy for the collard greens. It was a star on my family's Thanksgiving table just a few weeks later and is now requested every year.

4 servings

¼ cup apple cider vinegar
1 medium tart, crisp apple
1 medium watermelon radish
1 medium head bok choy
1 teaspoon kosher salt
½ teaspoon freshly ground black pepper
¼ cup extra virgin olive oil

Place the apple cider vinegar in a medium bowl. Slice the apple vertically into 4 equal quarters. Place each quarter cut side down, with the seeds facing your knife. With the blade at a 45-degree angle, slice away the core and seeds from each quarter.

Thinly slice the apple quarters either on a mandoline or by hand. Julienne the apple slices into matchsticks. Thinly slice the watermelon radish on a mandoline or by hand, then cut the thin slices into matchsticks; add to the bowl with the apple. Trim the bok choy by removing the core at the base. Separate each leaf and rinse well. Cut each leaf lengthwise down the center of the rib. Lay the trimmed leaves one on top of another and cut them crosswise into thin pieces. Add the leaves to the bowl, season with salt and pepper, and toss with the olive oil.

PEARS POACHED IN WHITE WINE AND ROSEMARY

Here's an easy way to put up a bumper crop of pears without pulling out the canning equipment. Depending on the size, ripeness, and variety of the pears, they may take more or less time to cook, so keep an eye on them in the pot. Serve with cheese, as a component of a dessert, or sliced in a salad. Piney, evergreen rosemary imparts an intriguing overtone.

8 servings

1 bottle medium-dry white wine
2 cups sugar
6 sprigs rosemary
Pinch salt
4 firm ripe pears

In a large saucepan, combine the wine, sugar, rosemary, and salt. Slice each pear vertically into equal quarters. Place each quarter cut side down, with the seeds facing your knife. With the blade at a 45-degree angle, slice away the core and seeds from each quarter. Add the pear quarters to the pan. Simmer over medium-low heat until the pears become just tender with a hint of translucence, but still retain their shape, 30 to 40 minutes. With a slotted spoon, carefully remove the pears from the liquid, and cool them separately to stop the cooking. Discard the rosemary stems. Let the liquid cool slightly and then chill it in the refrigerator. Recombine when they are both completely cooled. Store covered in the refrigerator for up to 2 months.

PEAR, BLUE CHEESE, WALNUT, BACON, AND WATERCRESS SANDWICH

People often take sandwich making for granted, but it is an art and there is a lot of nuance to the process. The way ingredients are layered, spread onto the bread, and positioned is very critical. This sandwich, once a staple on the menu at Watershed, where I worked for almost a decade, is a perfect example of this artistry. The cheese mixture serves as the glue to hold both the pears and the walnuts in place, while the other ingredients layer in between. This savory-sweet-salty combination might sound more like a salad, but between two slices of bread it makes a sophisticated handheld lunch. Make this when you have a pear that is neither too soft nor too hard, still crisp yet ripe.

2 sandwiches

2 ounces blue cheese, crumbled
2 ounces soft, fresh chèvre
1 medium ripe, crisp pear
1 lemon wedge, seeds removed
Kosher salt
4 slices rustic bread, toasted and buttered on the inside
½ cup walnut halves or pieces, toasted
4 slices cooked bacon
1 large handful watercress
Hilda's Icebox Pickles (page 140)

In a small bowl, blend together the blue cheese and chèvre and set aside.

Slice the pear vertically into equal quarters. Place each quarter cut side down, with the seeds facing your knife. With the blade at a 45-degree angle, slice away the core and seeds from each quarter. Slice each quarter lengthwise into ¼-inch-thick pieces. Place the pear slices in a small bowl and squeeze the lemon wedge over them to prevent browning. Sprinkle lightly with salt and set aside.

Lay the bread on a cutting board buttered side up. For each sandwich, the bottom slice should be next to the top slice, and the slices lined up so that they fit properly when pressed together. Divide the cheese mixture among all 4 slices and spread evenly. For each sandwich, press ¼ cup walnuts into the cheese on the top slice of bread, and arrange the pear slices neatly over the cheese on the bottom slice of bread. Press down lightly on the walnuts and the pears. Lay 2 pieces of bacon across the pears and divide the watercress over the bacon. Carefully press each sandwich together. Slice each sandwich in half and serve with Hilda's Icebox Pickles.

BROCCOLI, CAULIFLOWER, AND BRUSSELS

Broccoli, cauliflower, and Brussels sprouts belong to the genus *Brassica*, which also includes mustards, kale, turnips, and cabbage. I've singled out these three because they have similar dense, meaty textures that complement fall flavors especially well. They are all vegetables that are commonly considered to be more healthful than flavorful, and people tend to eat them out of guilt rather than for enjoyment. When boiled with no seasoning or no regard to cooking time, these vegetables do not taste good. If lightly roasted, sautéed, blanched, or pureed into a soup, they can actually be eaten for pure enjoyment, and the health benefits simply become an added bonus.

BROCCOLI: Timing is everything when it comes to preparing broccoli. All too often this emerald green vegetable disintegrates into a squishy, stinky mess. I find it bland when raw or undercooked, and unpleasantly pungent when cooked too long. The trick is to cook it just long enough to tenderize its fibers and maximize its sweetness and crunch. Broccoli florets mop up any kind of moisture, and this trait can be a bonus because they will soak up a flavorful sauce. Steaming or blanching preserves broccoli's vibrancy and retains nutrients. Once it reaches the crisp-tender stage, serve immediately, or shock in ice water to stop the cooking. Pat the florets dry in a cotton towel. To protect its green color, wait until the last minute to add an acid like lemon or vinegar to broccoli.

Look for broccoli with firm stalks and stems and bright green, tightly closed floret clusters. Cut ends should be completely closed; open ends are likely to be woody. When prepping, be sure to trim off the dried or weathered end first. Do not wash broccoli until ready to use. Besides the standard green broccoli that we all know, there are many hybrids and crosses, in shades of green and purple. The green Italian variety, Calabrese, has larger, loose florets that look more like flowers. Broccoli rabe (rape) is a bitter, peppery cross between broccoli and turnip. One of my favorites, broccolini, can be served whole and unpeeled because it has a long, tender stem and a small floret. Broccoflower is a hybrid of broccoli and cauliflower, which looks like cauliflower with a greenish tint. Romanesco may be one of the most gorgeous vegetables on earth, with tiny spirals of endless fractal patterns in the florets and a pale electric-green color.

BRUSSELS SPROUTS: In 2008, a national survey gave Brussels sprouts the prize as the most hated vegetable in America. But they are one of my personal favorites, and I embrace the challenge of showing their best side. Brussels sprout varieties come in shades of green and purple. Most are harvested from the bottom of the plant to the top, as not all the sprouts ripen at the same time. But newer hybrids have been bred so that the entire plant can be harvested at once. This plant dates back to the sixteenth century in Europe, where it was cultivated and named for the capital of Belgium. French settlers brought Brussels sprouts to Louisiana, but they grow best in cooler areas. Like other brassicas, Brussels sprouts may develop a mustardy or horseradish taste if grown in hot or dry conditions. Store covered and unwashed in the refrigerator, away from light and dry air.

CAULIFLOWER: Generally speaking, the darker and more brightly colored a fruit or vegetable, the higher its vitamin content. This rule, however, does not apply to pigment-free cauliflower. The coarse, dark green outer leaves shield its inner creamy-white head from the sunlight that would enable it to produce chlorophyll, but it is just as healthful as its cousins. Besides having high levels of vitamin C and other nutrients, cauliflower is a more nutritious substitute for potatoes or dairy products when pureed, adding a rich taste and creamy texture from natural starch, without extra fat or calories. However, cauliflower comes not only in standard white, but also in stunning shades of light green, yellow-orange, and purple. Size doesn't affect the flavor or texture of cauliflower, so purchase one that best suits your needs. Store in the refrigerator, unwashed, covered or tightly wrapped in plastic.

BROCCOLINI WITH WHOLE WHEAT FETTUCCINE

Broccolini, a hybrid of Asian and Western broccoli varieties, has a thinner stalk and is more tender and sweeter than the woodier bunches we are more accustomed to. Because it needs no peeling, you can make a quick and easy vegetable side dish by simply sautéing it with olive oil and a few key ingredients. Toss with a nutty whole wheat pasta, and in minutes you have a complete meal.

2 entrée or 4 side servings

2 bunches broccolini, about 1 pound
Kosher salt for pasta water and seasoning
½ pound whole wheat fettuccine
3 tablespoons extra virgin olive oil
2 garlic cloves, thinly sliced
⅛ teaspoon crushed red pepper flakes
Freshly ground black pepper
1 tablespoon unsalted butter
Juice of 1 lemon
2 tablespoons freshly grated Parmigiano-Reggiano

Wash the broccolini. Cut into 1-inch pieces, separating the stems from the florets, and set aside.

Over high heat, bring a large pot of salted water to a boil. A good ratio is about 1 teaspoon kosher salt per 1 cup water. Add the pasta; cook, stirring often, until the texture is al dente. Remove ¼ cup of the pasta water and reserve for later use, then drain the pasta in a colander and set aside.

Place a large skillet over medium-high heat; put in the olive oil. Add the broccolini stems, garlic, and red pepper flakes; sprinkle with salt and pepper; and sauté 2 minutes. Add the florets; sauté 1 to 2 minutes or until the vegetables are tender. Add the butter, lemon juice, and 2 tablespoons of the reserved pasta water.

Stir to coat the vegetables, then add the cooked pasta. Toss well to combine and add more reserved pasta water as needed to moisten. Remove from the heat and transfer to a serving vessel. Top with Parmigiano-Reggiano.

FRIED RICE WITH BROCCOLI AND MUSTARD GREENS

We make fried rice for a staff meal at least once a week. The key ingredient is cold leftover rice, which we almost always have on hand at the restaurant. From there almost anything goes. One of my favorite choices is broccoli. When thinly sliced, it sautés beautifully and stands up to the bold flavors of soy sauce, ginger, garlic, and scallion. In this version, I supplement it with the carrots I pickled in the spring and, for an unexpected twist, pungent mustard greens. Easy as fried rice is to make, there is a bit of strategy. It's important to organize your prep in advance, as each step requires ingredients to be at the ready. Portion out everything into bowls and place them by the stove. I cook the ingredients in stages and then remove each from the hot skillet as soon as it is done.

4 entrée servings

2 cups broccoli florets (about 1 small head)
½ cup thinly sliced celery (about 1 rib)
½ cup thinly sliced raw carrots (about 2; or Pickled Baby Carrots, page 18)
1 bunch scallions, roots trimmed, white and light green parts thinly sliced
5 garlic cloves, minced
2 tablespoons minced fresh ginger
1 small hot pepper, seeded and minced
1 bunch mustard greens (about ½ pound), trimmed, washed, and roughly chopped
5 large eggs
5 cups cooked rice, chilled
3 tablespoons soy sauce, or more to taste
1 tablespoon sriracha sauce (or Hot Sauce, page 210)
Juice of ½ lime
4 tablespoons peanut oil

Wash and trim the broccoli florets and thinly slice lengthwise. In a medium bowl, combine the broccoli, celery, and carrots. In a small bowl, combine the scallions, garlic, ginger, and hot pepper. Place the mustard greens in a separate bowl. Crack the eggs into a medium bowl and lightly whisk. Break up the cold rice in a medium bowl. In a small bowl, combine the soy sauce, sriracha, and lime juice. Set all of these bowls near your stove.

In a large wide skillet or wok, heat 1 tablespoon peanut oil over high heat. When the oil begins to shimmer, add the broccoli mixture to the pan and quickly toss to coat. Add about one-third of the scallion mixture, and toss well. Add one-third of the soy, sriracha, and lime mixture and toss well. Remove all from the pan and spread out in a wide dish in a single layer to cool. Do not pile the vegetables in a mound, or they will to continue to cook.

With the skillet or wok still on high heat, put in another 1 tablespoon of the peanut oil. Add the mustard greens to the hot pan, and add one-third of the scallion mixture and one-third of the soy mixture. Toss well to coat and spread out over the broccoli mixture.

With the skillet or wok still on high heat, put in another 1 tablespoon peanut oil. Add the eggs to the pan and quickly swirl them against the hot surface with the back of a spoon or spatula to make as thin a layer as possible. Remove the egg as soon as it solidifies, and add to the vegetable mixture.

With the skillet or wok still on high heat, put in the remaining 1 tablespoon peanut oil. Add the cold rice to the pan. Add the remaining scallion mixture and soy mixture to the rice, and stir frequently to prevent sticking. When the rice is hot, return the cooked ingredients to the pan and stir well to combine. Serve immediately.

GRILLED BROCCOLI WITH WALNUTS AND LEMON

One of the most satisfying ways to eat broccoli is cooked over hot coals on a grill. The florets absorb the smoky flavor and the sizzling-hot grates char the outside slightly.

4 servings

2 garlic cloves, minced
Zest and juice of 1 lemon
2 tablespoons extra virgin olive oil
1 large head broccoli, trimmed into 2- to 3-inch pieces (about 3 cups)
Kosher salt
Freshly ground black pepper
½ cup chopped walnuts, toasted

Heat the grill to highest heat and keep the lid closed until ready to use. In a large bowl, stir together the garlic, lemon zest and juice, and olive oil. Toss the broccoli pieces in the bowl, then season lightly with salt and pepper. With tongs, transfer the broccoli to the hot grill and cook for 1 minute on each side. Toss with the chopped walnuts and serve.

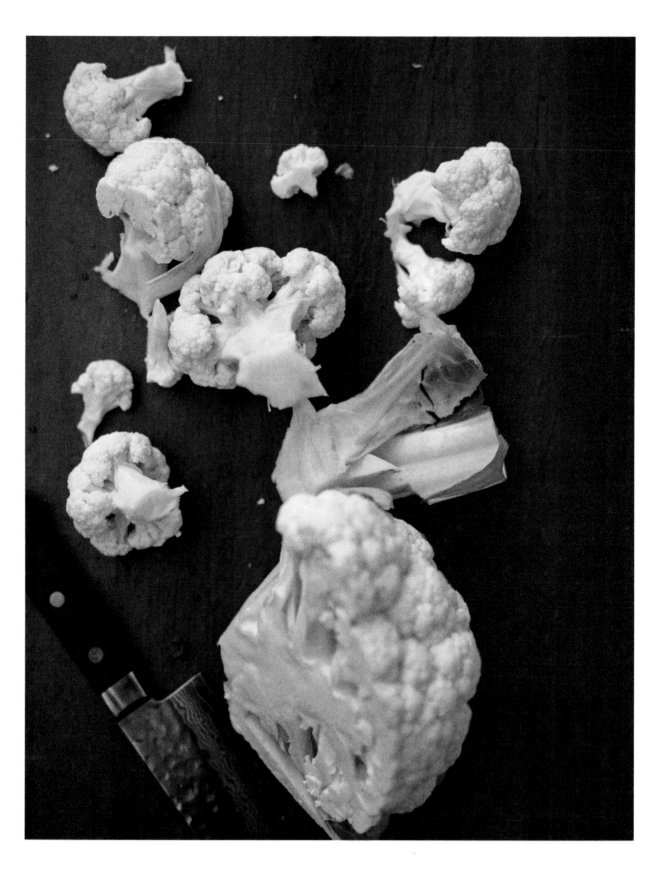

CAULIFLOWER AND TURNIP SOUP

This velvety soup seems decadent, yet it contains not a speck of cream and less than a tablespoon of butter per serving. Pureed cauliflower and turnip give body and depth, and the thyme, nutmeg, and bay leaf accentuate the essence of these earthy vegetables.

12 servings

8 tablespoons (1 stick) unsalted butter
1 medium onion, roughly chopped
1 shallot, roughly chopped
2 garlic cloves, halved
1 teaspoon kosher salt, plus more to taste
1 medium head cauliflower, trimmed, washed, and cut into 2-inch pieces
2 to 3 medium purple-top turnips, peeled and cut into 1-inch pieces
6 to 8 cups chicken broth
1 teaspoon fresh thyme leaves
1 bay leaf
Freshly ground black pepper
Whole nutmeg for grating

In a large saucepan or Dutch oven over medium heat, melt the butter until foamy. Add the onion, shallot, and garlic; season with salt; and cook until translucent about 5 minutes. Add the cauliflower, turnips, thyme, bay leaf, and 6 cups of the broth, and stir to combine. Bring to a simmer and cook until the cauliflower and turnips are tender, about 20 minutes. Taste for seasonings and adjust as needed. Remove the bay leaf and, using an immersion blender or working in small batches with a countertop blender, blend to a smooth consistency. If the soup is too thick, add some of the remaining stock. Taste again for seasoning and adjust as needed. Finish with black pepper and a pinch of freshly grated nutmeg when serving.

BRUSSELS SPROUTS LEAVES WITH PEAR, BACON, AND PECANS

There's a Southern tradition of making a wilted salad with a boiled dressing made from the fatty drippings of cooked bacon (see page 37). Though young spring lettuces are typically the base, the leaves of Brussels sprouts offer a toothsome texture, especially in combination with other fall flavors. Bosc or Anjou pears are my favorite for this salad.

6 to 8 servings

½ cup pecan pieces
6 thick slices bacon
12 fresh sage leaves
1 firm-ripe pear
¼ cup apple cider vinegar
Kosher salt
Freshly ground black pepper
1 pound Brussels sprouts

Heat the oven to 300°F. Spread the pecan pieces on a baking sheet and toast until lightly browned and fragrant, about 8 minutes. Transfer to a dish to cool. In a wide skillet over low heat, cook the bacon until crisped on both sides. Remove the bacon from the skillet and set on paper towels. With the heat still on low, add the sage leaves to the bacon fat and lightly fry until crisped but not browned, 1 to 2 minutes. Remove the leaves and drain on a paper towel. Turn the heat off and allow the fat to cool slightly.

Slice the pear vertically into equal quarters. Place each quarter cut side down, with the seeds facing your knife. With the blade at a 45-degree angle, slice away the core and seeds from each quarter. With the core side down, cut each quarter crosswise into thin slices. Place the sliced pears in a nonreactive dish with the vinegar, and season with salt and pepper. This will keep them from turning brown.

Trim the stem end off the Brussels sprouts and, with your hands, pull the leaves apart. Rinse the leaves and then dry them in a salad spinner. Roughly chop the leaves and place in a mixing bowl. Pull the pears out of the seasoned vinegar and set aside. Chop the crisped bacon and set aside. Lightly crush the fried sage and set aside. Heat the bacon fat in the skillet and add the seasoned vinegar. Bring to a boil, and then pour over the Brussels sprouts leaves. Toss immediately. Taste for seasoning. Then add the pears, bacon, and sage, and toss well. Sprinkle with the toasted pecans and serve.

ROASTED BRUSSELS SPROUTS WITH SHALLOTS AND GARLIC

Most people who say they do not like Brussels sprouts base their judgment on a former encounter with sprouts that were boiled until they were mushy. Roasted, Brussels sprouts are almost like another vegetable. The dry heat of the oven crisps and caramelizes the edges and concentrates the sugars, while the olive oil seeps into the crevices between the leaves.

6 to 8 servings

1 pound Brussels sprouts
4 garlic cloves, thinly sliced
2 shallots, thinly sliced into crescents
¼ cup extra virgin olive oil
Kosher salt
Freshly ground black pepper

Preheat the oven to 400 °F. Wash the Brussels sprouts in cool water, trim off the stem ends, and cut in half—or quarters if they are large. Add the garlic, shallots, olive oil, salt, and pepper. Toss well, and spread on a shallow baking dish in a single layer. Roast until the sprouts are just tender, about 10 minutes. Serve immediately.

MUSTARD-ROASTED CAULIFLOWER

Cauliflower and mustard are both members of the genus *Brassica*, so it's not surprising that the seed of the mustard plant is compatible with its big-headed cousin. Try it for yourself in this incredibly simple vegetable roast, which makes a terrific side dish with fish or fowl and is also hard to stop eating straight out of the pan. If you come across the orange, green, or purple cauliflower varieties, mix them together for a stunning presentation.

4 to 6 servings

2 tablespoons whole-grain mustard
1 small garlic clove, minced
1 teaspoon kosher salt
½ teaspoon freshly ground black pepper
2 tablespoons extra virgin olive oil
1 medium head cauliflower, washed and trimmed into bite-size florets

Heat the oven to 400°F. In a large mixing bowl, stir together the mustard, garlic, salt, and pepper. Whisk in the olive oil. Toss the cauliflower in the mustard mixture to coat. Spread in a baking dish in a single layer and roast until the cauliflower is just tender and lightly browned on the edges, 20 to 25 minutes.

CHICORIES

Bitterness is not a flavor that most Americans seek. As one of the five basic tastes on the tongue, though, it does have its place. A very strong, bitter taste can warn you that what you are eating may be poisonous. Mildly bitter foods, however, can offer a bright, palate-cleansing counterpoint to sweetness, richness, and salt. Chicories are a hardy annual or biennial plant originally cultivated from a wild form native to Europe, Africa, and western Asia. They are a cool-weather crop that can bolt and turn unpleasantly bitter if temperatures warm, and this trait makes them perfect for growing in autumn.

There are two cultivated varieties: root chicory and salad chicory. Medieval monks grew the plants to dry the roots and grind them into a coffee additive, and this use is still popular in Europe and New Orleans. But my focus on chicories is above the ground, with the edible leaves: endive, escarole, frisée, radicchio, and sugarloaf.

ENDIVE: Belgian endives are palm-size, oblong, compact heads with crisp and juicy white to pale green leaves. They are grown in fields in late fall and winter and covered with dirt to stop chlorophyll from forming. Belgian endive came about in 1830 when a Brussels farmer stored chicory roots in his cellar to later dry and roast for coffee. When he returned from serving in the Belgian War of Independence, he discovered that the roots had sprouted small white leaves, which were crunchy and delicious. The popularity of Belgian endive spread to Paris, and by the 1870s this vegetable was known as white gold. It is grown in cooler climates, and its crunchy petals must be protected from light and moisture. If not, they will turn brown or slimy. Red endive looks like a crimson-tipped form of white Belgian endive, but actually it is a miniature version of radicchio and the two can be used interchangeably. Curly endive has lacy emerald-edged leaves and a prickly texture.

ESCAROLE is milder than endives in flavor and looks like a head of lettuce. It can be eaten raw or cooked and is often used in Italian cooking.

Escarole is a natural pairing with sautéed onions and garlic, olive oil and butter, or sweet or hot peppers. Escarole leaves are delicious wilted into cooked lentils or a bean stew, or sautéed and mixed with roasted fall squash. The darker outer leaves are more bitter, and the lighter leaves inside are sweeter. For best flavor, look for heads with lots of light-colored leaves. Store escarole like lettuce in the crisper, loosely wrapped in a damp towel or plastic.

FRISÉE grows in small heads with curly, frilly leaves that are darker green around the outer edges and a beautiful light chartreuse near the base and the center. Frisée is used in many fall and winter salads, and dressing intertwines nicely in its lacy leaves. One of the most famous French uses for frisée is a salad called *frisée aux lardons*. The leaves are lightly dressed in a vinaigrette and served with small bits of bacon and a poached egg. The runny yolk is sopped up by the leaves and becomes part of the dressing. Avoid heads that have lots of dark green leaves, which taste more bitter, or leaves that are turning brown or withered.

RADICCHIO: There are two main types of radicchio—the more common Chioggia, which forms a tight head and looks similar to red cabbage; and the longer-leafed Treviso, which grows upright and resembles a head of romaine lettuce. It adds color and bitterness to salads and is delicious grilled, braised, or sautéed. The deep red color turns to grayish-purple when cooked. Look for heads that are firm and not limp. Avoid any signs of deterioration, like browning or soft spots.

SUGARLOAF: This is a conical head that grows like an erect cabbage. Its leaves are extremely large and wrap around the core. When unfolded, they can be up to two feet wide. The flavor of this chicory is sweet and the leaves are crisp. I love tossing chopped sugarloaf with thin slices of watermelon radish, lemon juice, flaky sea salt, and walnut, or olive oil for a simple, quick salad that goes nicely with grilled or sautéed fish. Look for heads that are firm and crisp and avoid any with browning or wilted outer leaves.

ESCAROLE, APPLE, AND WATERCRESS SALAD

On its own, raw escarole might be too bitter for some people, but it's easily tamed by tossing it with tart-sweet apples, spicy watercress, and a mustardy vinaigrette. Look for crisp apple varieties for eating out of hand, such as Cameo, Crispin, or Pink Lady. This recipe is everything I want from a salad: cool, juicy, tangy, crisp, and refreshing, with just the right balance of bitterness.

4 to 6 servings

1 medium head escarole
2 small bunches watercress
1 medium tart-sweet apple, quartered and cored (see page 250)
A few leaves radicchio (optional)
Shallot Vinaigrette (see recipe)

Remove the outer leaves of the escarole if bruised or yellowing. Remove the root end and slice the head in half lengthwise. Lay the cut sides down and cut into 1-inch-square pieces. Transfer the chopped escarole to a large bowl of water and agitate with your fingers to wash away any dirt. Remove the escarole from the water and transfer to a salad spinner. Discard the used water. Spin dry and set aside. Trim any thick stems off the bottom of the watercress and discard them. Wash and spin dry. Repeat with the radicchio leaves, if using.

Thinly slice the apple quarters lengthwise and then place in a large bowl. Add the escarole, watercress, and radicchio leaves. Stir the Shallot Vinaigrette first, then spoon about 4 tablespoons around the inside of the bowl, dressing the bowl, not the greens. Gently lift the salad ingredients upward, repeatedly, until all the leaves are well coated. Taste and add more dressing if needed. Serve immediately.

SHALLOT VINAIGRETTE

With its sharp acidity and zippy flavor, this is my go-to dressing for bitter greens.

About 1 cup

3 tablespoons finely diced shallots
1 tablespoon Dijon mustard
1 teaspoon kosher salt
Freshly ground black pepper
2 tablespoons apple cider vinegar
2 tablespoons sherry vinegar
¾ cup extra virgin olive oil

In a medium bowl, combine the shallots, mustard, salt, pepper, and vinegars. Slowly drizzle in the oil and whisk quickly to emulsify. Taste for seasoning. The vinaigrette can be stored covered and refrigerated for up to 1 week.

WILTED ESCAROLE

Often thought of as a bitter salad green, escarole also takes well to cooking. As most Italian cooks will tell you, braising, sautéing, or wilting it tempers the bitterness and brings out its sweeter side. This quick preparation can be incorporated into any pasta dish, or served alongside fish, chicken, or slow-simmered beans.

4 to 6 servings

1 teaspoon unsalted butter
1 tablespoon extra virgin olive oil
½ cup diced onion (about ½ medium onion)
1 garlic clove, minced
Kosher salt
Crushed red pepper flakes
1 medium head escarole, washed and cut into 1-inch-square pieces
¼ cup chicken or vegetable stock
Juice of ½ lemon

In a large skillet over medium heat, melt the butter with the olive oil. Add the onion, garlic, salt, and a pinch of red pepper flakes; sauté until all the onion is translucent, about 5 minutes. Add the chopped escarole and sauté briefly, about 2 minutes. Add the stock and stir until the escarole is slightly wilted, 1 to 2 minutes. Squeeze the lemon over the cooked greens, taste for seasoning, and serve immediately.

GRILLED AND BRAISED RADICCHIO

Much of traditional Southern cooking parallels Italian peasant cuisine. Consider cooked radicchio with polenta. It is not dissimilar to our grits and greens. I like to get some char on the leaves before braising, for an extra meaty flavor.

6 servings

2 large heads round radicchio or 3 to 4 heads medium Treviso radicchio
2 tablespoons extra virgin olive oil
Kosher salt
Freshly ground pepper
2 cups chicken or vegetable stock, heated
½ cup balsamic vinegar
1 recipe creamy polenta (see page 135)
Parmigiano-Reggiano, optional

Heat the oven to 350°F. Trim the root end of the radicchio, leaving the core intact, then quarter lengthwise. On a hot grill or over an open flame, lightly char each cut side of the quarters. Arrange the charred radicchio in a pan to fit snugly. Drizzle with the olive oil and season with salt and pepper. Add the hot stock, then cover with a layer of parchment paper, followed by a layer of aluminum foil. Fold the parchment and foil over the edge of the pan to seal tightly and place in the oven. Cook the radicchio for 15 to 20 minutes or until tender. The firm and dense round varieties of radicchio need longer cooking than the light and leafy radicchio di Treviso.

Meanwhile, make the balsamic syrup. Place the balsamic vinegar in a small saucepan. Cook on medium heat until reduced by half.

To serve family style, spoon the polenta onto a wide platter, and then place the cooked radicchio, including its cooking liquid, on top. Drizzle with the balsamic syrup and serve hot. Garnish with Parmigiano-Reggiano if desired.

FALL GREENS

Every season has its greens, but at no time are greens more plentiful and varied than in fall. They start out growing in warm weather, but as the nights turn chilly and the season rolls on they get better. A cool snap creates sweeter-tasting green leaves and adds to their crunch. The greens featured in this section are more delicate than hardy greens like kale and collards, and cannot withstand the colder temperatures of winter. Look for perky greens that are not wilted or blemished and ribs that are healthy and not cracked or browning. Store wrapped loosely in a damp towel or in a plastic bag in the refrigerator for three to four days.

CHARD: With its large, ruffled leaves and taut, brilliantly colored stems, chard is so beautiful it is often used as a decorative plant in lawns and office parks. It is called Swiss chard, not because it hails from Switzerland but because the botanist who named it was Swiss. Chard is sometimes called "spinach beet" and is in fact related to both beets and spinach, in the chenopod family. Another name for chard is "sea kale," as it is prevalent in Mediterranean regions. Chard's crisp, fibrous rib and tender spinach-like leaf should be separated, for they cook at highly different rates. The leaves wilt easily and can be used any way that spinach can, although they have an astringent beet-green taste when served raw. There are long strings in the rib, as in celery. Slice or dice the stems crosswise into small pieces to break up the fibers. They can be used for sautéing or pickling, or made into a relish.

MUSTARD GREENS: The most bitter and sharpest member of the mustard family is considered the mother of the brassicas. Bite into a raw mustard leaf, and at first it tastes mildly sweet and vegetally green. But then your palate fills with a spicy, fresh mustard flavor that can be as strong as Dijon, horseradish, or even wasabi. Often, the larger outer leaves are harvested first, allowing the smaller center leaves to grow. This might account for its bitter taste, as the darker green leaves in the mustard family tend to harbor more bitterness. Though it does not form a true head, the leaves grow from a central stem, as in all of the cruciferous brassica greens. There are many types of mustard greens, from curly green to flat with purple tips or even delicate mustard frills. Mizuna and arugula are also versions of this plant, and are highlighted in spring.

TURNIP GREENS: See **TURNIPS** (page 351).

ASIAN GREENS: When you think of Southern greens, bok choy or tatsoi probably isn't what comes to mind. That being said, both have cropped up in many local growers' fields. They grow extremely well in our humid conditions and rich soil. Americans first got their taste for these delicately crunchy vegetables decades ago from exploring Asian markets or restaurants in urban areas. It is now very common to see these and other Asian greens on farmers' availability lists throughout the country, in fall and sometimes in the spring as well.

Large, oblong-shaped Napa cabbage, or Chinese cabbage, is the variety most familiar to Americans. It is the key ingredient in kimchi, and it is often used in place of Western cabbage in slaws, salads, and stir-fries. I am especially partial to both mature and baby bok choy—also known as pak choi or Chinese chard. Bok choy has a high water content, with a crisp base and tender, sweet leaves. It is succulent and surprisingly meaty when cooked, releasing flavorful juices in every bite. Tatsoi is a close cousin, with rounder leaves that look more like baby spinach, and the two can easily be interchanged. Komatsuna, also called Asian mustard greens, has brilliant reddish-purple-tinged green leaves with a sweet mustard flavor and spicy finish. I particularly like to use komatsuna raw in salads rather than cook its delicate leaves.

GLAZED BOK CHOY WITH CITRUS AND STAR ANISE

One of the qualities I love about bok choy is how easily the crisp rib absorbs the flavors of whatever it is cooked with. If it is not closely monitored, however, its tender leaves wilt quickly and the rib may turn mushy. I address this issue by quickly pulling the bok choy from the pan when it just begins to turn tender and succulent, allowing the sauce to reduce and intensify on its own. This recipe is perfect with a rice dish, or with a delicate fish that could be poached in the cooking liquid for a full meal.

4 servings

1 cup chicken or vegetable stock
1 orange, quartered, seeds removed
1 lemon, quartered, seeds removed
2 tablespoons unsalted butter
4 star anise pods
12 black peppercorns
1 teaspoon kosher salt
4 small bok choy, halved and washed

Simmer the stock in a large, wide skillet or shallow braising pan over medium heat. Squeeze the citrus into the pan, then drop in the peels. Add the butter, star anise, peppercorns, and salt and bring back to a simmer. Place the halved bok choy cut side down in the pan in a single layer. Continue to simmer over medium heat until the bok choy is tender but still has texture and bright color, about 4 minutes. With a slotted spoon remove the bok choy and set aside, but leave the citrus peels and spices in the pan. Continue to simmer until the broth is reduced by half or more. Taste the sauce for seasoning, then at the last minute, return the cooked bok choy to the glaze and reheat all the way through.

TATSOI AND ASIAN PEAR SALAD

Sweet, delicate, mild tatsoi is similar to spinach in taste but it is more closely related to turnips and mustards botanically. Tatsoi mingles happily with a gingery dressing accented with shallot rings and grain mustard. While other pears would work in this salad, I love the juicy snap of the Asian pear, which is often found in Southeastern farmers' markets. If you can't find tatsoi, you could substitute baby spinach in a pinch.

4 servings

1 Asian pear
3 tablespoons rice wine vinegar
½ pound tatsoi leaves
Juice of ½ lime
1 teaspoon soy sauce
1½ teaspoons whole-grain mustard
¼ teaspoon minced garlic
2 teaspoons grated fresh ginger
1 teaspoon honey
6 tablespoons grapeseed oil or other neutral vegetable oil
1 small shallot, peeled and sliced into thin rings
Kosher salt and freshly ground pepper to taste

Slice the pear vertically into 4 equal quarters. Place each quarter cut side down, with the seeds facing your knife. With the blade at a 45-degree angle, slice away the core and the seeds from each quarter. Thinly slice the pear quarters lengthwise either on a mandoline or by hand. Pour the vinegar over the pear slices to prevent browning while you prepare the other ingredients.

Fill a large bowl with water and submerge the tatsoi leaves to wash them. Remove the leaves from the water and spin in a salad spinner to dry. Place them in a large mixing bowl and set aside. Remove the pear from the vinegar and set aside. To the vinegar, add the lime juice, soy sauce, mustard, garlic, ginger, and honey. While whisking, drizzle in the oil and then add the shallot rings and return the pear slices to the dressing. Season with salt and pepper to taste. Spoon the dressing, pears, and shallots over the tatsoi and toss to combine.

SAUTÉED RAINBOW CHARD WITH STEMS

Beautifully colored chard stems are often discarded. This is such a waste—they can be astringent and fibrous, but if finely diced and tempered with cooking, they are a delicious complement to the tender leaves. This recipe embodies the true idea of root-to-leaf cooking.

4 servings

1 large bunch rainbow chard
2 tablespoons butter
2 tablespoons diced yellow onion
Kosher salt
Freshly ground black pepper

When cleaning the chard leaves, run your fingers on either side of the base of the stem, upward, to tear away each leaf from its stem. Fill a large mixing bowl with water and submerge and agitate the leaves in the water. Remove the leaves from the water and transfer them to a salad spinner to spin dry. Roughly chop the leaves and set aside. Wash the stems under cold running water, sliding your thumb and fingers over the length of the stem to remove any small particles of sand or dirt. Pat the stems dry and dice them to ¼ inch.

In a wide skillet, over medium heat, melt the butter. Add the onion and the diced chard stems to the pan. Season lightly with salt and pepper and let cook for 3 to 5 minutes until the onion is translucent and the chard stems begin to turn tender. Increase the heat to medium-high and add the leaves. Season lightly with salt and pepper. Using tongs, turn the leaves often, until wilted. Taste for seasoning and serve immediately.

CHARD STEM RELISH

When preparing chard, you may find that you have more stems than you know what to do with. This ruby-toned sweet-and-sour relish is an easy solution. Serve it with cheese, game birds, or charcuterie. You can also use this same recipe for beet stems.

1 cup

2 cups diced chard stems
1 cup red wine
½ cup red wine vinegar
½ cup sugar
1 teaspoon kosher salt
½ teaspoon freshly ground black pepper

Combine all the ingredients in a medium saucepan. Bring to a simmer over medium heat. Cook until the stems are tender, 8 to 10 minutes. Remove the stems with a slotted spoon and reduce the liquid by half, about 5 minutes. Let the stems and liquid cool separately and then combine. Serve chilled or at room temperature. Store covered and refrigerated for up to 4 weeks.

GREENS, FIELD PEA, AND CORNBREAD CASSEROLE

I love the combination of bitter mustard greens and creamy field peas in this hot and crusty cornbread bake. Make it using the Slow-Simmered Field Peas recipe, but if fresh peas are past their season, you can use dried and soaked peas or frozen fresh peas in their place. Typically, I see fresh field peas in our markets through October.

8 to 10 servings

2 tablespoons butter, melted; plus more, softened, for greasing pan
1 recipe Slow-Simmered Field Peas (page 198)
1 tablespoon extra virgin olive oil
1 large bunch mustard or other fall greens, washed, stemmed, and chopped
  (about 1 pound trimmed)
½ cup Crème Fraîche (page 181) or sour cream
2 to 4 tablespoons Hot Sauce (page 210), to taste
1 cup fine cornmeal
1 teaspoon kosher salt
½ teaspoon baking soda
1½ cups buttermilk
1 large egg

Heat the oven to 400°F. Lightly grease a 9 x 13-inch baking dish and set aside. Heat the batch of cooked peas and set aside. In a large saucepan or a Dutch oven over medium-high heat, warm the olive oil. Add the mustard greens and season lightly. Cook, turning with tongs, until the greens are wilted and tender, about 8 minutes. You may need to add a bit of liquid from the cooked peas to help wilt the greens. Remove from the heat. Pour off most of the cooking liquid from the peas and reserve. Add the cooked peas to the wilted greens. Stir the crème fraîche and hot sauce into the field peas and greens mixture, adding a little of the reserved pea cooking liquid to make a smooth sauce. Spread the peas and greens mixture in the prepared baking dish and check the level of liquid. Add more of the reserved cooking liquid from the peas, if needed, to come about halfway up the solids, and gently stir to combine. Keep the mixture hot while you make the cornbread topping.

In a medium mixing bowl, combine the cornmeal, salt, and baking soda. In a small bowl, whisk together the buttermilk and egg. Whisk the buttermilk mixture into the dry ingredients, then whisk in the 2 tablespoons melted butter. Carefully pour the cornmeal mixture evenly over the hot peas and greens mixture, covering the entire surface. Bake until the cornbread topping is set and lightly browned, about 30 minutes.

ATLANTA IS A LUSH, GREEN CITY AND URBAN FARMERS MAKE THE MOST OF OUR HUMID, TEMPERATE CLIMATE TO GROW CLEAN, ORGANIC FOOD FOR THE SURROUNDING COMMUNITY.

FALL SQUASH

If there is a handbook out there for organizing a fall festival, the first instruction must read, "Spread some hay into a pile and stack fall squashes on top." Their beautiful colors, shapes, and sizes are truly a sign of the season. They can easily stick around through the winter with their hard, protective skins, and are sometimes called winter squash, but their true season is autumn. There are many varieties to choose from. These are just a few.

ACORN SQUASH is indeed shaped like an acorn, with a deeply ribbed rind. Because its flesh is starchier and less sweet than that of other squashes, I roast acorn squash with a little water in the pan to steam it from below and glaze it with maple syrup, honey, or sorghum.

BUTTERNUT is probably the most recognizable squash next to pumpkin. Butternut squash has dense, sweet flesh with butterscotch notes. This bell-shaped squash has a thinner skin than most and is somewhat easier to peel owing to its smooth surface. It roasts well and is delicious on its own or stirred into other roasted fall vegetables or blended into a soup.

DELICATA has a nice combination of starchiness and sweetness, and is often called the sweet potato squash. This pale yellow, green-striped, ribbed heirloom squash is actually one of the few that have edible skin.

HUBBARD SQUASH is very large, with a tapered top, and comes in different colors. The seeds are thick and woody, and the flesh is dense, thick, and starchy, but if cooked properly this can be the meatiest of all the squashes, with a deep sweetness.

PUMPKINS are large and rounded and usually orange, but come in a range of colors from white to green to speckled and striped. They vary in texture and sweetness as well. Besides the iconic pie, pumpkin is a popular ingredient in cheesecake, custard, soup, and purees. For these recipes I prefer sugar pie pumpkin, white pumpkin, or cheese pumpkin.

The other fall squashes make great fillings for pastas or fried pies, since pumpkins have a higher water content. If necessary, the liquid can be drained out after cooking by suspending the flesh in cheesecloth over an empty bowl.

SPAGHETTI SQUASH: This has a unique fiber structure that, if the squash is cooked properly, can unravel into long strands resembling spaghetti. It is less sweet and milder than other squashes, and I love to cook with it in ways that accentuate its pasta-like strands.

Sometimes, cutting a whole squash or pumpkin can be a challenge, especially if it is large or oddly shaped. Place it on a stable flat surface and in a position where it won't rock or slip. Use a large, long knife that can span most of the surface area, and slowly wedge the blade into the squash to split the squash in half. Once halved, continue to break down the squash to manageable pieces. Then scoop the seeds from the center and reserve for roasting if desired. You may want to peel the squash whole or in sections, depending on shape and size.

When working with fall squash or pumpkin, if the seeds are relatively small, you can turn them into a crunchy, healthful snack or a flavorful oil that is great for swirling into pureed soups or drizzling on vegetables. Heat the oven to 350°F. Place the seeds and stringy flesh along with an equal amount of water in a bowl and add a tablespoon of salt. Stir together and let it sit for at least 30 minutes. Strain off the liquid, then transfer the solids to a roasting pan. Roast until the seeds are golden brown, stirring occasionally. Let cool and then separate the seeds from any clinging flesh. To make roasted squash seed oil: Place an equal amount of dry roasted seeds and canola or other neutral-flavored oil in a blender, along with any of the roasted flesh. Puree until smooth, then strain through a wire-mesh strainer. Pour the clarified oil into a separate container slowly, leaving the solids behind. Store covered and refrigerated.

SQUASH AND MUSTARD
FRILLS TOASTS

I love the contrast between roasted squash and bitter greens. This duo works well not only on a dinner plate, but also as a rustic canapé for passing or as a simple lunch. Mustard frills, a delicate type of mustard green, make it decidedly fancy, if you can find them. If not, some chopped mustard greens, dressed with a little lemon and olive oil, will taste just as good.

8 servings

1 small winter squash (delicata, acorn, or kabocha), peeled and seeded, diced into
   ½-inch pieces
3 tablespoons extra virgin olive oil
2 teaspoons kosher salt
2 garlic cloves, thinly sliced
8 slices rustic bread
1 small handful mustard frills, or mustard greens if frills are not available
Flaky sea salt
Freshly ground black pepper
Shaved Parmigiano-Reggiano

Heat the oven to 350°F. Toss the squash with 2 tablespoons olive oil, 1 teaspoon salt, and thinly sliced garlic. Transfer the squash mixture to a roasting pan. Roast until the squash is very tender and slightly caramelized, about 35 minutes. Lightly brush the bread on both sides with the remaining 1 tablespoon olive oil and bake directly on an oven rack until lightly toasted. Spread the cooked squash on the toasts. Top with mustard frills or chopped dressed mustard greens, and garnish with sea salt, pepper, and Parmigiano-Reggiano.

ROASTED BUTTERNUT SQUASH AND APPLES

Butternut squash possesses qualities that take well to roasting: firm, moist flesh with fresh pumpkin and butterscotch notes. To accentuate its savory side, I toss in some red onion and fall herbs. The dry heat of the oven brings out the natural sugars of both the diced squash and the apples, caramelizing the corners and sealing in the flavors. I separate the squash and apples when roasting because they cook at different rates, and then combine them when finished.

4 to 6 servings

1 large butternut squash or 2 small
1 red onion, cut into ½-inch dice
½ teaspoon each roughly chopped fresh thyme, sage, and rosemary leaves
2 tablespoons extra virgin olive oil
Kosher salt
Freshly ground black pepper
2 large or 3 small apples
2 tablespoons unsalted butter, melted

Position two racks in the oven, one-third above the bottom and one-third below the top. Heat the oven to 375°F.

With a Y-shape peeler, remove the outer skin of the squash. With a long knife, slice off about ½ inch of the stem end and the base end. Place the squash base side down on a cutting board, so that it stands up on its own. Carefully insert the blade of the knife across the diameter of the squash and slowly rock the knife until it is fully inserted. With both hands, carefully push down through the squash until your blade reaches the cutting board and the squash is bisected. Remove the seeds and discard or save for another use.

With each half-squash cut side down, separate the wider, hollow base from the solid upper section. Cut the hollow pieces lengthwise radially into long, 1-inch-wide strips. Trim each strip into 1-inch cubes. Cut the solid upper pieces into 1-inch cubes also. Place all of the cubed squash in a large mixing bowl. Add the onion, thyme, sage, rosemary, and olive oil. Season liberally with salt and a few turns of the pepper mill. Toss well to combine and transfer to a parchment-lined baking sheet. Roast until the squash is tender, 20 to 25 minutes.

While the squash is roasting, peel the apples. Slice the apples vertically into 4 equal quarters. Place each quarter cut side down, with the seeds facing your knife. With the blade at a 45-degree angle, slice away the core and the seeds from each quarter. Slice each quarter into three pieces lengthwise, then cut the pieces in half crosswise. Transfer the apples to a bowl, and toss with melted butter and season lightly with salt. Turn the apples out onto a parchment-lined baking sheet, and roast until the apples are tender, 10 to 15 minutes. When both the squash mixture and the apples have finished roasting, combine and taste for seasoning before serving.

MAPLE-ROASTED ACORN SQUASH WITH PECANS AND ROSEMARY

Starchier and less sweet than other fall squashes, acorn squash needs some assertive partners to overcome its blandness. Fresh rosemary, maple syrup, and buttery pecans do the trick. This recipe is so filling and satisfying that it could be served as a main vegetarian entrée.

2 to 4 servings

1 large acorn squash
2 teaspoons fresh rosemary leaves
½ cup maple syrup
Kosher salt
Freshly ground black pepper
2 tablespoons unsalted butter
¼ cup chopped pecans

Heat the oven to 375°F. Place the squash stem side up on cutting board. Using a large, sharp knife, cut the squash in half through the stem. Cut each half again, leaving four quarters. Scoop out the seeds and discard. Using a vegetable peeler, remove the skin. If any skin remains in the crevices, remove it with a paring knife.

Place the squash quarters in a baking dish, hollow side up, and add ¼ inch water to the bottom of the dish. Sprinkle the rosemary leaves over each quarter. Drizzle with the maple syrup, taking care to completely cover the squash surface. Season generously with salt and pepper. Bake, uncovered, until the squash is tender, about 1 hour. The water should evaporate by the end of the cooking time. But if it does so too quickly, the squash might scorch on the bottom. To prevent this, check halfway through the cooking time and add water as needed. Top each quarter with ½ tablespoon butter and 1 tablespoon pecans. Return to the oven and cook until the butter is melted and the pecans are golden, about 10 more minutes.

CREAMED SPAGHETTI SQUASH

Delicately flavored spaghetti squash needs only a very light sauce. The secret to showcasing its elongated spaghettilike strands is to cut it crosswise, not lengthwise. The strands grow in a spiral that wraps around the seed center. Once cooked, simply flake the strands out of the skin with the tines of a fork.

8 servings

1 medium spaghetti squash
1 tablespoon unsalted butter
½ cup heavy cream
½ cup chicken or vegetable stock
1 teaspoon kosher salt
¼ teaspoon chopped fresh thyme
4 or 5 fresh sage leaves, thinly sliced
Pinch freshly grated nutmeg

Position an oven rack one-third above the bottom, and leave the upper area of the oven open. Heat the oven to 375°F. Cut the squash in half crosswise and remove the seeds. Place both halves cut side down in a baking dish. Add ¼ inch water to the pan to keep the squash from burning on the bottom. Cook until the outside of the squash yields when pressed firmly, 30 to 40 minutes. Note that overcooking the squash causes the strands to lose their shape and become mushy. Remove from the oven and let rest until the squash is cool enough to handle.

To remove the flesh, run a fork in circles around the inside of each half. You should have about 4 cups of spaghettilike strands.

In a large skillet, melt the butter over medium-high heat. Add the cream, stock, salt, and herbs and simmer for 30 seconds. Add the squash and gently stir to warm and coat with the cream mixture. Finish with the nutmeg.

GINGERED PUMPKIN
CUSTARDS

I love pumpkin pie, but not a soggy crust, so I'm inclined to eat the filling and leave the crust behind. Preparing these in individual ramekins eliminates the crust from the get-go, and makes for a lovelier, more refined presentation.

4 servings

1 small baking pumpkin or other small fall squash
Butter for greasing ramekins
1 large egg
½ cup sugar
½ teaspoon ground cinnamon
⅛ teaspoon freshly grated nutmeg, plus more for garnish
Pinch ground ginger
Pinch ground cloves
1 teaspoon finely chopped fresh ginger
¼ teaspoon fine sea salt
¾ cup heavy cream
½ cup Whipped Sweetened Crème Fraîche (page 181)
Nutmeg for grating

Heat the oven to 350°F. Using a large knife, cut the pumpkin in half through the stem. Scoop out the seeds and fiber and discard. Place the pumpkin halves cut side down in a roasting pan and pour in ¼ inch water. Roast until the shell is easily pierced with a fork, about 40 minutes. When the cooked pumpkin is cool enough to handle, use a spoon to scoop the flesh from the shell. Transfer to a food processor and puree until smooth. Measure out 1 cup of the puree. If any puree remains, save it for another use.

Increase the oven heat to 400°F. Butter four 5-ounce ramekins.

In a medium bowl, whisk the egg until frothy. Whisk in the pureed pumpkin. Then whisk in the sugar, cinnamon, nutmeg, ground ginger, cloves, fresh ginger, and salt. Whisk in the heavy cream.

Pour into the prepared ramekins. Place the ramekins in a baking pan and set on the middle rack in the oven. Carefully pour boiling water into the baking pan until it is halfway up the sides of the ramekins. Bake until the custard is just set, 20 to 25 minutes. Cool completely. To serve, top with Whipped Sweetened Crème Fraîche and freshly grated nutmeg.

GREEN TOMATOES

As summer days recede into fall, tomatoes may still be clinging to their vines, but they will not manage to ripen in the shorter, cooler days before the first frost. Often the farmer, or the gardener, needs to use this land for other crops, so the plants will be dug up and the unripe fruit harvested. This is what I call "green tomato season." Though some might discard the green tomatoes, they are edible and quite delicious. Because I treat them so differently from a ripe tomato, I wanted to highlight them as a different fruit and emphasize the benefit of enjoying them in the fall.

Green tomatoes can appear in stores and farmers' markets throughout the entire tomato-growing season, as growers often pluck some from vines overburdened with fruit. A good time to use them is at that moment in autumn when you can support the farmer best. In the South, this bonus tomato season can last from September up to December. Perhaps that is why we have the largest consumption of green or unripe tomatoes in our foodways. Fried green tomatoes, served as a snack or in a sandwich, are a Southern specialty, but the flavorful fruits can also be cooked into a casserole, roasted, or sautéed—even baked in a mock-apple pie. I encourage shoppers to use green tomatoes as a savory Thanksgiving side dish.

Except for their lower sugar content and higher acidity, green tomatoes carry much of the same nutritional value as ripe tomatoes. They are low in calories and sodium, and they are a very good source of vitamin C. There is some evidence to suggest that tomatine, an alkaloid found in green tomatoes, may help reduce cholesterol and inhibit the growth of some human cancer cells.

Green tomatoes may be available year-round in warmer climates, such as Florida and southern Texas. The largest green tomato harvest is toward the end of the growing season, when the weather cools and the daylight shortens, slowing the ripening process. Select green tomatoes that are firm and feel dense for their size. Avoid fruit with puckered or shriveled skin, which may indicate that the vine started to die before the tomatoes were harvested. Any sign of blush or pink on the skin indicates ripening.

Green tomatoes must be stored chilled, for they will ripen at room temperature. Store away from light in a cool dry place, like the crisper of your refrigerator. Wash green tomatoes in cool water and trim as needed. If cutting into chunks, quarter and remove the top where the vine was attached. Because the fruit is unripe and the seeds are not as developed, the seed pockets are typically eaten.

Some simple ways to prepare green tomatoes are as follows.

Raw: Thinly sliced and seasoned with salt and pepper, green tomatoes add a crisp, juicy texture and an acidic counterpoint to a salad or a sandwich.

Broiled: Cut into thick slices, season with salt and pepper, place in a roasting pan, and drizzle with olive oil. Broil until bubbling and lightly caramelized. Serve hot.

Sautéed: Cut into bite-size wedges, and sauté on high heat with olive oil, salt, pepper, and thyme. Add Vidalia onions and roasted eggplant for a hearty side dish. Toss with cooked pasta to turn it into a meal.

Fried: Cut into thick slices, and season liberally with salt and pepper. Allow the slices to sit on a draining rack for 20 minutes. Pat dry and dip in beaten egg, then in fine bread crumbs to coat. Panfry in ¼ inch vegetable oil or bacon grease, on medium heat, until browned on each side. Drain on paper towels.

GREEN TOMATO GRATIN

This dish is essentially a sophisticated riff on the kitschy casseroles that begin with opening a can of cream-based soup. I start mine instead with an aromatic celery-infused cream. After layering thinly sliced, salted, and drained green tomatoes in a casserole dish, I cover them with stale bread crumbs and then pour the flavored cream over the whole thing. By the time the green tomatoes are tender, the wet bread mixture has crisped completely without burning, and the casserole is hot, bubbly, and ready to serve.

6 to 8 servings

2 tablespoons unsalted butter, room temperature
1½ to 2 teaspoons kosher salt
6 large or 8 medium green tomatoes
1 cup bread crumbs made from day-old baguette
2 cups celery cream (page 406), warmed

Butter a 9-inch baking dish. Measure out the salt into a small bowl and set aside. Slice off and discard the tip of the bottom of each tomato. Cut each tomato into ⅛-inch-thick slices. Layer the tomato slices across the bottom of the prepared pan, overlapping slightly. Sprinkle lightly with some of the salt. Continue layering and lightly salting until all the slices are used. Place a similarly sized and shaped dish or plate that fits just inside the baking dish to cover the surface of the tomatoes. Weigh down the top dish and let rest for 30 minutes. Meanwhile, heat the oven to 350°F.

Remove the weights, and holding the two dishes together, invert them to drain off the liquid that has been drawn out. Apply enough pressure so that the tomatoes stay in place, while you press out as much of the liquid as possible.

Sprinkle the bread crumbs evenly across the top of the tomatoes. Carefully pour the celery cream over the bread crumbs, making sure to soak them evenly, but not displace them. Bake until the bread crumbs are crisp and toasted and the tomatoes are bubbling, about 1 hour. Cool 15 minutes before serving.

THYME-ROASTED GREEN TOMATOES WITH CORNBREAD CROUTONS

Day-old cornbread gets a second chance when made into toasty croutons and tossed with roasted green tomatoes. The recipe is easily halved.

8 servings

½ recipe Skillet Cornbread (page 131)
4 tablespoons (½ stick) unsalted butter, melted
5 to 6 medium green tomatoes
½ yellow onion, diced
1 tablespoon chopped fresh thyme leaves
Kosher salt
Freshly ground black pepper

Heat the oven to 350°F. Cut the cornbread into 1-inch cubes and place them in a baking dish. Drizzle the cubes with about 2 tablespoons butter and toss well to coat. Quarter and core the tomatoes, and cut into 1-inch pieces. Toss them in a second baking dish with the diced onion, thyme, salt, and pepper. Drizzle with the remaining 2 tablespoons butter. Place both dishes on the center rack of the oven and bake until the cornbread is lightly browned and the tomatoes are tender, 30 to 40 minutes. Note that the croutons might be ready before the tomatoes. When both baking dishes are out of the oven, mix the croutons and tomatoes together and taste for seasoning.

HILDA'S CHOWCHOW

Old-fashioned chowchow is something my grandmother always had on her canning shelves. Though rooted in Pennsylvania Dutch country, this American classic spread throughout the Eastern United States, eventually migrating down South. Made with the fall crops of green tomato and cabbage, this zesty relish complements any Southern vegetable plate. Recipes vary, depending on family traditions and on what is abundant, but all follow the same technique. Before being cooked, the vegetables are always chopped into tiny bits, traditionally with a meat grinder, but if you do not have one, a food processor works just as well. If you end up with a bumper crop of green tomatoes, this is an excellent way to put some up for later.

4 quarts

3 medium yellow onions, about 4 cups chopped
1 small head green cabbage, quartered, cored, and roughly chopped
4 green bell peppers, trimmed, seeded, and roughly chopped
4 red bell peppers, trimmed, seeded, and roughly chopped
1 small jalapeño or serrano pepper, roughly chopped
4 medium green tomatoes, cored and roughly chopped
½ cup kosher salt
1 cup sugar
1 tablespoon celery seed
2 tablespoons mustard seeds
1½ teaspoons ground turmeric
4 cups apple cider vinegar

In a large bowl combine the onion, cabbage, bell peppers, jalapeño pepper, and green tomatoes. Pass them through the food grinder or process them in batches in a food processor. Add the salt to the vegetable mixture and stir well. Let rest 30 minutes. Transfer the vegetable mixture to a large saucepan or Dutch oven and add the sugar, celery seed, mustard seeds, turmeric, and cider vinegar. Over medium-low heat, simmer, stirring occasionally, until thickened, about 1 hour. Transfer to sterilized quart jars and process in a boiling water bath for 15 minutes, following the canning procedures recommended by the jar manufacturer, or if you choose not to process, simply refrigerate the jars.

MUSHROOMS

Mushrooms are mysterious. Unlike plants, which owe their structure to cellulose, fungi contain chitin, a protective substance also found in the exoskeletons of insects and shellfish. Mushrooms have been called the liver of the woods, or the oyster bed of the forest, because they are filters for unwanted decay. The root system actually thrives on decaying plant matter as a source for food, recycling what is dead into a new life-form. The cap of the mushroom, the part that we eat, is considered the fruit of the fungus. The cap grows in size by absorbing moisture in the air. Foragers often travel great distances, deep into the woods, to find these hidden treasures. In addition, several varieties are cultivated by mushroom growers as well. Wild or cultivated, mushrooms are prized by chefs and culinary enthusiasts alike.

CHANTERELLES: These are found only in the wild and have a light fruity aroma and delicate flavor. They appear in the South around June but in other parts of the country through summer and fall.

CREMINI: These are like darker, deeper-flavored versions of the common white button mushroom, though actually they are young versions of portobellos and are sometimes sold as "baby bellos," or "baby bellas."

HEDGEHOG: With a flavor akin to a mild chanterelle, these mushrooms get their name because they have small toothlike projections on their lower cap surfaces rather than gills.

HEN OF THE WOODS: These delicate, rich-tasting mushrooms look like flowers and grow at the base of trees, especially oaks. They are also called *maitake*, which means "dancing mushrooms" in Japanese.

LION'S MANE: These globular-shaped mushrooms grow up in the limbs of trees and have vertical teeth-like spines. Their flavor has been compared to lobster or shrimp, and they are as prized for their medicinal properties as for their taste.

MORELS: These honeycomb-webbed mushrooms with cartoon-like caps pop up in the wild in springtime only and are a prized delicacy.

OYSTER MUSHROOMS: These are shaped like little fans, with white, pale brown, gray, yellow, blue, or reddish caps and white stems. They are velvety-textured and have a mild peppery undertone that becomes sweeter when they are cooked. They can be found in the wild or cultivated by mushroom growers.

PORCINI: Similar to portobellos, these nutty mushrooms are a staple of Italian cuisine in both fresh and dried form. When dried they make a strongly flavored dark broth that can enhance soups, stews, and braises.

PORTOBELLO: These deeply flavored mushrooms are actually overgrown cremini, and are frequently grilled whole as an entrée. The woody stem can be used for stock, but the dark brown gills under the cap should be removed. The gills can easily be scraped away with the side of a spoon.

SHIITAKES: First popular in Asia, these meaty-textured mushrooms have round, brown caps and tough stems that should be removed before cooking. Shiitakes add a smoky, umami flavor to a variety of dishes, and the stems can be used to make a flavorful stock (see page 131).

Choose mushrooms with spongy, firm caps that are neither broken nor shriveled. Store in the refrigerator in a paper bag or in a container covered with a damp paper towel for up to a week. Clean mushrooms by brushing with a small paintbrush, or a clean soft-bristled toothbrush. If mushrooms are extremely dirty, you can rinse them quickly under cool water and dry immediately, right before using. Do not store after rinsing.

CHANTERELLES AND CAMEMBERT TOAST

In the cheese-making process, the bloomy white rind of Camembert is formed after it is misted with an edible mold spore that is derived from mushrooms. These simple but elegant toasts unify the mushroom theme, pairing wild delicate chanterelles with this soft-ripened cheese.

8 servings

1 tablespoon unsalted butter, plus more for the baguette slices
8 slices baguette, buttered and toasted
3 to 4 ounces good-quality Camembert, cut into thin wedges, room temperature
1 tablespoon extra virgin olive oil
2 cups chanterelle mushrooms, cleaned, trimmed, and torn into bite-size pieces
Kosher salt
Freshly ground black pepper
1 small shallot, minced
2 garlic cloves, minced
Juice of ½ lemon
½ teaspoon each finely chopped fresh parsley and thinly sliced chives

Heat the oven to 300°F. Arrange the buttered baguette slices on a baking sheet and bake until crisp but not hard, 4 to 5 minutes. Divide the cheese among the toasts and set aside.

In a medium skillet over high heat, melt the 1 tablespoon butter with the olive oil. Add the mushrooms, season with salt and pepper, and then toss to coat. Leave the mushrooms undisturbed for about 1 minute until lightly browned. Repeat on the other side. Add the shallot and garlic, toss to combine, and lightly season again with salt and pepper. Cook for 1 minute more, then add the lemon juice and herbs and remove from the heat. Top each slice of toast with some of the hot mushroom mixture. Serve immediately.

PRESERVED MUSHROOMS

These brightly flavored pickled mushrooms, when chilled, are wonderful on a warm chèvre toast. I also love them heated and served over a juicy grilled steak.

1 quart

1 pound mixed mushrooms, such as shiitakes, oyster, cremini, and chanterelles
1 cup white wine vinegar
1 cup dry white wine
1½ teaspoons kosher salt
Finely grated zest of 1 lemon
1 fresh hot pepper, thinly sliced
½ cup extra virgin olive oil

Slice the mushrooms into ¼-inch pieces and transfer to a small saucepan. Add the vinegar, white wine, and salt. Bring to a boil and then remove from the heat. Add the lemon zest, hot pepper, and olive oil and stir to combine. Transfer to a lidded container and refrigerate overnight or up to a day prior to serving. Store covered and refrigerated for up to 4 weeks.

ROASTED MUSHROOM FARROTTO

This recipe follows the basic risotto technique, but with a nontraditional grain. The nutty flavor and chewy texture of farro, the spelt equivalent of the wheat berry, are an unexpected delight with earthy, deep-flavored mushrooms both dried and fresh.

Makes 4 main-dish or 6 side-dish servings

1 small onion, roughly chopped
1 small carrot, roughly chopped
1 rib celery, roughly chopped
1 sprig fresh thyme
1 ounce dried mushrooms, porcini or other variety
2 pounds mixed fresh fall mushrooms
1 tablespoon minced fresh garlic
1 tablespoon finely diced shallot
¼ cup extra virgin olive oil
2 teaspoons kosher salt, plus more for seasoning
½ teaspoon freshly ground black pepper, plus more for seasoning
4 tablespoons (½ stick) unsalted butter
½ pound farro (about 1 rounded cup)
2 cups white wine

Heat the oven to 400°F.

In a medium saucepan, combine the onion, carrot, celery, thyme, and dried mushrooms. Cover with 4 cups water and place over medium heat.

Clean the fresh mushrooms, trimming off any woody stems. Add the stems to the simmering broth and cook for 25 minutes. Meanwhile, cut the cleaned fresh mushrooms into 1-inch pieces and transfer to a large bowl. Toss the mushrooms with the garlic, shallot, olive oil, salt, and pepper. Transfer the mushroom mixture to a baking sheet and spread in a single layer. Roast until slightly browned but not crisp, 12 to 15 minutes. Remove from the oven, let cool, and set aside.

When the mushroom broth is ready, place a wire mesh strainer over a large bowl and strain out the solids. When cool enough to handle, pick out the rehydrated dried mushrooms, roughly chop them, and set them aside. Discard the rest of the solids and reserve the broth.

In a wide skillet, over medium heat, melt the butter until foamy. Add the farro and season lightly with salt. Stir continuously until the farro is well coated and lightly toasted. Add ½ cup wine and stir until all of it is absorbed. Repeat the preceding step until all the wine has been absorbed. Repeat this same step using the mushroom broth, ½ cup at a time, until all the broth has been absorbed. Taste a few grains of the farro. If it is too firm, add water, wine, or broth, ½ cup at a time, until absorbed and the farro reaches the desired tenderness. Add the roasted mushrooms and the chopped rehydrated mushrooms to the farro and taste for seasoning.

NUTS

There are many tree nuts around the world, but the ones that I mainly focus on in this book are pecans and chestnuts. Both are available in the South, where I live, and from local sources.

PECANS: Though pecans are available year-round, their harvest season is the fall. Since I have been in the restaurant business, I have always worked with the folks at Pearson Farm in Fort Valley, Georgia. They grow the Elliott pecan, which has a small, round shape and perfect sweetness. The pecan is the only tree nut that is native to North America. Its origins can be traced back to the sixteenth century in central and eastern North America and the river valleys of Mexico. Pecans were revered not only for their taste, but because they were easier to shell than other nut species. The first U.S. pecan tree planting took place on Long Island, New York, in 1772. Around this time, settlers were also planting pecans along the Gulf Coast; and New Orleans, with its strategic location near the mouth of the Mississippi River, became a major center for distributing pecans throughout the world. Today they are mainly grown in Texas, Louisiana, Mississippi, and Georgia.

Pecans in the shell should be heavy for their size and should not rattle when shaken. Fresh pecans generally peak during the first few weeks after harvesting season in the fall. Unshelled pecans can be stored at room temperature for three months. Shelled pecans will keep for up to six months in the refrigerator in a sealed container. Because of their high oil content, they are better purchased in the shell or refrigerated if shelled.

CHESTNUTS: Unlike pecans or walnuts, chestnuts have sweet, starchy flesh that deteriorates rapidly, and they need to be used almost as quickly as they fall. There are three species of chestnut trees around the globe: Japanese, European, and American. But from 1900 to 1940, nearly all American species were wiped out by the "chestnut blight"—a parasite accidentally introduced by Japanese species imported to America. As a result, I never tried a chestnut until I lived abroad. When I studied in Paris for my final year of architecture school, I would often walk by a little old man peddling roasted chestnuts just around the corner from my apartment. One cold November morning, I decided to stand in line and see what everyone was waiting for. I remember the aroma: they had a smoky smell, from the smoldering shells that were cooked over an open flame in order to crack their seal. The piping-hot sweet chestnuts were served right off his cart into a brown paper bag. I soon became a regular in his line.

ROASTED CHESTNUTS: Peeled and cooked chestnuts can be purchased vacuum-packed, but their flavor pales in comparison with freshly roasted ones. Though chestnuts are undeniably tedious to peel, you can make this a group activity to lessen the burden. They should always be scored before roasting to allow steam and pressure to escape when they heat. If you happen to own a chestnut scoring knife (yes, these exist), by all means use it. However, you can easily get by without one by following the method below.

Heat the oven to 350°F. Place each chestnut flat side down on a cutting board. Hold a paring knife with one hand and with the other secure the chestnut firmly on the board with the pointed end, or crown, toward your knife. Score the crown vertically with the tip of the knife, making sure that the tip fully penetrates the outer hull. Turn the nut and repeat the same motion to form an X. Repeat until all the chestnuts are scored. Put the chestnuts in a single layer in a shallow baking dish, and roast on the middle rack of the oven for 20 to 25 minutes. Check the chestnuts periodically. They are ready when the hard outer hull begins to split. If a chestnut makes a popping sound while cooking, quickly remove the pan before more of them start to explode in your oven. Allow the chestnuts to cool for at least 15 minutes, then break off and peel away the outer hull. You may want to wear gloves, as the shells can have sharp edges.

CORNBREAD-PECAN DRESSING MUFFINS

The first year that Miller Union was open, I received a call that both thrilled and terrified me. A representative from the *Martha Stewart Show* invited me to be a guest on the Thanksgiving episode, the holy grail of media opportunities for any chef. It just so happened that I was already working on a recipe for cornbread dressing that I thought Martha would really like. Rather than cut unattractive hunks out of a casserole dish, I wanted to serve individual portions, baked in a muffin tin, that would give each diner the perfect balance of crusty edge to moist center. I added chopped pecans and dried fruit for crunch and tang. Nervous as I was under the bright lights of the soundstage, I began to relax when Martha bit into one muffin and raved on live TV.

12 muffins

2 tablespoons unsalted butter, plus more for greasing tins
1 recipe Skillet Cornbread (page 131), crumbled (8 cups)
¾ cup coarsely chopped dried sour cherries
¾ cup chopped pecan pieces
1 cup chopped onion
1 cup chopped celery
2 tablespoons chopped shallot
2 teaspoons finely chopped fresh sage
1½ teaspoons chopped fresh thyme leaves
1¾ cups chicken or vegetable stock
3 large eggs, lightly beaten
Kosher salt
Freshly ground black pepper

Heat the oven to 325°F. Grease a standard 12-cup muffin tin with butter; set aside. Crumble the cornbread into medium-fine pieces into a large bowl. Add the cherries and pecans and set aside.

Heat 2 tablespoons butter in a large skillet over medium-high heat. Add the onion, celery, shallot, sage, and thyme, and cook until the onion is translucent, about 5 minutes. Add the stock and let simmer for 5 minutes. Pour the vegetable mixture over the cornbread and mix to combine; let cool slightly. Stir in the eggs and season with salt and pepper.

Using your hands or a large spoon, place a heaping mound of the cornbread mixture in each muffin cup. Gently press and pat each mound into a domed shape. Keep in mind that this batter does not rise. Bake until set, 35 to 40 minutes. Let cool, then remove from the muffin tins. To reheat, wrap each muffin individually in aluminum foil and return to the oven until hot.

CHESTNUT, WATERCRESS, AND WILD RICE SALAD

Roasting and peeling chestnuts can be a daunting task, but you need only a small amount to enhance this autumnal rice salad. The base is a mixture of two distinctive regional grains: Southern coastal Carolina Gold rice and wild rice, a tea-flavored grass seed first discovered by Native Americans. The watercress in this rice salad is used more like an herb, and it happens to thrive in water, the same environment that rice needs to grow. Served at room temperature, this salad is an ideal candidate for the Thanksgiving table, an autumn picnic, or a potluck.

4 to 6 servings

2 tablespoons unsalted butter
1 cup Carolina Gold rice (or basmati, if Carolina Gold is not available)
½ cup wild rice
1 teaspoon salt, plus more as needed
3 cups stock or water, heated
1 tablespoon finely diced shallot
¼ teaspoon Dijon mustard
1 tablespoon Champagne vinegar
2 tablespoons extra virgin olive oil
¾ cup chopped roasted chestnuts (see page 331)
1 large handful watercress, roughly chopped

Place two small saucepans on the stove. Melt 1 tablespoon butter in each pan over medium heat. Add the Carolina Gold rice and ½ teaspoon salt to one pan and the wild rice and the remaining ½ teaspoon salt to the other pan. Stir both rices frequently until the Carolina Gold rice turns opaque and the wild rice becomes fragrant, about 5 minutes. Add 2 cups hot stock or water to the Carolina Gold rice pan, and 1 cup hot stock or water to the wild rice pan. Bring each mixture to a boil, then immediately reduce to the lowest simmer and cover. Cook the Carolina Gold rice until all the liquid is absorbed, about 15 minutes; and the wild rice until it reaches the desired tenderness, 40 to 45 minutes. Turn off the heat, let rest for 5 minutes, fluff with a fork, and then turn the rices out into a shallow dish together to cool.

In a small bowl, whisk together the shallot, mustard, vinegar, and olive oil to make the dressing. Add the chestnuts and watercress to the rice and then toss with the dressing. Taste and adjust seasoning as needed. Serve at room temperature.

PECAN-CARAMEL CHOCOLATE TART

I'm all about healthy eating, but sometimes I just want to indulge. This dessert is straight-up salted caramel, crunchy pecans, and dark chocolate with a sweet, gooey center—all housed in a crisp tart shell. I would take this inspired creation from Miller Union's pastry chef, Pamela Moxley, over the cloying corn syrup–laden cliché any day. The recipe can also be made into individual tarts (as shown in the photo here).

12 to 15 servings

1½ cups sugar
1 tablespoon light corn syrup
½ cup heavy cream
½ cup unsalted butter
1½ ounces unsweetened chocolate, chopped
1½ cups toasted and finely chopped pecans
¼ teaspoon salt
1 vanilla bean, split, seeds scraped, and pod reserved for another use
1 recipe Tart Dough (page 471)

In a 4-quart saucepan, combine the sugar, ¼ cup water, and the corn syrup. Place over high heat and stir with a wooden spoon until the sugar has dissolved. Once the sugar has dissolved, stop stirring and cook until the mixture turns a caramel color, 6 to 8 minutes. Remove from the heat and carefully add all of the heavy cream. It will bubble furiously. Whisk to combine. Add the butter, chocolate, pecans, salt, and split vanilla bean and seeds. Cool the mixture for at least 1 hour before baking. Remove the vanilla bean after cooling.

Preheat the oven to 350°F. Pour the caramel-pecan filling into a par-baked tart shell and bake until bubbly around the edges and halfway to the center of the tart, 30 to 35 minutes. Cool completely before unmolding.

CREAMY CHESTNUT PUREE

Chestnuts seem to go well with any type of bird, domestic or wild, and this is fitting, since they are most abundant during hunting season. To balance the chestnuts' distinct, naturally sweet flavor in this sauce, I cook them with savory ingredients like onion, garlic, and shallot. The result is a velvety puree with subtle sweet tones and a creamy thyme-laced finish. You may or may not end up incorporating all of the cooking liquid, depending on the starchiness of the chestnuts. If any liquid remains, you can use it as the base for cooking bitter greens, which I often pair with this sauce. Conversely, the puree can be thinned out with extra chicken stock to make a rich holiday soup.

About 1 cup

2 tablespoons unsalted butter
½ medium yellow onion, diced
1 small shallot, diced
2 garlic cloves, halved
1 teaspoon kosher salt
½ cup roasted chestnuts (see page 331)
1 sprig fresh thyme
1 cup chicken stock
1 cup heavy cream

In a medium saucepan over medium heat, melt the butter until foamy. Add the onion, shallot, and garlic and season with salt. Cook and stir until the onion turns translucent, 4 to 5 minutes. Add the chestnuts, thyme, stock, and cream. Simmer until the chestnuts are tender, 15 to 20 minutes. Remove from the heat and pull out the sprig of thyme. With a slotted spoon, transfer the solids to a blender. Add about half of the cooking liquid to the blender pitcher and turn the motor on at slow speed. If the mixture in the blender is too thick, add more liquid until the contents move around freely. Blend at medium speed until smooth and then taste for seasoning. The mixture should have the consistency of hummus or a thick sauce.

GRIDDLED CHICKEN

I learned this method of cooking boneless skin-on chicken when I staged in the kitchen at Chez Panisse one summer. Because the bones have been removed, the skin lies flat against the hot surface; the heat crisps it while rendering the fat within the skin. The resulting flavor of this nearly naked bird falls somewhere between roasted and fried, and it's simply delicious. I strongly recommend that you seek out a butcher who sells local farm-raised chickens that are not pumped with growth hormones or antibiotics. These free-roaming birds tend to have more developed leg and thigh muscles, which may require a longer cooking time. The breasts, however, are much smaller than those of commercially packaged factory birds and cook more quickly. If you are not comfortable butchering whole birds yourself, ask your butcher to do it for you. Here I've paired these cuts with escarole and chestnuts, but truly they will go with just about any vegetable side.

4 servings

2 free-range boneless skin-on chicken thigh-leg quarters (about 6 ounces each)
2 free-range boneless skin-on chicken breast halves (about 4 ounces each)
Kosher salt
Freshly ground black pepper
¼ cup extra virgin olive oil
1 recipe Creamy Chestnut Puree (page 340)
1 recipe Wilted Escarole (page 283)

Warm a large cast-iron skillet on medium heat for 5 minutes. Meanwhile, season the chicken with salt and pepper. Add the oil to the warm skillet and increase the heat to medium-high. Carefully place the chicken pieces in the oil, skin side down. Lower or raise the heat as needed to keep a constant medium-high temperature. Griddle without turning until the skin is golden and crispy, about 15 minutes. If the heat is too high, the skin can easily burn. When the skin is crisp, turn the chicken pieces over and cook through, about 10 minutes. Keep in mind that the breasts will be ready first and can be removed while the dark meat continues to cook. Let rest for 5 minutes after cooking, then serve whole or sliced with the chestnut puree and escarole.

SWEET POTATOES

Sweet potatoes thrive in hot, moist climates, which may explain why they have always been popular in the South. We whip them, soufflé them, candy them, and bake them, alone and in pies and other sweet desserts. Most traditional preparations rely on, or even enhance, their sugar content, sometimes making them too sweet to enjoy. I like to use them in sweet and savory ways, but always with some balance.

One easy way to cook them is to peel them, cut them into disks, and place them in a shallow pan. Pour in a syrup of equal parts water and sorghum with some lemon juice and nutmeg. Dot them with butter, sprinkle with salt, and bake until they are tender and caramelized. They are also incredible in a spicy curry or a savory soup. Sweet potatoes can be grated raw and stirred into muffins, pancakes, fritter batter, or cake batter. Anywhere you use them, you are adding not only flavor and depth but also deep nutrition.

Sweet potatoes can, under the right conditions, produce more pounds of food per acre than any other cultivated plant. And this was important in poor, agrarian areas, as they are filling, nutritious, and delicious. High in fiber and a rich source of antioxidants and beta-carotene, sweet potatoes are in fact one of the most nutritious vegetables around.

Sweet potatoes are not in the nightshade family at all, and are only a very distant relative of the potato. They are more closely related to the morning glory and belong to the family Convolvulaceae. We mostly eat the roots, but the greens are a nutritious and edible source of food, too. These pitchfork-shaped greens can be cooked just like spinach. Because the quick-growing greens need to be pruned from the plant, farmers tend to harvest the greens daily as the plant matures, so there is actually a brief sweet potato greens season in late summer or early fall. Though the greens are common in Chinese and Taiwanese cooking, Southerners, ironically enough, have been slow to develop a taste for them.

In midsummer, when the earth maintains a constant warm temperature, farmers plant sweet potato slips: stems that emerge from a sweet potato sprout. Once they take root, the vines spread widely, forming a thick ground cover that not only shades and cools the soil but also inhibits the growth of weeds. The tubers are dug up in early fall, before the soil gets cold, and are cured in a warm place for a week or two before being stored at temperatures above fifty-five degrees.

One of the oldest vegetables known to man, the sweet potato is as diverse as the potato. There are white, golden, orange, red, and purple-fleshed sweet potatoes. Some are starchier than others, depending on the variety, growing conditions, and how long they were cured.

Common varieties include these:

Beauregard, with its smooth skin and deep orange flesh, is the most commonplace commercial cultivar. It is versatile and lends itself to all kinds of preparations.

Garnet has a rough, reddish skin and a moist, orange-yellow flesh that's especially prized for pies.

Orange-skinned Jewel has tender, deep-orange flesh ideal for baking.

More unusual varieties include the nutty-flavored speckled purple sweet potato; the mild, pale orange heirloom called Envy; and the tan-skinned Hannah, which has dry, yellowish-white flesh that's great for mashing.

Even though sweet potatoes are harvested in cold weather, do not store them in the refrigerator. Moisture and light encourage them to sprout. Store them in a cool, dark place in a breathable situation.

CONFIT SWEET POTATOES IN DUCK FAT

Confit is the French technique of submerging an ingredient in warm fat and cooking it slowly. Think of this as gently poaching in fat instead of water. Butter is usually my go-to for enhancing sweet potatoes, but duck fat makes this nutritious tuber feel decadent. When the confit process is done, the sweet potatoes will seem a little soggy or limp because they were cooked at a low temperature. To remedy this, they will be cut into pieces and meet the fat again, this time in a hot skillet, to crisp and blister. If duck fat is not available, you could substitute butter or olive oil.

4 servings

4 small sweet potatoes, about 2 pounds
2 pounds rendered duck fat, about 4½ cups
Kosher salt for finishing

Choose a saucepan large enough to hold your sweet potatoes snugly, allowing space for the fat to fill in around them. Then remove the sweet potatoes and melt the duck fat over medium-low heat in that saucepan. Meanwhile, scrub the sweet potatoes under running water and then wipe them dry with a kitchen towel. Carefully place the potatoes in the warm fat, making sure that they are completely submerged. Cook on medium-low heat without stirring for 30 to 45 minutes, depending on their size. Test them from time to time with the tip of a paring knife. As soon as the flesh yields to the knife, remove the potatoes with a slotted spoon, transfer to a plate, and refrigerate. While the fat is still warm but not hot, reserve a few tablespoons, then strain it into a heatproof container and chill for later use.

Once completely cooled, slice the sweet potatoes crosswise into ½-inch disks. Heat a wide cast-iron skillet over medium heat and add 1 tablespoon of the reserved duck fat. Cook the sweet potato slices 2 to 3 minutes on each side in batches to avoid crowding the pan. Remove from the pan when crisped and blistered. Continue to add duck fat as needed for the other batches. Season with salt and serve hot.

SWEET POTATO–BUCKWHEAT PANCAKES

Buckwheat pancakes can be one of the most nutritious breakfasts you eat, but the strong, tannic flavor of this powerhouse grain often compels us to douse them in butter and maple syrup. I added some grated sweet potato to this batter for extra depth and natural sweetness and was amazed at how tender and light these pancakes turned out. It doesn't hurt that this recipe is ridiculously easy to make and happens to be gluten free. I tested these with honey, sorghum, and maple syrup, and honey was the winner.

4 cups batter; about 16 pancakes

1 cup buckwheat flour
1 teaspoon baking powder
1 teaspoon baking soda
½ teaspoon salt
1 large egg, room temperature
1½ cups buttermilk, room temperature
1 small sweet potato (4 to 5 ounces), peeled and grated, about 1 cup
4 tablespoons (½ stick) unsalted butter, melted and cooled, plus softened butter
  for serving
Honey for serving

Put the buckwheat, baking powder, soda, and salt in a medium bowl, and mix to combine. In a separate bowl, whisk together the egg and buttermilk. Add the dry to the wet ingredients and stir to combine. Stir in the grated sweet potato and melted butter.

Heat a wide skillet or griddle over medium-low heat. Drop ¼ cup of pancake batter onto the griddle, being careful not to let the edges of the cakes touch. Flip when the edges are set and bubbles form in the center of each cake, about 3 minutes. Cook about 2 minutes after flipping or until golden brown. To make sure that they do not get too dark, check the color by gently lifting with a spatula and taking a peek.

Stack on plates and serve warm with softened butter and warm honey.

ROASTED SWEET POTATOES IN THEIR JACKETS

Raw sweet potatoes may seem starchy and dry, but it is amazing how much moisture they actually hold. When they are roasted whole, this liquid steams the inside and converts the starches to sugars. Often some of this natural syrup oozes out onto the pan. That's your sign to yank them from the oven, split them open, and add dollops of butter, a sprinkling of coarse salt, and freshly milled black pepper. Eat them, jacket and all, and be sure to scrape some of that syrup off the pan with your fork, too. Resist the temptation to prick the potatoes with a fork before baking; you do not want to lose any of the caramelized juices that emerge from the inside.

4 servings

4 small to medium sweet potatoes, scrubbed clean
4 tablespoons (½ stick) unsalted butter, or to taste
Coarse salt
Freshly ground black pepper

Heat the oven to 350°F. Place the sweet potatoes in a shallow roasting pan and position in the center of the oven. Cook until tender, about 40 minutes. Remove the potatoes from the oven. While still hot, score lengthwise and crosswise with the tip of a knife. Holding each end of the sweet potato, gently push toward the center to release the steam and loosen the flesh. Immediately fill with pats of butter and season with salt and pepper.

CARDAMOM-WHIPPED SWEET POTATOES

Here's an exotic-tasting variation of the above recipe using fragrant, pungent cardamom. I prefer to grind the cardamom fresh, but if you already have some ground, by all means use it. A little goes a long way.

4 to 6 servings

4 medium sweet potatoes
4 to 6 tablespoons butter, room temperature
½ teaspoon ground cardamom
1 tablespoon kosher salt
1 teaspoon freshly ground black pepper
½ teaspoon freshly grated lemon zest
1 teaspoon freshly squeezed lemon juice

Follow the instructions above for Roasted Sweet Potatoes in Their Jackets. When they are cooked, remove the skin and place the flesh in a large bowl. Add the softened butter, cardamom, salt, and pepper and mix with a potato masher or a firm whisk. Add the lemon zest and juice, and stir to combine. Taste for seasoning.

TURNIPS

There is nothing glamorous about a turnip. It has long been a symbol of poverty and considered peasant food. But I find it to be a workhorse of a vegetable with its subtle versatility. Its starchy flesh yields creamy purees, peppery pickles, and hearty roasts. Turnip tops can be simmered slowly with fatback, wilted into a stew, or eaten raw. Because the green tops and the roots are usually sold separately, the farmer has the opportunity to sell two products from one plant; this give the turnip an economic edge over some other vegetables. Among the oldest and most commonly used crops, this member of the genus *Brassica* does best in cooler fall conditions, as warm temperatures give it a bitter flavor, characteristic of the mustard-related plants. Since the roots and greens are edible I will address them separately.

TURNIP ROOTS: Of all the turnip roots, the purple top is the most common and also the most dense. It requires cooking to capitalize on its flavor and texture. Its starch content is high, so if blended it can thicken a sauce or soup and add body and weight. Unless a purple top is very young and tender, the skin needs to be peeled away. The roots pop through the ground surface when they are ready, letting the grower know that it's time to pull them. Frost improves the flavor and the turnips can be stored in the ground until you are ready to use them—cover them to keep from freezing. Because the purple top is a storage root it will keep in the refrigerator for several weeks and still be good for cooking.

The scarlet turnip looks more like a radish but has a sweet turnip flavor. It has a higher water content and a perfumed aroma. The flavor is earthy with strong floral tones. I like to leave the beautiful magenta skin on, rather than peel it away, since it is relatively smooth and flavorful.

The hakurei turnip, also called Tokyo turnip or salad turnip, has the highest water content of all. It "eats" more like a radish, with a mild sweet turnip flavor. These turnips can be enjoyed raw or cooked. Because the starch is low, they can be cooked quickly and provide a juicy burst of flavor when roasted. They never require peeling, but may need a little scrubbing at the top where sand or dirt can collect around the base of the green stem. These are also great for pickling or fermenting and even make a good snack eaten raw.

TURNIP GREENS: Like the other fall greens, turnips do best in cool weather; but their tender tops cannot survive cold temperatures, and heat makes them bitter. One unique feature of the turnip is that if you trim the tops from the plant but leave some on the root while in the ground, more greens will regenerate up until the first frost. Because they typically grow in sandy soil, the leaves sometimes droop and can be very dirty. It is important to wash them several times to remove any sandy grit. All turnip roots form greens that usually are best when cooked, with the exception of baby turnips and hakurei turnips. When they are young and tender, the greens can be chopped and added to a salad or lightly wilted and eaten like spinach.

To make traditional stewed turnip greens, start with some chopped onion in a stockpot or Dutch oven. Cook the onion in olive oil, or in fat from a little smoked pork. Season the pot well, then fill halfway with water. Bring to a simmer and add the washed, chopped greens. Tasting as you go, simmer until tender. Serve with piping-hot cornbread. Be sure to serve some of the cooking liquid, or the pot likker, from the pan with the greens.

To select turnip tops, look for perky greens that are not wilted or blemished and ribs that are healthy and not cracked or browning. Store wrapped loosely in a damp towel or in a plastic bag in the refrigerator for three to four days.

TURNIPS AND THEIR GREENS WITH BACON

A lot of people do not realize that turnip greens and turnip roots are two parts of the same plant. This dish features the best of both. The starchier purple-topped roots are turned into a pillow of creamy puree, where lightly wilted greens and their roasted petite roots nestle with crispy bits of bacon. This study in turnips is easy to assemble. Just spoon the puree onto the plate and layer with the turnips, greens, and bacon.

4 servings

Purple top turnip puree

2 tablespoons butter
1 small onion, diced
2 medium purple top turnip roots, peeled and cubed, about 1 pound
1 teaspoon kosher salt
½ cup heavy cream
½ teaspoon fresh thyme leaves

In a wide skillet over medium heat, warm the butter until foamy. Add the onion and cook, stirring frequently, for 2 minutes. Add the turnips, season with salt, and stir to combine. Cover with a lid and turn the heat down to the lowest setting. Check after 5 minutes to make sure that the turnips are not sticking to the pan or caramelizing or burning. Stir again, then add the cream and cover. Cook until the turnips are tender, about 35 minutes, stirring occasionally. Transfer all to a blender and add the fresh thyme. Blend until smooth. Cool completely, then store covered and refrigerated for up to 5 days.

Roasted hakurei turnips

2 cups hakurei turnips, quartered, greens separated and reserved
½ teaspoon salt
1 teaspoon fresh thyme leaves
2 tablespoons extra virgin olive oil

Heat the oven to 425°F. In a small bowl, combine the turnips, salt, thyme, and oil. Toss well to combine, then transfer to a shallow roasting pan or rimmed baking sheet. Roast just until tender, 15 to 20 minutes.

Sautéed hakurei greens with bacon

8 slices thick-cut bacon, cooked
2 tablespoons bacon fat
¼ cup diced onion
½ teaspoon kosher salt
5 to 6 cups reserved turnip greens

Chop the bacon into bite-size pieces and set aside. In a wide skillet over medium heat, warm the bacon fat. Add the onion and salt to the skillet and cook for 3 minutes, or until translucent. Add the greens and sauté, turning with tongs until wilted, about 5 minutes. Taste for seasoning and adjust as needed.

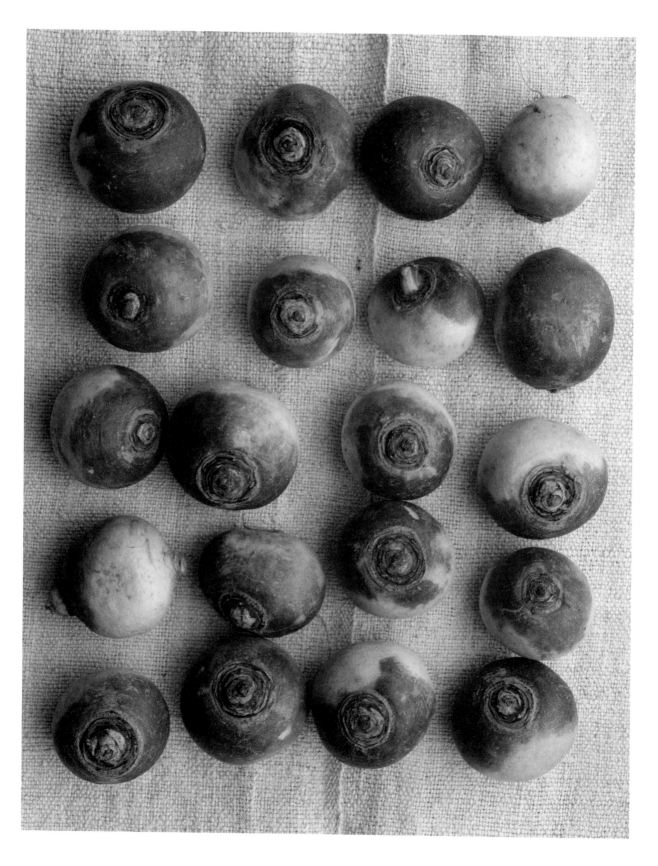

ROASTED SCARLET TURNIPS AND FENNEL

Turnips and fennel make a flavorful duo. The aromatic scarlet turnip has beautiful dark pink smooth skin that does not need to be removed. A dusting of fennel pollen adds a sweet anise accent, if you can find it, but is not crucial.

4 servings

4 medium scarlet turnips, greens removed for another use
1 fennel bulb, stems and fronds removed
¼ cup extra virgin olive oil
2 tablespoons wildflower honey
1 teaspoon kosher salt
Freshly ground black pepper
½ teaspoon fennel pollen, for garnish (optional)

Heat the oven to 375°F. Peel the turnips, cut into 1-inch cubes, and place in a medium bowl. Cut the stems and fronds from the fennel bulb and reserve for another use. Cut the fennel bulb into quarters lengthwise and cut out the solid core at the base. Slice into ½-inch pieces and add to the bowl. Drizzle with the olive oil, honey, salt, and pepper, and toss well to combine. Transfer to a shallow roasting pan and spread out in a single layer. Place in the oven on the center rack and roast until tender, about 30 minutes. Taste for seasoning. Serve hot and (if desired) garnish with fennel pollen.

GLAZED TURNIPS WITH BROWN BUTTER AND SHERRY VINEGAR

Most glazed root vegetables are coated with some kind of sugar or syrup while cooking. This technique instead uses vinegar and browned butter to balance the natural sugars of the hakurei or Tokyo turnip.

6 to 8 servings

2 bunches hakurei turnips
4 tablespoons (½ stick) unsalted butter
¼ cup sherry vinegar, plus more if needed
1 teaspoon kosher salt, or more to taste

Trim off the tops from the turnips and reserve for another use. Wash and trim the turnip roots. Slice them in half if small, or quarter them if large, and set aside.

In a wide skillet over medium-low heat, cook the butter until foamy. When the foam subsides, watch closely as the bits of milk solids on the bottom of the pan begin to brown. When lightly browned, immediately remove the skillet from the heat and set it on a cool surface to stop the cooking.

Add ¼ cup vinegar to the browned butter and return the skillet to the stove over medium-high heat. When the mixture begins to sizzle, add the turnips and season with salt. Keep the turnips moving either with tongs or by shaking the pan so that they cook evenly on all sides. When they begin to brown and the sauce is reduced to a glaze, taste for seasoning and adjust as needed. If the butter separates, just add a splash of vinegar, and it should come back together.

OTHER FALL FRUITS

Robby Astrove, an environmental educator, park ranger, and urban forager, frequently brings me wild edibles. We took a tour with him one fine autumn day and harvested wild persimmons, pomegranates, and muscadines all within a mile of my city home, close to downtown. He, along with other dedicated urban fruit seekers, formed a group called Concrete Jungle, which highlights ripe fruit and nut trees within the city limits. Because these are items that are not necessarily found at farmers' markets, I've included them here.

MUSCADINES: Muscadines are one of the only true American grapes. They are native to the South and grow in every Southern state from Florida to Texas to Arkansas to Maryland. They range in size from marble to pinball and in color from yellow-green to bronze to deep purple. "Scuppernongs" is the colloquialism for the green varieties. As with a plum, the skin is tart and slightly tannic and the fruit is sweet. Some people eat the skin and some don't, but all muscadines are full of seeds. Though some folks make muscadine wine, I do not consider the muscadine a wine grape. It is far more suited for the table or for cooking.

Besides making muscadine jam, jelly, or chutney, I like to juice the grapes and use the juice in sauces or cocktails. If you have a centrifugal juicer, you can drop muscadines in whole and the machine will separate the solids from the liquid. Since muscadines' fruit is sweet and the skins are tart, you get the best of both of these flavors. If you don't have a juicer, cut the grapes in half, remove the seeds, and put the grapes through a citrus press or toss them into the blender and strain the solids out.

PERSIMMONS: Persimmon trees have long been a part of the American landscape. The persimmons are typically deep orange in color, but wild varieties can also be a dusty purple. There are actually two types: astringent and nonastringent. The astringent kind needs to be soft and ripe before being eaten. If it is pulled from the tree too early, you will get a very unpleasant mouth-puckering surprise. The nonastringent kind can be eaten firm or soft. Hachiya persimmons are an example of an astringent variety, and Fuyu persimmons are nonastringent. Persimmons were part of something called pemmican—the original "energy bar," used by explorers and Native Americans. Pemmican is basically dried meat (jerky) mixed with wild nuts and berries and pressed into a bar. Persimmons usually fall by the first frost and are gone by winter.

POMEGRANATES: I was surprised to learn that pomegranates can grow right here in Georgia. Though not widely seen, they do exist and are usually planted. The name "pomegranate" comes from the Latin *pomum granatum*, meaning "seeded apple." For more than four thousand years, these smooth-skinned crimson fruits have symbolized hope and prosperity. In more recent years they have been acclaimed for their potent nutritive value. High in antioxidants and vitamin C and a host of other nutrients, pomegranates now make their way into juices and concentrates and all kinds of health-fortifying products. Once available only from late summer to early winter, they are now imported from other parts of the world to keep up with demand year-round. Pomegranates grow best in arid climates and don't do well in humidity. However, occasionally you'll spot an ornamental—as my friend Robby did—that indeed bears fruit.

The crisp white seeds surrounded by individual juicy, crimson seed pockets are entirely edible and are wonderful to have on hand for dressing up a salad, a dessert, or just about anything else. They must be removed from the bitter white pith first, however. The easiest way to do this is to cut the pomegranate in half and then submerge it in a bowl of water. With the fruit under the water, break the half into pieces and let the seeds fall to the bottom. This reduces mess and makes it easy to retrieve them.

MUSCADINE CHUTNEY

I was asked to create a lunch saluting the late, great Southern chef Edna Lewis at the Southern Foodways Alliance's annual symposium in Oxford, Mississippi. It was a particular honor to be asked to do this because I had the privilege of knowing her, and even cooking for her, when she was living in Atlanta. I chose an autumn Emancipation Day menu based on one featured in her classic cookbook, *The Taste of Country Cooking*. In addition to guinea fowl, green bean and tomato salad, and wild rice, her menu called for yeast rolls with homemade grape jelly. Knowing her love of chutneys, I took the liberty of serving this gingery muscadine relish in its place. I feel sure she would have approved.

1½ cups

½ cup apple cider vinegar
½ cup sugar
1 pound muscadines, quartered and seeded
1 shallot, finely diced
2 tablespoons grated fresh ginger
1 jalapeño or serrano pepper, seeds removed, finely diced
4 teaspoons mustard seeds
2 teaspoons kosher salt

In a wide skillet over medium heat, combine the vinegar and sugar and bring to a simmer. Add the grapes, shallot, ginger, jalapeño pepper, mustard seeds, and salt. Cook, stirring often, until the syrup is reduced and thickened, about 20 minutes. When cooled, transfer to a container with a lid and store for up to 2 months, refrigerated.

WHISTLING DIXIE

Miller Union bartender Stuart White came up with this clever cocktail using fresh-pressed muscadine juice. The acid in lemon and tamarind balances the intense sweetness of the grape juice, which would be cloying on its own.

1 cocktail

1½ ounces Kentucky bourbon
1 ounce muscadine juice (see page 358)
½ ounce freshly squeezed lemon juice
¼ ounce Royal Rose tamarind syrup
¼ ounce simple syrup (see the Pimm's Patch, page 101)
Muscadines or scuppernongs skewered on toothpicks, for garnish

In a shaker, combine the bourbon, muscadine juice, lemon juice, tamarind syrup, and simple syrup. Add ice and shake until the outside of the shaker is frosty. Strain into an ice-filled glass and garnish with skewered muscadines or scuppernongs.

PERSIMMON PUDDING

The wild persimmon or the cultivated Hachiya is best for this recipe. Before you make this dessert, wait until the fruit has ripened past its astringent phase and begins to blacken on the outside and soften on the inside. A heady mix of cinnamon, nutmeg, and brandy gives this English-style pudding a comforting, familiar tone that suits the first cold night of autumn and is a reminder that holiday merriment and cheer are just around the corner.

12 servings

4 tablespoons (½ stick) unsalted butter, melted
2 cups very ripe persimmon pulp (from about 5 large or 10 small persimmons, peeled and seeded)
1½ cups sugar
2 large eggs
1½ cups buttermilk
¼ cup heavy cream
1 cup unbleached all-purpose flour
1 teaspoon baking soda
1 teaspoon baking powder
½ teaspoon ground cinnamon
¼ teaspoon freshly grated nutmeg
⅛ teaspoon fine sea salt
2 tablespoons brandy or cognac
Brandied Crème Anglaise (see recipe)

Heat the oven to 300°F. Brush a 9 x 13-inch baking dish with 1 tablespoon of the melted butter. In a large bowl, whisk together the persimmon pulp and sugar. Add the eggs, buttermilk, and cream and whisk to combine. In a small bowl, whisk together the flour, baking soda, baking powder, cinnamon, nutmeg, and salt. Add the dry ingredients to the wet ingredients and stir just until incorporated. Stir in the brandy and the remaining melted butter and transfer to the baking dish. Bake until set in the center but still very moist, about 1½ hours. Serve warm or room temperature, with Brandied Crème Anglaise.

BRANDIED CRÈME ANGLAISE

2½ cups

2 cups whole milk
1 vanilla bean, split
½ cup sugar
⅛ teaspoon fine sea salt
¼ cup brandy
Freshly grated nutmeg
4 egg yolks

Set a large fine-mesh strainer over a medium bowl and set the bowl in a shallow pan of ice water. In a large saucepan, combine the milk and vanilla bean, and cook over moderately low heat just until small bubbles appear around the rim, about 5 minutes. In another medium bowl, whisk together the sugar, salt, brandy, nutmeg, and egg yolks. While whisking, pour in half of the warm milk in a thin stream, to temper the eggs. Pour the egg mixture back into the saucepan with the remaining milk and stir constantly with a wooden spoon or rubber spatula over moderate heat. Cook until the sauce has thickened slightly, 4 to 5 minutes. When the sauce coats the back of a spoon, immediately pour it through the strainer into the bowl that is resting in the ice water. Either serve at room temperature, or cover with a layer of plastic wrap and refrigerate to serve chilled.

CRANBERRY-PERSIMMON SAUCE

Tart cranberries need a lot of sugar to tame their astringent taste, but the addition of ripe persimmon adds natural sweetness. This makes it possible to lower the amount of sugar needed, adapting to personal taste.

2¼ cups

12 ounces cranberries
2 large ripe Fuyu persimmons or 8 ripe wild persimmons (about ½ cup persimmon pulp)
Zest and juice of 1 orange
½ cup turbinado sugar, or more to taste
⅛ teaspoon ground allspice
Pinch salt

Wash and drain the cranberries and set aside. Peel the persimmons and separate the flesh from the seeds. In a medium saucepan over medium heat, combine the cranberries, persimmons, orange zest and juice, sugar, allspice, and salt. Cook the mixture, stirring frequently, until the cranberries burst and the sauce thickens, about 5 minutes. If a thinner consistency is desired, add water as needed.

QUAIL WITH MUSCADINES, GRITS, AND REDEYE GRAVY

Redeye gravy gets its name from the caffeine jolt of coffee added to country ham pan drippings to make a down-home sauce spooned over grits. Rather than ham, my version begins with quail, and it ends with fresh muscadines—both found in abundance in the wilds of my home state during the fall months. The sweet grape juice and fresh ginger cut the bitter bite of the coffee. Country ham is still present but is used as a seasoning instead of the foundation.

4 entrée or 8 appetizer servings

8 whole quail, semi-boneless if available
4 tablespoons (½ stick) unsalted butter
Kosher salt
Freshly ground black pepper
3 tablespoons finely diced country ham
1 tablespoon minced fresh ginger
1 cup strong coffee
½ cup fresh-pressed muscadine juice (page 358)
1 recipe grits (page 135)
Fresh muscadine halves for garnish, seeds removed
Snipped fresh chives for garnish

Rinse the quail, pat them dry, and set aside. In a wide skillet, over medium-high heat, melt 2 tablespoons butter. Season the quail lightly with salt and pepper on both sides and then tuck their wing tips behind the backbone. Place 4 of the birds in the skillet breast side down, without crowding. Sear the quail until browned, gently shaking the skillet from time to time to keep them from sticking, 3 to 4 minutes. Turn the birds over and cook on their other side until browned on the outside, an additional 3 to 4 minutes. They can be slightly pink in the center. Remove the cooked quail from the pan and drain on paper towels. Repeat with the remaining butter and quail.

Without wiping the hot pan, add the country ham, ginger, coffee, and muscadine juice. Simmer over medium-high heat until reduced by half, 10 to 12 minutes. Place the quail on the cooked grits and spoon the redeye gravy over the top. Garnish with fresh muscadines and chives.

NEXT SPREAD
FALL VEGETABLE FEAST (clockwise from top left): Cornbread-Pecan Dressing Muffins; Roasted Sweet Potatoes in Their Jackets; Roasted Brussels Sprouts with Shallots and Garlic; Hilda's Chowchow; Apple, Bok Choy, and Radish Slaw; Chestnut, Watercress, and Wild Rice Salad; Sautéed Rainbow Chard with Stems; Green Tomato Gratin; (center of table, left to right) Muscadine Chutney; Cranberry Persimmon Sauce

WINTER

After the bustle of the holidays, I fill a cooler with winter produce and drive down to the coast, where I can cook at a relaxed pace. The cold, short days make growing difficult, but the harvest is still rich with flavor and possibility.

BEETS

Beets have not always been a favorite in America. Raised in the era of canned foods, I assumed they came only that way. I began to see them in a different light in the 1990s while working at Floataway Café, where Anne Quatrano was roasting beets with vinegar and serving them with fresh cheese, arugula, and olive oil. They were so popular that we were roasting and peeling beets every day to keep up with the demand. Almost every restaurant serves a beet dish today, and it is nice to see this vegetable get the attention that it deserves. It is a versatile plant that has many delicious applications. And with the increasing demand for fresh, locally grown food these days, beets have become a popular mainstay for chefs, home cooks, and growers alike. Beet greens, or "beet tops," are the delectable other half of this earthy plant.

Beets are native to Northern Africa and the Mediterranean, where they grew wild as a coastal plant. They were first cultivated for their greens, much like spinach, their cousin. The roots came into vogue a lot later in their culinary history, in the 1800s in Western Europe. Prior to that, the root was mostly used for medicinal purposes or as the base of a dye. Beets can be harvested once the greens are about six inches high or taller, when the top of the root begins to emerge from the ground. They love cool weather and grow best in deep, loose soil. I prefer beets harvested young, with roots just slightly larger than a golf ball, for tenderness and flavor. Look for beets with healthy intact greens as a sign of freshness, and plan to use both the root and the leaf.

There are several heirloom varieties of beets. They range in hue, shape, and size, but all have a similar flavor and red is the most common color. Less common are the beautiful pink-and-white-striped beets called Chioggia; and there are yellow, golden, orange, and white varieties as well. Beets are chenopods, most of which are weeds that are salt- and drought-resistant. But the edible chenopods include spinach, chard, quinoa, and beets.

Beets are one of the most healthful foods on our planet. The pigments in beet roots provide powerful antioxidants and are thought to be potent cancer fighters. Beets are rich in folate, which promotes a healthy heart and is essential for healthy tissue growth. Beetroot has been prescribed by nutritionists as a liver tonic and blood purifier. Beets are high in potassium and iron, but surprisingly, beet greens score higher than the roots in calcium, vitamin A, and vitamin C.

Remove the leaves from the roots and store in the refrigerator in a plastic bag. Do not wash the roots before refrigerating, as any excess dirt can help hold moisture in and protect the roots from drying out. If beets are washed and water is clinging to the skin or trapped in the bag with the roots, it can eventually cause water rot. If roots are well protected from the dry air of the refrigerator, they can last several weeks, but remember that the nutritional value decreases over time as the vegetable deteriorates. Beet greens are best washed and spun dry or towel-dried, then stored in a plastic bag or wrapped in a damp cotton towel.

If young and tender, the greens can be a delicious addition to a seasonal salad. Slightly more mature leaves are best enjoyed as a quick sauté, with some olive oil and garlic for instance. The stems can also be used in sautéing. Simply cut the stems crosswise and put them in the skillet first, as they take a little longer to cook than the leaves. Beets are easier to peel after cooking or roasting. A kitchen towel that you don't mind staining might be the best for rubbing the skins away. You may want to wear latex gloves to protect your hands from staining. Besides being roasted, beets can be shaved raw or grated into a salad, pickled, sautéed, or grilled. Sometimes I like to highlight the naturally sweet flavor with honey, agave, or even chocolate. To bring out the savory side, use ingredients like garlic, shallots, ginger, vinegar, citrus, nuts, or herbs.

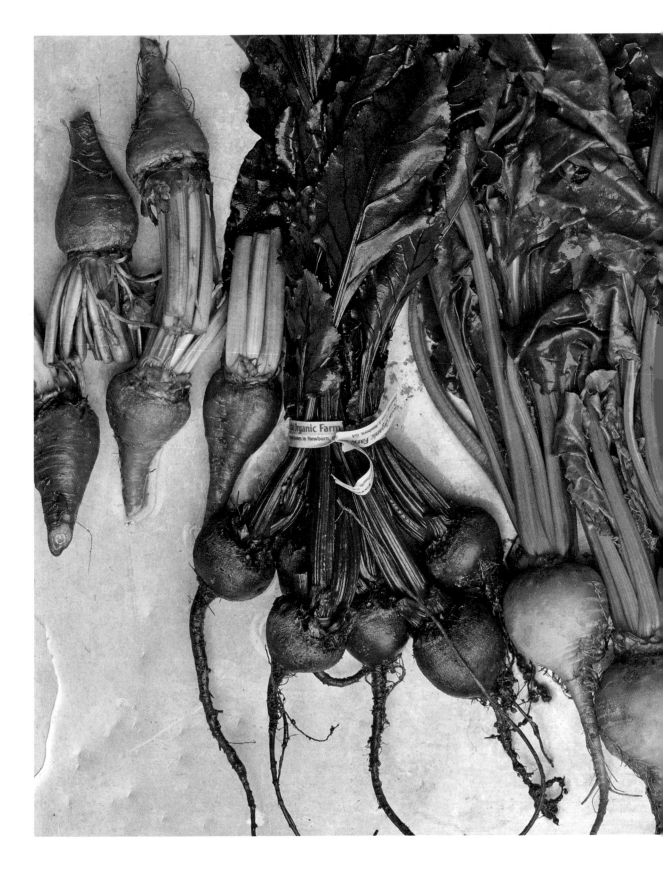

SIMPLE ROASTED BEETS

The liquid in this recipe is important, as it steams the beets from the bottom of the pan during roasting, cooking them evenly and keeping them moist. Though they are great on their own, roasted beets are even better in a vinaigrette, pickled, sautéed, pureed, spiced, or even added to a smoothie.

4 to 6 servings

4 to 6 medium beets, stems and greens trimmed and reserved for another use
1 tablespoon olive oil
2 tablespoons white wine vinegar
2 teaspoons kosher salt
½ teaspoon freshly ground black pepper

Heat the oven to 350°F. Wash the beets and place in a shallow roasting pan wide enough to hold them snugly in a single layer. Pour ¼ inch of water into the pan. Drizzle the beets with olive oil and vinegar and then season with salt and pepper. Cover the pan with parchment and foil and wrap the foil tightly around the lip of the pan. Roast the beets until tender, 45 to 60 minutes. To test for doneness, insert the tip of a paring knife into the flesh of a few beets. If they pierce easily, remove the beets from the oven. If not, cook a little longer. Let the beets cool slightly and peel them while they are still warm. With a towel, wipe the skin off each beet until the surface is smooth. Slice the beets and serve as a side dish or use in other preparations.

SAUTÉED BEETS WITH ORANGE AND WALNUTS

Once you have roasted your beets, you can use them in many ways. This is one of my favorite combinations.

Serves 4

½ cup walnut halves or pieces
1 tablespoon extra virgin olive oil
4 medium beets, roasted, peeled, and sliced ⅓ inch thick (see recipe above)
½ teaspoon kosher salt
Freshly ground black pepper
Zest and juice of 1 orange

Heat the oven to 300°F. Place the walnuts on a baking sheet on the middle rack of the oven. Roast until lightly browned, about 10 minutes. Meanwhile, put a wide skillet over medium-high heat. Put in the olive oil and heat until shimmery. Add the beets and season with salt and pepper. Toss the beets frequently so that they do not burn. Sauté for 4 to 5 minutes, then add the orange juice and zest. Cook a few minutes more until the juice has reduced. Transfer to a serving dish and then add the toasted walnuts. Garnish with more orange zest if desired. Serve hot or at room temperature.

BULGUR WHEAT WITH ROASTED BABY BEETS AND THEIR TOPS

Outside of Middle Eastern cuisine, bulgur wheat often conjures images of 1970s health food stores and poorly made versions of tabbouleh. With all the buzz about whole grains these days, this nutty-flavored, par-cooked cracked wheat might be ready for a comeback. Combined with beets in this recipe—which uses every part of the plant—it is a true *Root to Leaf* meal that is delicious and incredibly healthful.

4 servings

4 small beets with tops
1 cup bulgur
2 cups vegetable broth or water, heated
Kosher salt
2 tablespoons extra virgin olive oil
1 shallot, diced
Freshly ground black pepper
Juice of ½ lemon
4 ounces fresh cheese, such as farmers' cheese or chèvre, crumbled

Trim the tops from the beets and reserve. Wash the roots and roast according to the instructions on page 380. (This can be done a day or two in advance, if desired.)

Wash the tops well and separate the stems from the leaves. Reserve the leaves. Slice the stems crosswise to make small dice, and set aside.

Place the bulgur wheat in a medium bowl. Pour the hot broth over the bulgur and add a pinch of salt. Cover and let sit until the grains swell and become tender, 15 to 20 minutes. Taste for seasoning and set aside.

In a medium skillet over medium-high heat, warm 1 tablespoon olive oil. Add the shallot and beet stems and season with salt and pepper. Cook until the shallot and beet stems are tender, 2 to 3 minutes, and add the beet greens. Using tongs, turn the leaves several times until wilted. Remove from the heat and set aside.

Peel the roasted beets, slice them into quarters, and set aside.

In a large bowl, mix together the cooked bulgur and the sautéed beet greens and stems and stir until combined. Taste for seasoning. Divide the grain mixture among 4 serving bowls. Toss the roasted beets with the lemon juice, salt, and the remaining 1 tablespoon olive oil. Divide the dressed beets among the serving bowls. Divide the cheese among the bowls and serve.

BEET RED VELVET CAKE

I started tinkering with the idea of a classic red velvet cake using naturally red beets in the cake batter and fresh chèvre in the frosting, but when it comes to baking tests I am not the most patient. So I posed this challenge to Miller Union's pastry chef, Pamela Moxley. She made several versions, in her scientific, pastry chef way, and discovered the best combination. Both light and tender, the cake is incredibly moist and not too sweet, with just the right amount of beet flavor. Not only is this version nutritionally superior to the sugary, artificially colored original, but it also tastes better. When beets are in season, we have this on the dessert menu, and it was even featured in *The New York Times*.

Makes a 2-layer, 9-inch cake

3 medium beets, tops and taproots removed
12 tablespoons (1½ sticks) unsalted butter, room temperature, plus more for
  greasing the pans
¾ cup buttermilk
Juice of 1 large lemon
2 teaspoons distilled white vinegar
1½ teaspoons vanilla extract
2 cups sifted cake flour
3 tablespoons cocoa powder
1 teaspoon fine sea salt
1⅛ teaspoons baking powder
½ teaspoon baking soda
1¾ cups granulated sugar
3 large eggs
Fresh Chèvre Frosting (see recipe)

Heat the oven to 400°F. Wash the beets and place on a sheet of parchment. Fold the parchment around the beets. Place the parchment on a sheet of aluminum foil and wrap the foil tightly around the parchment to make a packet. Bake until the tip of a knife slides easily into the largest beet. Cool until the beets can be handled, then peel.

Butter two 9-inch round cake pans. Line the bottoms of the pans with parchment, and butter the parchment. Set aside.

Lower the oven temperature to 350°F. Place the beets in a food processor and process until finely chopped. Remove the beet mixture from the processor and measure out 1 cup. Reserve any remaining chopped beets for another use. Return the measured 1 cup beets to the food processor. Add the buttermilk, lemon juice, vinegar, and vanilla, and process until smooth.

Into a medium bowl, sift together the flour, cocoa, salt, baking powder, and baking soda. Set aside.

In the bowl of a stand mixer, beat the 12 tablespoons butter until soft. Slowly add the sugar, and beat until creamy. Beat in the eggs one at a time. After each addition, stop the motor and scrape down the sides of the bowl.

Alternate adding dry and wet ingredients to the butter mixture, beginning and ending with the dry ingredients. After each addition, beat for 10 seconds, and then scrape the bowl. Divide the batter between the prepared cake pans, smoothing the tops. Bake until a cake tester inserted in the cake comes out clean, about 20 minutes. Cool completely in the pans on a wire rack.

To assemble, place a serving platter upside down on top of one of the pans. While holding the pan and the plate, invert the pan, allowing the cake to drop out onto the plate. Lift off the pan, and peel away the parchment.

Put 1 cup Fresh Chèvre Frosting on the center of the cake. Using a flat spatula, spread the frosting evenly over the top. Invert the second cake onto a plate, remove the parchment, then invert again onto a flat plate. Carefully ease the second cake, flat side down, centered on top of the frosted layer. Cover the top and sides of the cake with the remaining frosting. Serve immediately or store covered at room temperature for 2 to 3 days.

FRESH CHÈVRE FROSTING

Enough frosting for one 2-layer cake

6 tablespoons unsalted butter, room temperature
1½ cups sifted confectioners' sugar
Pinch salt
½ teaspoon vanilla extract
8 ounces cream cheese, room temperature
8 ounces creamy goat cheese (chèvre), room temperature

In the bowl of a stand mixer, beat the butter until soft. Beat in the confectioners' sugar, salt, and vanilla, and continue beating until creamy. With the motor running on low, add pieces of the cream cheese one at a time. Stop the motor and scrape down the sides of the bowl. With the motor running, add pieces of goat cheese, and beat until creamy. Store at room temperature until ready to frost the cake layers.

PICKLED BEETS

Most recipes for pickled beets require that the beets be either roasted or boiled first. Thinly slicing them when raw circumvents this step. The hot liquid gently cooks the beets, while leaving a bit of crunch. When pouring the boiling brine over the beets, I strain out the spices to keep them from clinging to the pickles. This makes the pickles easier to serve and eat later.

2 quarts

6 medium beets, peeled and thinly sliced on a mandoline
2½ cups red wine vinegar
6 tablespoons honey
3 tablespoons kosher salt
1 teaspoon each coriander seeds, yellow mustard seeds, black peppercorns, allspice berries, green cardamom pods, and fennel seeds
1 whole clove
1 bay leaf
1-inch knob ginger, sliced (may leave skin on)

Place the beets in a glass container large enough to hold them and the liquid. In a medium saucepan over high heat, combine all the other ingredients with 2½ cups water and bring to a boil. Remove from the heat and then pour the hot brine through a strainer or wire-mesh sieve over the beets. Cover and let cool completely, then refrigerate. Pickled beets can be stored refrigerated for up to 4 weeks. Serve cold or at room temperature.

CABBAGE AND KOHLRABI

Cabbage and kohlrabi are both members of the very broad genus *Brassica*. Together they represent one of the most familiar and one of the most unrecognized vegetables from the same spectrum. Kohlrabi, also called cabbage turnip, its literal translation from German, has a long history in Europe but is still relatively obscure in the United States. It grows remarkably well here and is often seen in local farmers' markets in the colder months of harvest. Cabbage, on the other hand, has a rich history in almost every culture in the world, with endless applications and varieties.

CABBAGE: I served a creamed cabbage and mushroom toast as a starter one winter and a guest asked to have it with just the mushrooms and no cabbage. We tried to explain that they were mixed together and she promptly let us know that lowly cabbage and high-priced mushrooms did not belong in the same dish. Her prejudice against what she considered peasant food stopped her from enjoying one of my favorite wintertime bites. Although cabbages are, in many ways, the ragamuffins of the vegetable world, they are grown and appear on tables in nearly every-region around the globe. Throughout the British Isles, cabbages have been notoriously stewed for hours on end in similar preparations, usually with a bit of pork. A key ingredient in borscht and the national food of Russia, cabbage is stuffed, pickled, and simmered in soup throughout Eastern Europe. In Germany, it's turned into sauerkraut. Thai cuisine utilizes cabbage leaves as a wrap. In Korea cabbage becomes kimchi. The Chinese dry cabbage leaves for the winter and rehydrate them for soups.

Cabbage has been prized throughout history not only for its versatility, but also for its sturdiness, economy, and nutritional virtues. The dark green, crinkly savoy cabbage has a tender texture and is particularly meaty when cooked. Red and purple cabbages have anti-inflammatory effects and contain flavonoids that are powerful antioxidants and fight free radicals. Cabbage is also high in fiber and aids in digestion.

When growing, cabbage starts off as open leaves. As the core develops, a small head begins to form and the leaves fold in on one another. Once the cabbage has fully headed, it is harvested and it can be stored for many weeks. Cabbage grows best in fall or spring, and in milder climates without hard freezes, it can be harvested throughout the winter season as well. Frost makes it sweeter and sometimes leaves a purple or reddish mark on the tips of the leaves. Store cabbage refrigerated in the crisper.

KOHLRABI: Our first dining room manager at Miller Union was Hungarian and was simply in love with kohlrabi. Knowing this, I brought her a few bulbs from the farmers' market one day and she cradled them in her arms like an overjoyed mother holding a baby.

I do not like the flavor of fully cooked kohlrabi, which is similar to that of overcooked broccoli or cabbage. I stick to simple preparations and enjoy kohlrabi raw and shaved thin in a salad with other winter vegetables or cooked simply in butter and lemon with salt. It also makes great pickles and can ferment nicely as a kraut.

Kohlrabi looks somewhat like a turnip, but it is not a root. It is a bulbous stem that grows just above the ground with leafy stalks protruding in an alternating pattern from the sides of the bulb. Kohlrabi comes in white, light green, or purple varieties, which are relatively interchangeable. I often describe the texture and flavor of kohlrabi by comparing it to a broccoli stem. It is sweet and crisp with a slight cabbage flavor.

Look for bulbs three inches or less in diameter (about the size of a medium turnip). They are more tender and delicate in flavor and do not necessarily require peeling. Large bulbs tend to be tough and woody, with a hard outer layer that must be removed. If the leaves are still intact, they should be used first. The kohlrabi bulb will store for several weeks in the crisper of your refrigerator.

BASIC SAUERKRAUT

A fermenting crock is a good-quality ceramic cylinder made just for sauerkraut and other fermented foods. Often such crocks come with porous weighting stones that are designed to fit tightly inside and hold the vegetables underneath the layer of liquid, a key step in the art of fermentation. There are also makeshift ways to ferment but none more foolproof. It takes a minimum of a week for cabbage to reach the deliciously sour stage, so you may want to prep more than one head at a time.

So how does sauerkraut work? Salt draws liquid out of the cabbage to create the brine. If cabbage is stored at room temperature and away from free-flowing oxygen, the natural lactic acid–producing bacteria that exist on the leaves are allowed to thrive and grow, creating a biochemical change that softens the vegetable and produces a pleasant sour taste. The salt inhibits the growth of unwanted bacteria. A good ratio to follow is this: for every head of cabbage, use about 1 tablespoon kosher salt.

4 quarts

3 large heads cabbage, about 9 pounds
3 tablespoons kosher salt
Distilled water, if needed

Cut the cabbages into quarters, remove any outer damaged leaves, then cut away the core at the base. Shred the cabbage thinly on a mandoline or by hand with a knife. Transfer the shredded cabbage to a large bowl, sprinkle with the salt, and toss. Let sit until the cabbage has wilted and begun to appear translucent, about 1½ hours.

Working in batches and with clean hands, squeeze the salted cabbage over a large bowl with aggressive force to release the natural liquids. Be sure to capture all the liquid that is released in this process. Transfer the cabbage and its liquid to the bottom of a fermenting crock. Place weighting stones or a plate that fits inside the crock on top of the cabbage, and push down until the liquid rises above the weight by about 1 inch. If there is not enough liquid in the crock, add just enough distilled water to reach the level needed (do not use chlorinated tap water).

Cover with a lid, and if your crock is designed with a lid trough, fill the trough with water. Check every couple of days and taste. It is safe to try the cabbage at any time during the fermentation process. Let it sit until it reaches the level of sourness you prefer, from 3 days to 2 weeks. If a layer of mold forms on the top, just skim it away; then rinse the weight and put it back in place. Don't be concerned if white foam or bubbles appear. This is a natural part of the fermentation process. When the sauerkraut is as sour as you like, skim off any white foam that may be present, transfer the sauerkraut to a storage container with a lid, and refrigerate to stop the fermentation. It will keep refrigerated for up to 3 months.

CREAMED SAVOY CABBAGE WITH MUSHROOMS AND BUCKWHEAT PASTA

Like the little ridges in penne rigate that are designed to soak up sauce, the crinkly leaves of savoy cabbage catch every creamy, earthy drop as well. Cabbage, often regarded as poor people's food, feels luxurious in this mushroom-laden entrée. Here I like to use a combination of shiitake, oyster, and cremini mushrooms, but almost any fresh mushroom will work fine.

6 entrée servings

2 ounces dried porcini or other dried mushrooms
Kosher salt
4 tablespoons (½ stick) unsalted butter
1 pound fresh mushrooms, trimmed and thickly sliced
1 shallot, finely diced
2 garlic cloves, minced
1 small yellow onion, diced
Freshly ground black pepper
1 small head savoy cabbage, quartered, core removed, and cut into ¼-inch strips
1 pound buckwheat penne rigate
¼ cup heavy cream
1 teaspoon fresh thyme leaves
Freshly grated Parmigiano-Reggiano for garnish

Cover the dried porcini mushrooms with 1 cup of boiling water and steep for 15 to 20 minutes. Remove the rehydrated mushrooms and set aside. Pour the remaining liquid through a fine-mesh sieve set over a bowl to catch any sand or dirt, and reserve the liquid. Finely dice the rehydrated mushrooms and set aside again.

Set a large saucepan of water seasoned with 2 to 3 tablespoons salt over high heat. Meanwhile, in a large skillet over medium-high heat, melt the butter until foamy. Add the dried and fresh mushrooms to the skillet and sauté until browned. Add the shallot, garlic, and onion and season with salt and pepper. Cook until the onion is translucent, about 5 minutes, stirring occasionally. Add the dried mushroom broth and the cabbage to the pan and season lightly. Reduce the heat to low, cover the skillet, and cook until the cabbage is tender, 7 to 8 minutes.

Meanwhile, add the pasta to the boiling water and cook until al dente, 7 to 8 minutes. Place a colander in the sink and drain the pasta. Toss several times to cool, then set aside.

While the pasta cools, add the cream and thyme to the cabbage mixture, and cook until the liquid is reduced in volume and slightly thickened. Add the cooked pasta to the skillet and toss until well coated. Transfer to serving bowls and garnish with Parmigiano-Reggiano.

SAUTÉED KOHLRABI

If kohlrabi is cooked just until tender, it can be delightful, but if it is cooked too long it tastes and smells like overcooked broccoli stems. A quick flash in the pan, in a single layer, is my favorite way to tenderize this sweet and underused brassica bulb. If any leaves happen to still be attached, chop them up and add to the pan at the last minute. Do not overcrowd the pan. It may be necessary to cook the kohlrabi in batches, depending on the size of your skillet.

4 to 6 servings

2 tablespoons unsalted butter
2 tablespoons extra virgin olive oil
2 large or 4 small kohlrabi bulbs, peeled and cut into 1/8-inch-thick slices
Kosher salt
Freshly ground black pepper
Juice of 1 lemon
Juice of 1 orange

In a wide skillet over medium heat, melt the butter with the olive oil. Add the kohlrabi slices in a single layer across the bottom of the pan and season lightly with salt and pepper. Cook on one side for 1 minute. With tongs, turn each piece over and cook on the opposite side for 1 minute. Then add the lemon and orange juices and cook until the kohlrabi pieces are tender but still have a little crunch. Remove from the pan and repeat if cooking in batches.

KOHLRABI, CELERY ROOT, TANGERINE, AND POMEGRANATE SALAD

Winter roots and dense bulbs are generally considered for cooking only, but if shaved paper thin, they can take on new meaning. Kohlrabi is a great example, particularly in this crunchy and refreshing mélange of celery root, tangerine, and pomegranate. If I happen to have an orange around too, it could easily end up in the mix. For this recipe it is best to use kohlrabi that is young and tender, as it does not need to be peeled and can fit easily whole on a mandoline. If you have a larger kohlrabi bulb, peel it first and cut it in half or into quarters before slicing.

4 to 6 servings

1 small to medium kohlrabi bulb, thinly sliced and quartered
1/4 celery root, peeled, thinly sliced, and quartered
2 to 3 tablespoons Shallot Vinaigrette (page 282)
Kosher salt
2 to 3 tangerines, peeled and sectioned, seeds removed (page 429)
1/2 cup pomegranate seeds

In a large bowl, combine the kohlrabi, celery root, and vinaigrette. Toss well to combine and season lightly with salt. Divide among salad plates or bowls. Scatter the tangerines and pomegranate seeds across each salad and serve.

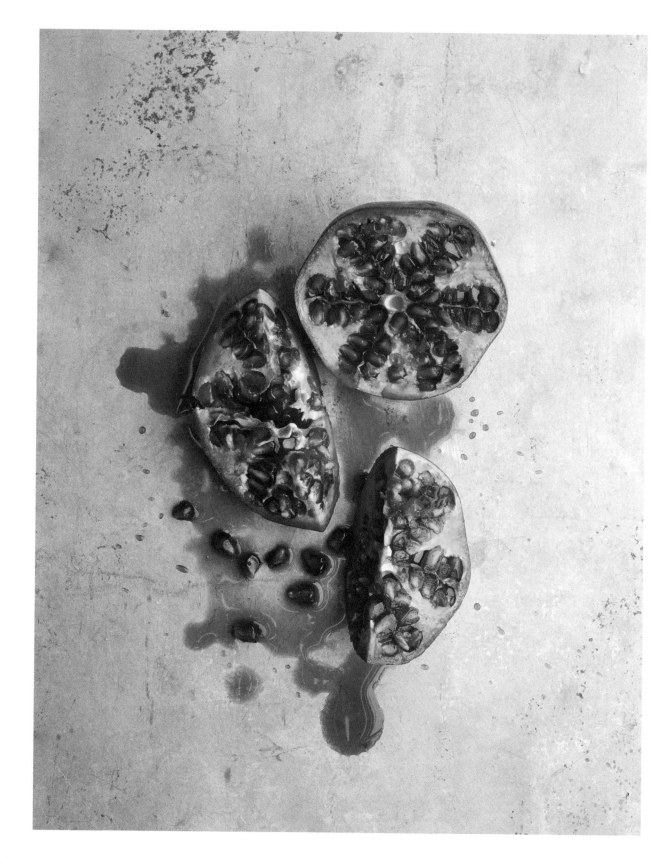

CELERY AND CELERIAC

There are three main types of celery. The type that is grown for its stalks is what most people recognize, with the majority of it being grown in California. There is also a type called leaf or cutting celery that used to be the most widely grown in its early days of cultivation, but is more rare now and mostly seen in farmers' markets. Then there is the type that is grown for its root, called celeriac, which has a dense ivory-fleshed center with a gnarly, warted skin. All are cousins of anise, carrots, parsley, and parsnips and have similar flavor profiles but vastly different uses.

CELERY: The Pascal variety of celery is the most commonly recognized and widely grown on the West Coast. All varieties have the signature dark green leaves at the top of their canopy, but the ribs can come in different colors including white, light green, dark green, golden, red, and purple. Cutting celery has the most intense flavor and is best used more sparingly, like an herb—it can be an accent in salads, soups, braises, and stews. Celery has a distinct flavor that is grassy, sweet, and slightly salty. It has a fibrous texture with boomerang-shaped ribs in cross section and strings that run their length. Celery has such a high fiber and water content and such a low calorie count that the energy spent digesting a stalk is about the same as the calories consumed. Celery is a culinary aromatic, adding deep flavor to whatever it is cooked with. Its unique taste cannot be duplicated and it is a vitally important ingredient in both the French mirepoix of onion, carrot, and celery and the Cajun holy trinity of onion, bell pepper, and celery. Celery is rarely seen as a feature and is often taken for granted as a common vegetable, but there is no substitute for this water-based crispy stalk.

One of the most popular dishes on the dinner menu at Miller Union is a farm egg baked in celery cream. This dish relies on the flavor of celery, and it makes me proud to think that my celery creation has brought new respect to one of the most underrated vegetables in the produce bin.

Celery loves cold weather. During several weeks of the winter months we are lucky enough to get locally grown cutting celery, with its bitter leaves and intensely flavored ribs. I like to use this variety with braised beef, or with a full-flavored fish. It also adds an extra kick to a winter Bloody Mary or a crudités plate. Keep celery cold in the crisper wrapped in plastic or in a container with a lid. It wilts easily in the dry air of the refrigerator. If celery ribs are cut, they can be stored in water to retain their crispness. You can easily remove dirt or sand by rubbing your finger down the length of the rib under running water.

CELERIAC OR CELERY ROOT: The celery plant grown for its root, called celeriac, grows long stalks like the other varieties, but the main purpose for its cultivation is its enormously large and knotty root, found underground. Its dense, creamy flesh is an excellent alternative to potatoes or other starches, and when cooked needs very little seasoning, owing to its naturally savory flavor. Though not widely used in the United States, it has been popular in Europe for ages and grows well in any cool region. It is the main ingredient in the cold French salad céleri rémoulade, in which the root is peeled, grated, tossed in lemon, and dressed with a mustardy mayonnaise. Celeriac can be stored for months after harvest in a root cellar or under refrigeration. It can be eaten raw if thinly sliced and used sparingly, but is mostly used for cooking. It makes a velvety puree, creamy soup, or hearty stew, and is delicious when grated into fritters or savory pancakes. It has a long growing period, taking three to four months for the root to fully form, and is generally harvested in the winter, when the cold converts the starches to a sweeter flavor.

To peel celeriac, first square off the top and the bottom to create a flat surface. Because the skin is thick and bumpy, it is better to use a chef's knife to remove the outer layer and then clean it up with a Swiss Y-shaped peeler. Rinse well to remove any dirt that may still be present, then cut into equal cubes if cooking or shave on a mandoline if serving raw.

FARM EGG BAKED IN CELERY CREAM

"Celery cream" is a simple idea: Steep cream with celery, aromatics, and herbs, then strain. This is the basis for one of Miller Union's signature dishes: we serve it as a first course, but it also makes an outstanding breakfast or brunch entrée at home. Its power is in its simplicity, but timing is everything. A farm egg is cracked into a ramekin or shallow bowl and doused in the warm celery-infused cream, then baked until the white is cooked through—and not a second longer. The briny hint of celery permeates the thickened cream as it becomes one with the egg white. The best way to eat it is to puncture the runny yolk with a corner of your bread and drag it straight through the molten mixture of savory cream and just-set white on the way to your mouth. Although we serve this year-round, in the winter we add some of the freshly harvested celery from our local farms.

6 servings

1 tablespoon butter, plus more for buttering ramekins or bowls
6 ribs celery, including leaves, roughly chopped
1 shallot, including skin, sliced
½ small onion, including skin, sliced
12 black peppercorns, crushed
1 teaspoon kosher salt
1 small bay leaf
4 sprigs fresh thyme
2 cups heavy cream
6 large, farm-fresh eggs
6 slices crusty bread
Extra virgin olive oil

In a small saucepan over medium heat, melt 1 tablespoon butter until foamy. Add the celery, shallot, onion, peppercorns, salt, bay leaf, and thyme. Cook the vegetables, stirring frequently, until the onion is translucent, about 5 minutes. With a wooden spoon, smash the cooked vegetables against the bottom of the pan to release more of their flavors. Add the cream to the pan and heat until it begins to simmer. Remove from the heat and let steep for 20 minutes. Strain the cream into a medium bowl, gently pressing on the solids. Discard the solids and reserve the flavored cream, keeping it warm.

Heat the oven to 350°F. Lightly butter six 5-ounce ovenproof ramekins or bowls and place them on a baking sheet. Crack one egg into each ramekin or bowl, being careful not to break the yolk. Spoon ¼ cup of the warm celery cream over each egg. The cream should just cover the egg but with the yolk slightly protruding across the top. Slide the baking sheet with the ramekins or bowls onto the middle rack of the oven.

Bake the eggs and check them after 5 minutes. As soon as the whites start to set around the edge of the ramekin or bowl, pull the eggs from the oven and put aside. The eggs may be slightly undercooked but will continue to cook with the residual heat for few minutes.

Turn the oven setting to broil. Brush the bread on both sides lightly with olive oil. Broil the bread for 1 to 2 minutes on each side, until warm and toasted.

Because heat radiates from the source at the bottom of the oven, the whites of the eggs may need to cook a little longer. You can run the eggs under the broiler briefly, but take extra precaution not to overcook the yolks. With the broiler on and the oven door propped open, position the ramekins 8 to 10 inches below the heat source. Watch carefully while the surface of the egg begins to cook. It is fine if the whites brown slightly, but the goal is to keep the yolks runny. Serve immediately with the warm, toasted bread.

CELERY ROOT PUREE

This creamy puree can be used as a pasta filling or as a sauce underneath roasted winter vegetables, or served with fish, meat, or fowl. Whatever remains freezes well for future use. Because this root has a savory quality, I usually do not add salt.

4 to 6 servings

1 medium celery root
About 4 cups whole milk

Peel the celery root until it is smooth and unblemished. Cut into 1-inch pieces and place in a medium saucepan. Pour the milk into the pan, just up to the level of the celery root pieces. Cook on low heat for 40 to 50 minutes or until tender. Transfer the solids to a blender and blend in batches. Add just enough of the cooking liquid to allow the solids to move around freely and puree until smooth.

CELERY SALSA VERDE

Classic Italian salsa verde (green sauce) is an olive oil–based sauce with fresh herbs that varies from region to region. It is typically made with anchovies, or sometimes capers, but because I am serving this with an oily fish, I have chosen to omit both. Instead, I include the crisp, astringent leaves of celery to balance the full flavor of Spanish mackerel.

½ cup

1 small garlic clove, minced
Zest of 1 lemon
1 teaspoon Dijon mustard
½ teaspoon kosher salt
¼ cup chopped celery leaves
2 tablespoons chopped fresh parsley
2 tablespoons chopped fresh mint
⅓ cup extra virgin olive oil

In a small bowl, combine the garlic, zest, mustard, and salt. Stir in the celery leaves, parsley, mint, and olive oil. Taste for seasoning and adjust salt as needed.

SAUTÉED SPANISH MACKEREL

Spanish mackerel is a small fish found in the Gulf of Mexico and Southern Atlantic waters. It follows warmer currents and stays fairly close to the shore. The flesh is flaky and white with a full, briny flavor. Because this is an oily fish, be sure to buy it fresh and cook it soon thereafter, as it is more perishable than some other species. This is a wonderfully simple first course, or it can be made into a fuller entrée served with Kohlrabi, Celery Root, Tangerine, and Pomegranate Salad (page 399), or Sea Island Red Pea Hoppin' John (page 442).

2 fillets

2 medium Spanish mackerel fillets (5 to 6 ounces each), skin removed
Kosher salt
Freshly ground black pepper
2 teaspoons extra virgin olive oil
1 lemon wedge
Celery Salsa Verde (see recipe above)

Pat the fillets dry with a paper towel and season with salt and pepper on both sides. In a large skillet, warm the olive oil over medium-high heat. Carefully lay the fillets in the hot oil, lightly brown them on one side, and turn off the heat. When ready to serve, flip the fillets over and let sit for 30 seconds, then transfer to dinner plates. Finish with a squeeze of fresh lemon and a drizzle of Celery Salsa Verde.

CELERY, APPLE, PECAN, AND WATERCRESS SALAD

I love using the last of the local fall apples and pecans with the first of the winter celery in this updated Waldorf salad. Watercress adds a crisp, peppery spice and lots of dark-green nutrition. A simple dressing of crème fraîche, lemon, and honey makes it feel decadent and coats well, so you don't need to drench the produce with mayonnaise like some of the church-supper horrors of yesteryear.

6 to 8 servings

⅔ cup pecan halves
1 tart, crisp apple
2 to 3 ribs celery
½ cup Crème Fraîche (page 181)
Juice of ½ lemon
1 tablespoon honey
½ teaspoon kosher salt
Freshly ground black pepper
1 bunch watercress, thick stems removed

Heat the oven to 300°F. Place the pecans on a baking sheet on the middle rack of the oven. Roast until lightly browned, about 10 minutes. Let cool. Meanwhile, cut the apple into quarters lengthwise and remove the seeds and core from each quarter. Slice each quarter into three pieces lengthwise, then cut in half crosswise.

Trim the ends from the celery ribs, wash the ribs, and slice crosswise into ¼-inch-thick pieces. In a large bowl, combine the apple, celery, and pecans. In a small bowl, mix together the crème fraîche, lemon juice, honey, salt, and pepper. Spoon the dressing into the celery mixture and stir well to combine. Toss with the watercress just before serving. Taste for seasoning.

CITRUS

Citrus is a large category that encompasses the flowering evergreen trees of the rue family. Living in Georgia, I have direct access to an impressive array of citrus fruits from nearby Florida. In the middle of winter, when everything is looking drab and bleak, and there are mostly greens or roots to work with, citrus goes into full swing and brightens our short days with candy-stripe colors and refreshing acidity. Citrus fruits mature in cool weather and produce bright colors: orange, yellow, pink, red, and green. Their tangy juice wakes up our palates and provides lots of immunity-building vitamin C.

ORANGES: Lower in acid and sweeter than the other citrus fruits, oranges come in many sizes and shapes—and in many colors besides their namesake orange. Navel oranges have a small second fruit that forms at the blossom end and bulges slightly with a concave center, looking like a belly button. The fruit is sweet with low acid and has a thick skin, making it easy to peel. Cara cara, the pink navel, has the lowest acid of all the oranges and beautiful pink grapefruit-colored flesh. There is also a red navel with slightly darker flesh color, like a ruby red grapefruit. Valencia is the number one choice for fresh-pressed juice, with a higher acid level and a larger yield from squeezing than other oranges. The blood orange has a distinctive, sweet-tart, raspberry-orange flavor. The Moro variety, with dark, purple-red flesh and a red blush on the skin, is the most widely planted and the first of the season to ripen. Sour orange is a small- to medium-size fruit, also known as a Seville orange; it has a bitter rind and very tart flavorful fruit that is prized for marmalade. The tangelo is a cross between a pomelo and a mandarin orange. Tangelos have a tangerine flavor but are a larger fruit, about the size of your fist. The tangerine is a small, dark orange fruit with a smooth, easy-to-peel skin and a deep orange color. Tangerines have a tangy, sweet flavor and are easy to pull apart because of their naturally formed segments. The satsuma is a seedless, easy-to-peel orange also known as a mandarin orange. The kumquat resembles an orange but is about the size and shape of an olive. It has large seeds and very little fruit. Once the seeds are removed, the entire kumquat is edible, skin and all.

LEMONS: These are extremely tart and high in acid. Lemons are usually mixed with sugar for beverages or desserts. They are used often in cooking to add acidity, brightness, and character to a sauce, soup, sauté, or salad dressing. Meyer lemons are a cross between a lemon and a tangerine. They are golden yellow with lots of juice and a slightly sour taste. The acid is lower, so Meyer lemons can be eaten without making your face pucker. The skin has a sweet flavor and a strong aroma.

LIMES: These are a green citrus with sour-tasting juice and pulp and a distinctive flavor. Limes have a stronger presence in Asian and Mexican cuisine; here we tend to use them more in cocktails. Key limes are a very small green citrus from the Florida Keys that tastes like lime but is much more sour. The skin is thin and aromatic and the fruit is very seedy.

GRAPEFRUIT: This is a sour to semisweet fruit and comes in a range of sizes and colors. Grapefruit are larger than other citrus fruits and have a high juice yield. They grow in clusters on the tree, resembling grapes, hence the name. The white grapefruit is generally more acidic and tart, while the pink and ruby red varieties have more sugar and less acid. Pomelos are the largest form of a grapefruit, with a fragrant skin, very thick rinds or pith, and flavorful, low-acid juice.

You'll get more juice out of citrus fruit if you bring it to room temperature and then roll it with your palm before pressing. Most people think of using just the fruit, but the skins also have a distinctive flavor. Citrus zest can be added to just about anything. An easy way to zest citrus is by running the skin across a microplane grater. All citrus is best stored refrigerated until you are ready to use it.

GRAPEFRUIT, AVOCADO, AND ESCAROLE

I have a vivid memory of the first time I ever tasted avocado and grapefruit together. They were served in a salad at an early 1980s dinner party given by my "city" grandparents, and that dish left an impression of sophistication on my preteen palate. My grandfather, M. B. Satterfield, was an architect in Atlanta and designed their beautiful modern house. My grandmother, Frances Gibson, or "Gibby," introduced all of us to the continental cuisine of that era. Avocados were still considered an exotic delicacy in Georgia, and the lighter, less creamy Florida varieties were the only ones we came across. Pleasantly bitter, cool-weather escarole provides a nice backdrop for the zippy grapefruit.

4 to 6 salads

1 large head escarole
1 small pink grapefruit
1 small white grapefruit
1 large ripe Florida avocado (or Hass avocado)
1 teaspoon sea salt, plus more for seasoning
2 tablespoons Champagne vinegar
1 tablespoon minced shallot
1 teaspoon Dijon mustard
½ teaspoon freshly ground black pepper
⅓ cup extra virgin olive oil

Remove the outer leaves of the escarole if bruised or discolored. Remove the stem end, trim off 1 inch of the top, and slice the escarole in half. Lay cut side down and then dice into roughly 1-inch pieces. Transfer the chopped escarole to a large bowl of water and agitate with your fingers to wash any dirt away. Dry the escarole in a salad spinner. Transfer to a large bowl and set aside. Make grapefruit "supremes" (see page 429) and place the sections and juice in a separate bowl. Set aside.

Slice the avocado in half, and remove the pit and peel. Cut the avocado into 1-inch pieces and transfer to a separate bowl. Spoon a little bit of the reserved grapefruit juice over the avocado to keep it from browning, and season with a little salt.

To make the vinaigrette, in a small bowl whisk together the vinegar, shallot, mustard, 1 teaspoon salt, and black pepper. While whisking, drizzle in the olive oil. Add the avocado and grapefruit to the bowl with the escarole and dress with just enough of the vinaigrette to coat evenly. Taste for seasoning and adjust as needed.

KUMQUAT AND PICKLED BEET RELISH

Sweet and sour kumquats may be tiny, but they make a big impact. One fun way to use these is to combine them with thinly sliced pickled beets in a relish that is phenomenal with Melting Pot Braised Pork (below).

About 1½ cups

1 cup whole kumquats
½ cup Pickled Beets (page 387)

Thinly slice the kumquats with a sharp paring knife or small serrated knife. Remove any seeds, then place the kumquat slices in a medium bowl. Arrange the beet slices one on top of another and cut into thin matchsticks. Toss the beets with the kumquats and serve.

MELTING POT BRAISED PORK

After brining for two days, this fatty cut of meat slow-cooks to fork-tenderness. The cooked vegetables in the braise can be served with the pork if desired (pictured)

12 servings

1½ cups kosher salt
5 pounds boneless pork shoulder
1 carrot, thickly sliced
1 small fennel bulb, quartered
2 ribs celery, thickly sliced
2 onions, quartered
½ cup dried porcini mushrooms
6 garlic cloves, halved
4 star anise pods
2-inch piece ginger, sliced
2 bay leaves
1 cup white wine
4 cups chicken stock

In a large container, whisk together the salt and 1½ gallons ice water until the salt is completely dissolved. Put the pork into the brine, making sure that it is completely submerged. Cover and refrigerate for 36 to 48 hours.

Heat the oven to 300°F. Remove the pork from the brine and place in a deep roasting pan or Dutch oven. Add the carrot, fennel, celery, onions, dried mushrooms, garlic, star anise, ginger, bay leaves, white wine, and chicken stock to the pan. Cover with a tight-fitting lid or with parchment and foil and place on the lower rack of the oven. Cook for approximately 5 hours. Take the pork out of the oven and remove the lid or foil. Let cool.

Remove the pork from the pan and strain the solids from the braising liquid. Skim off the fat from the reserved cooking liquid. Remove any large pockets of fat from the pork, and slice before serving.

CITRUS MARMALADES

This recipe is applicable for most citrus fruits and can be generalized among varieties. I have made a few suggestions below. The technique is relatively easy, but requires a very sharp knife and a watchful eye. The result is extremely rewarding. I make various marmalades every winter and use them on everything from cheese plates to desserts to just a Sunday morning buttered English muffin.

2 to 3 pints

4 navel, Valencia, or blood oranges; or 3 white or pink grapefruit; or 6 lemons, tangerines, or Meyer lemons (or a combination)
Sugar
Kosher salt

Slice each fruit across its "equator" (not end to end). With a citrus press or a reamer, squeeze the juice over a strainer into a medium bowl to catch any seeds, then discard the seeds and reserve the juice. Do not discard the fruit peel. Slice the peels into quarters and then remove any excess white pith around the base or top of the fruit, where the skin is often thicker. Flatten out the peels on a cutting board and, with a very sharp knife, slice them as thin as you possibly can across the shortest length. You may not need all of the skin. When the volume of sliced skin becomes as great as the volume of juice, you can stop. Add the sliced skins to the fruit juice and measure the total volume. Add an amount of water equal to that volume. Measure the new volume of the juice, skins, and water, and add an equal volume of sugar.

Transfer the mixture to a wide saucepan. Over medium-high heat, bring to a rapid simmer. While the marmalade is cooking, add a pinch of salt. With a small ladle or a wide spoon, remove any foam that rises to the surface. The rinds will begin to turn translucent while the liquid clarifies. When larger bubbles begin to form, remove from the heat. Let cool completely and check for the consistency. If the mixture is too thin, return to the heat until large bubbles form again, and then remove and cool once more. Do not overcook, as the sugars could caramelize and scorch the fresh citrus flavor.

Transfer to a container with a lid and refrigerate for up to 3 months. Or for shelf storage, follow the canning procedures recommended by the jar manufacturer.

KUMQUAT MARMALADE

Kumquats are exceptional in marmalade. They have a sharp taste, but unlike other oranges, they carry their sweetness in the skin. Kumquats do not produce enough juice to make the master Citrus Marmalades recipe (opposite page), so I add orange and lemon juice to compensate without losing flavor.

3 cups

½ pound fresh kumquats (about 2 cups), washed, thinly sliced, and seeds removed
1 cup freshly squeezed orange juice
½ cup freshly squeezed lemon juice
3 cups sugar
Pinch salt

In a wide saucepan, combine kumquats, orange juice, lemon juice, 1½ cups cold water, and sugar, and follow the cooking instructions for Citrus Marmalades.

LEMON BUTTERMILK ICE

No ice cream machine is needed to make this easy and refreshing treat, which I think of as a cross between a sherbet and a granita, the classic Italian fork-flaked frozen dessert.

7 cups

3 cups buttermilk, preferably full fat
1 cup heavy cream
1½ cups sugar
Zest and juice of 1 lemon
Pinch kosher salt

In a medium bowl, whisk together the buttermilk, cream, sugar, lemon zest and juice, and salt until the sugar is completely dissolved. Pour into a 9 x 13-inch pan. Cover and freeze for at least 4 hours, scraping with a fork several times during freezing. When fully frozen and ready to serve, scrape one more time right before serving. (If the scraping gets away from you and the mixture freezes solid, scoop into a food processor in batches and process until smooth, adding a little more buttermilk if necessary.)

PRESERVED LEMONS

The most critical ingredient in this recipe is time. The method could not be easier but you need to be prepared to wait a good three months—better yet, five or six—before using. Cut lemons into quarters, layer with salt, and then forget about them. When you are ready to use them, just pull out a wedge or two, and leave the rest behind for later use. Combine with any flavor like olive, feta, mint, oregano, fish, or poultry. Originally Moroccan, these add a briny lemon oil flavor to anything they mix with. I omit the traditional spices and keep this recipe neutral to mix in with any of my Southern ingredients. Since the skin is mostly what is eaten, purchase organic lemons whenever possible.

Makes 2 to 3 cups preserved lemons

12 organic lemons, washed
3 pounds kosher salt

Quarter the 12 lemons lengthwise and set aside. Cover the bottom of a gallon container with 1 inch of salt and then put a layer of lemons across the salt. Cover with more salt and repeat with another layer of lemons. Continue until all the lemons are completely covered with 1 inch of salt. Allow to sit in the back of your refrigerator for a minimum of 3 months or until they have softened and become translucent. When ready to use, rinse well. Then remove the fruit portion of the lemon and discard. Drop the rinds into boiling water for 30 to 60 seconds. Remove from the boiling water and transfer to an ice bath. Remove from the ice bath and then cut away any remaining white pith with the edge of a sharp knife. Thinly slice or dice the remaining lemon peel and add to soups, stews, sauces, or vegetable sautés.

Note: One lemon quarter yields about 2 teaspoons diced lemon peel.

ENGLISH BLOODHOUND

The Greyhound is a classic cocktail with gin or vodka and freshly squeezed grapefruit juice. Salt the rim and you have a Salty Dog. The English Bloodhound is yet another version, with London dry-style gin and a splash of Campari, giving it a vibrant scarlet hue that brightens a chilly winter day. Serve with a swipe of grapefruit peel and lots of cheer.

1 cocktail

1 ounce London dry-style gin
½ ounce Campari
1½ ounces freshly squeezed pink or white grapefruit juice
Ice cubes for shaker, and more for cocktail if desired
Grapefruit peel for garnish (optional)

In a cocktail shaker, combine gin, Campari, grapefruit juice, and ice and shake well to combine. Strain into a cocktail coupe or over ice in a cocktail glass. Garnish with a grapefruit peel if desired.

BLOOD ORANGE AMBROSIA
RICE PUDDING

Rice pudding is one of those old-fashioned desserts that you don't see too often, but when it's done right, it is stunning. Though it is typically served chilled, like any pudding, I like to eat it when it is still warm from the stove. The blood orange, coconut, and almond topping adds an unexpected twist to this classic creamy treat.

6 servings

4¼ cups whole milk
½ cup sugar
½ cup white rice, preferably Carolina Gold
2 blood oranges
2 tablespoons unsalted butter
2 tablespoons local honey
⅛ teaspoon fine sea salt, plus a pinch
1 egg
1 teaspoon vanilla extract
¼ cup skin-on sliced almonds, toasted
¼ cup shredded sweetened coconut, toasted

In a saucepan over medium-low heat, combine 4 cups milk, the sugar, and the rice. Simmer, covered, 1 hour, stirring frequently. Remove the pan from the heat and let rest 10 minutes.

Turn the oven setting to broil and position a rack 4 inches from the broiler. Zest 1 of the oranges and set the zest aside. "Supreme" both oranges (see page 429) and set aside.

In a small saucepan or microwavable dish, melt the butter with the honey and a pinch of salt. Pour over the orange segments; carefully turn the segments to coat. Spread out in a single layer on a rimmed baking sheet. Broil on the top rack until the segments begin to brown, about 5 minutes. Carefully turn the segments and return to the broiler until the other sides begin to brown, about 3 minutes. Transfer the segments and pan juices to a bowl. Set aside.

In a small bowl, whisk together the egg, the remaining ¼ cup milk, vanilla, reserved zest, and ⅛ teaspoon sea salt. Stir into the rice mixture and return the pot to low heat, stirring constantly, until the mixture begins to thicken, about 2 minutes.

To serve, spoon the warm rice pudding into individual dishes. Divide the orange segments and juices among the bowls. Top with the toasted almonds and coconut. If you prefer to serve chilled, cover the portions with plastic wrap and refrigerate for 2 hours prior serving.

HOT TODDY WITH LEMON, ORANGE, HONEY, AND AMARO

When I'm down with a nasty cold, a hot toddy is my kind of remedy. The booze numbs, the citrus fortifies, the honey soothes, and the amaro just makes you feel warm and fuzzy—whether you're under the weather or not. Amaro is a bitter digestif made with barks and herbs, and Fernet Branca is one of my favorites.

1 cocktail

1 ounce Kentucky bourbon
1 ounce Fernet Branca, or other Italian amaro
1 to 2 tablespoons honey
½ ounce lemon juice
½ ounce orange juice
2 whole cloves
Orange or lemon wedge for garnish

In a tall mug, combine the bourbon, amaro, honey, lemon and orange juices, and cloves. Stir well, and add boiling water to fill the mug. Garnish with an orange or lemon wedge. Serve hot.

MEYER LEMON SAUCE

This unique sauce, made from a whole Meyer lemon, thickens in the blender because of the natural pectin found in the skin. The skin is sweet, not bitter, and the fruit is lower in acid than a regular lemon, so this sauce is balanced and not too tart. It can be used on almost anything where you would want to add a hint of brightness and acid, including fish, shellfish, meats, vegetables, and salads.

½ cup

1 Meyer lemon, quartered and seeds removed
1 stalk green garlic or 1 garlic clove
½ teaspoon fine sea salt
4 tablespoons extra virgin olive oil

Combine lemon, garlic, salt, and olive oil in a blender and blend until smooth.

CITRUS SUPREMES

Eating citrus can be messy, but there is a technique that removes all of the seeds and membrane, leaving only the juicy segments behind. It's called the supreme. Cut off both ends of the fruit. Place cut side down, in either direction, and with a sharp slicing knife carve away the skin and pith, following the natural curve of the fruit. Using the tip of the knife and a slight sawing motion, cut away the pith and peel from the fruit, until all of the fruit is exposed. This makes for a prettier presentation.

Hold the peeled fruit in your hand over a bowl to catch any juices, and with the top third of the knife, separate the fruit from the membrane. When you have segmented the entire fruit, squeeze out any remaining juices from the membrane into the bowl. Store the supremes in the fruit juice, refrigerated, until ready to use.

COLLARDS AND KALE

Collard greens and kale are both leafy greens from the large genus *Brassica*. Both have leaves growing from strong ribs that sprout off one central columnar stem. They can sometimes be used interchangeably, with the exception that mature collards are generally cooked, whereas kale is eaten raw or cooked, no matter the size. Collards have a long history in the South as a poor man's mainstay simmered in large quantities on the stove all day long, creating the flavorful but smelly "mess o' greens" we have all come to love. Kale, on the other hand, has become the trendy superfood of our time, devoured by health nuts, models, actors, paleo dieters, and common folk alike.

Before they earned their respective statuses, both collards and kale were cultivated by the Romans. These are among the oldest hardy greens known to man. They have a dusty coating of natural wax that seals the outside and protects the cell walls. You can see this when you plunge them into cold water and then remove them. The water is repelled and cannot cling to the surface. This makes them extra sturdy to survive through a frost and protects them from the cold. Both collards and kale are in season from early fall through spring but usually in separate plantings. The greens cannot survive a harsh winter but can thrive through the winter in milder climates or in a greenhouse.

COLLARDS: A time-honored tradition in Southern kitchens, collard greens have held an important place on the table for ages, and there is no other vegetable that is quite so characteristic of the region. The traditional way to cook greens is to simmer them slowly with a piece of salt pork or ham hock for a long time, tempering the tough texture and any bitter flavor, until they are very tender. Typically, the greens are served with freshly baked cornbread to dip into the pot likker—the highly concentrated, vitamin-filled broth that results from the long cooking of the greens. But there are many other ways to enjoy collards, and chefs and home cooks alike experiment with them for new interpretations of Southern cooking like slaw, salad, kraut, kimchi, and more. Though the leaves can grow up to three feet long, I prefer young, tender leaves, which are more versatile for cooking or eating raw. The thick fibrous stem is usually removed and discarded but can be used if chopped finely. Rinse collard greens well when ready to use and remove any blemishes or browning when prepping.

KALE: Ever-popular kale is well liked for good reason. Its dark green cruciferous leaves are packed with vitamins and minerals. Kale is touted as a panacea with claimed benefits such as lowering blood pressure, improving bone health, fighting cancer, reducing the risk of diabetes, and decreasing symptoms of asthma. Besides the health benefits, it is a delicious green that has very little bitter flavor and, if kissed by a frost, a crisp sweetness. There are many varieties of kale that range widely in texture and color. Curly kale was once the most available and has tender leaves with a crisp rib. Lacinato or dinosaur kale is a deep green wrinkly leaf with a rigid rib and a sweet flavor. Red Russian has an even sweeter flavor and a thinner green leaf that is scalloped on the edges with beautiful purple stems. Winterbor kale has a flat leaf with ruffled edges and comes in a dark purple variety called redbor. Siberian kale has a large leaf with white ribs and veins that resembles a collard green leaf.

Kale can be sautéed, simmered, fried, baked, juiced, cultured, or eaten raw in salads, in slaw, or in smoothies. It is one of the most versatile greens and because people greet it with enthusiasm, perhaps they are more willing to try it in different ways. Store kale covered in the crisper of your refrigerator and wash it well when ready to use. It is better to remove the stems first and then wash; this makes them less rigid and easier to move around when submerged in water.

COLLARD GREEN AND
TURNIP ROOT KIMCHI

The Korean condiment kimchi is traditionally made with Napa cabbage and daikon radish. But two basic Southern ingredients from the early winter harvest—collards and turnips—easily adapt to this classic Asian technique. The zesty, racy flavor wakes up simple fish or rice dishes, or the kimchi can be added to hot chicken broth to make a comforting cold-weather soup. When you first lift the lid from this quickly fermenting concoction, don't be put off by the strong odor that will be released after gases build up; it is normal to have a strong smell.

2 quarts

1 bunch collard greens, about 1½ pounds
¼ cup kosher salt
1 small head garlic, peeled and finely chopped
One 2-inch piece ginger, peeled and finely chopped
¼ cup fish sauce
2 teaspoons ground arbol chile
1 teaspoon honey
1 bunch scallions, cut into 1-inch pieces
1 medium purple top turnip, peeled, thinly sliced, and quartered

Separate the collard green leaves from their stems. Chop the leaves into bite-size pieces and slice the stems into ½-inch pieces. In a large bowl, whisk together 1 gallon water and ¼ cup salt until the salt is dissolved. Put the chopped collard greens and stems into the salted water and let sit for 2 hours. If necessary, place a weight on top to keep the greens submerged.

In a separate large bowl, combine the garlic, ginger, fish sauce, ground chile, and honey. Add the scallions and turnip and toss with the spice mixture. Remove the collards from the salted water. Rinse and squeeze out excess water. Add the collard greens to the rest of the mixture, and toss well to combine. Put the finished mixture into a large glass or ceramic container with a tight-sealing lid. Store in a cool, dark place at room temperature for 2 to 3 days, opening the lid daily to let the gases escape and to assess the flavor. Store covered and refrigerated for up to 2 months.

KALE, ORANGE, AND POMEGRANATE SALAD

When the kale salad craze first began, I was slow to jump on the bandwagon. The early versions I tried had some serious textural issues. I got the nutritional aspect of it right away, but I spent more time chewing than enjoying. The way to work around this is to massage the dressing into the leaves. This gentle pressure, combined with the exposure to fat and acid, tenderizes the kale while neutralizing its raw, chalky mouthfeel. To enjoy this salad throughout the winter, experiment with different combinations of kale and winter fruits to keep it interesting.

4 salads

1 large bunch kale (about ½ pound), washed, stemmed, and roughly chopped
4 to 5 tablespoons Crème Fraîche Dressing (see recipe)
Kosher salt
Freshly ground black pepper
2 oranges, "supremed" (see page 429)
½ cup pomegranate seeds

Place the kale in a large bowl. Toss with the dressing. Make sure your hands are very clean; then gently massage the leaves with the dressing. Taste for seasoning and adjust as needed. Divide the kale among 4 serving bowls or plates. Divide the orange sections and pomegranate seeds evenly over each salad.

CRÈME FRAÎCHE DRESSING

½ cup

1 tablespoon minced shallots
½ teaspoon kosher salt
Pinch finely grated orange zest, plus 2 teaspoons freshly squeezed orange juice
½ teaspoon freshly squeezed lemon juice
¼ teaspoon freshly ground black pepper
½ cup Crème Fraîche (page 181)

In a small bowl, stir together the shallots, salt, orange zest and juice, lemon juice, and pepper. Add the crème fraîche and stir to combine. Taste for seasoning. If the dressing thickens after being stored in the refrigerator, thin it with a little water.

SAUTÉED BABY COLLARDS

Young, tender collard greens are practically a different species compared with their elephant-ear-size older siblings, which take hours to cook and are notorious for stinking up the kitchen. These early-harvest greens can be eaten raw, chopped into a slaw, steamed, or sautéed. I like to spike them with fresh ginger, garlic, and dried hot chiles. Serve these with the Sea Island Red Pea Hoppin' John that follows (page 442), and the Melting Pot Braised Pork (see page 420) as an updated New Year's Day feast.

4 servings

1 pound baby collard greens
1 tablespoon sesame oil
½ teaspoon minced fresh ginger
½ teaspoon minced garlic
¼ teaspoon crushed red pepper flakes
½ teaspoon fine sea salt
Stock or water for the pan
Toasted sesame seeds for garnish (optional)

Trim the stems from the greens and wash the leaves thoroughly. Roughly chop the leaves and set aside. The stems can be washed and thinly sliced to be cooked with the leaves, or set aside for another use.

In a 12-inch skillet, warm the sesame oil over medium-high heat. Add the ginger, garlic, red pepper flakes, and salt. Sauté for 1 minute, then add the greens. Add a tablespoon or two of stock as needed to steam the leaves and keep the ginger and garlic from browning. With tongs, turn the greens frequently until completely wilted, 3 to 4 minutes, adding stock as needed. Taste for seasoning and adjust. Garnish with toasted sesame seeds if desired.

WHITE BEAN STEW WITH KALE AND SAUSAGE

Though this recipe might sound like a cliché, I can think of few things more comforting on a cold winter's day than a pot of beans and greens simmering on the stove, filling the house with savory aromas and anticipation. I like to save the stems from the kale leaves and dice them up with the other vegetables, adding an extra dose of fresh produce to the mix.

8 to 10 servings

1 pound dried white beans
2 large bunches kale, about 1½ pounds
6 tablespoons extra virgin olive oil
1 large yellow onion, diced
4 ribs celery, diced
1 fennel bulb, diced
6 garlic cloves, minced
4 teaspoons kosher salt, plus more to taste
8 cups chicken stock or water
2 bay leaves
1 teaspoon crushed red pepper flakes
½ teaspoon freshly ground black pepper
1 teaspoon fresh thyme leaves
1 tablespoon vegetable oil
1½ pounds mild Italian or other fresh unsmoked pork sausage

In a large bowl, cover the beans with cold water by 3 inches. Put a lid on the bowl and set aside at room temperature for 8 hours or overnight. Drain the soaked beans, rinse, and set aside.

Remove the stems from the kale, wash the leaves, and set aside. Rinse the stems, then slice them crosswise the same length as their thickness, and set aside.

In a large pot or Dutch oven, warm the olive oil over medium-high heat. Add the onion, celery, fennel, kale stems, garlic, and salt. Sauté until the onion is translucent, about 5 minutes. Add the drained beans and cover with stock by 2 inches. Add the bay leaves, red pepper flakes, black pepper, and thyme, and bring just to a boil. Skim any foam off the surface and discard. Reduce the heat and simmer, stirring occasionally, until the beans are tender, about 1½ hours. Taste for seasoning and adjust as needed. Remove and discard the bay leaves.

Roughly chop the kale leaves and stir them into the beans. Cook for 20 minutes. Meanwhile, in a large skillet, warm the vegetable oil over medium-high heat. Add the sausage to the skillet and brown on all sides until crisp. Remove the sausage and let cool 10 minutes. Slice the sausage into ¼-inch-thick pieces and add to the pot. Taste for seasoning. Ladle the stew into bowls and serve with hot Skillet Cornbread (page 131) or warm crusty bread.

SEA ISLAND RED PEA HOPPIN' JOHN

Throughout the South, hoppin' John and collard greens are served together on New Year's Day to ensure good luck and fortune for the coming year. The peas represent coins and the greens, dollar bills. Hoppin' John is a mixture of peas and rice believed to have originated the mid-1800s in the coastal plains of the Southeast. The blackeyed pea is more commonly seen now, but the red pea was the true original in this historic mixture.

8 servings

Peas

2 cups dried red peas or blackeyed peas
2 to 3 slices diced raw bacon
1 tablespoon butter
1 tablespoon extra virgin olive oil
¼ cup diced yellow onion
¼ cup diced celery
¼ diced green bell pepper
1 small fresh serrano or other hot pepper, seeded and chopped
½ teaspoon chopped garlic
½ teaspoon chopped fresh thyme
Kosher salt and freshly ground black pepper
6 cups chicken or vegetable stock or water, plus more if needed

Rice

2 tablespoons unsalted butter
2 cups Carolina Gold rice
½ teaspoon fine sea salt
4 cups chicken stock or water, heated

Place the peas in a large bowl and cover with at least 2 inches of cold water. Put a lid on the bowl and let soak overnight, then drain, rinse, and set aside.

In a medium saucepan over medium heat, sauté the bacon in the 1 tablespoon butter and olive oil. Add the onion, celery, bell pepper, serrano, garlic, and thyme and sauté for 5 to 6 minutes. Season lightly with salt and pepper. Add the drained and rinsed peas and cover with stock. Allow to cook slowly for 1 to 2 hours. Taste the broth for seasoning halfway through cooking, and adjust as needed. Add stock as needed to keep the peas covered with cooking liquid the entire time.

Meanwhile cook the rice. In a medium saucepan over medium heat, warm the 2 tablespoons butter until melted and foamy. Add the rice and salt and cook, stirring frequently, until the rice turns golden but not brown. Add the warmed chicken stock and cook until the stock starts to simmer, then turn the heat down to the lowest setting and cover tightly with a lid. Set a timer for 15 minutes.

When the timer goes off, gently fluff the rice with two forks and then cover again for 5 minutes. Turn out gently into a serving dish, being careful not to break the grains. When ready to serve, spoon the cooked peas over the rice.

OTHER WINTER ROOTS

Among produce bins filled with beauty and vibrancy, these are the ugly ducklings. Drab in color and irregular in shape and form, parsnips, rutabagas, and sunchokes are among the easiest to pass by. In part, there is just less general knowledge about what they are and what to do with them than about others in the vegetable world.

PARSNIPS: Parsnips are among the most cold-hardy of all vegetables, and in fact only get better as the temperature drops, causing their starches to convert to sugar. These pale yellow to ivory-colored roots are harvested after the first frost and can be stored in the ground over the winter season, covered if necessary to keep them from freezing. Their sweet, nutty flavor stands on its own if they are roasted, sautéed, or boiled and pureed. But they harmonize exceptionally well with other roots in wintry dishes, especially in soups and stews. Given their similar appearance, it's not surprising that parsnips and carrots are closely related. In ancient times, they often went by the same name and were used interchangeably. Rich in vitamin C, potassium, and other nutrients, they have long been inexpensive sustenance in Europe, and before sugar became widely available they were commonly used to sweeten desserts and jams. Parsnips play well with their other cousins—fennel, parsley, celeriac, and so on. They also pair nicely with pears, citrus, nutmeg, and savory herbs such as rosemary and thyme. Choose parsnips that are smooth, medium-size, and free of blemishes. Uncooked, they'll keep in a loose plastic bag in the refrigerator for several weeks or longer. Irregularly shaped parsnips are just as flavorful but may be trickier to clean and peel.

RUTABAGAS: These homely-looking members of the genus *Brassica* are a cross between a wild cabbage and a turnip, with a flavor that is milder than either. Rutabagas look like fat, overgrown turnips, with rough skin that is mottled with purple, yellow, and brown. Their thin skins are easy to peel, and their crisp, golden flesh is less starchy than a potato, yet still rich-tasting. Rutabagas can be mashed like potatoes, cooked into stews, and even peeled and thinly sliced or grated and eaten raw. They originated in Northern Europe, and in Britain and other parts of Europe they are also known as Swedish turnips, or "swedes." Though popular for centuries, the rutabaga lost its appeal after World War I, when it was one of the few fresh foods people had to choose from. It has struggled to shake its reputation as a "famine food" ever since. But it has many virtues that make this vegetable worthy of another chance: it is high in beta-carotene and potassium, easy to prepare, and versatile. Choose rutabagas that are heavy, firm, and free of holes and bruises. A rutabaga will keep at least several weeks in the crisper drawer or months in a root cellar.

SUNCHOKE: This knobby, mildly nutty-tasting tuber also called Jerusalem artichoke is not an artichoke at all but belongs to the same genus as the sunflower. Sunchokes are native to North America and were discovered by a French explorer who found them growing in Cape Cod in the early 1600s. Native Americans are said to have prepared them for Lewis and Clark in 1805. One theory explaining how they came to be known as "Jerusalem artichokes" is that Jerusalem is a corruption of *girasole*, the Italian word for sunflower. To avoid confusion, they are often marketed as sunchokes. Beware, though: in recent years they have earned the nickname "fartichokes," because they contain a polysaccharide called inulin (also found in garlic and onions) that can cause gas and bloating in people who are sensitive to it. However, inulin levels in sunchokes, and reactions to inulin, vary, so don't dismiss the sunchokes—just don't go overboard. The good news is that their high fiber and nutritional profile make them good for the gut, the heart, the bones, and pretty much everything else. Sunchokes can be extremely dirty, so use a clean toothbrush or vegetable brush to scrub them under running water to release dirt or sand that may be trapped in their crevices. Thought they are gnarled and creviced, sunchokes do not have to be peeled. As long as the skin is clean, it is edible, nutritious, and delicious. Store sunchokes in a plastic bag in the crisper and do not wash until ready to use.

OYSTER STEW WITH SUNCHOKES AND CELERY

In its purest form, oyster stew is little more than oysters, butter, cream, and maybe a little onion. In this version, the naturally sweet sunchoke adds texture and body to the creamy base, while the salinity of celery echoes the briny oysters. I like to serve this on Christmas Eve with the savory oyster crackers that follow. If you can't find sunchokes, parsnips work remarkably well as a substitute.

8 servings (8 cups)

2 dozen shucked oysters with liquid
3 cups whole milk
1 cup heavy cream
6 tablespoons unsalted butter
1 large yellow onion, finely diced (about 2 cups)
2 ribs celery, finely diced (about 1 cup)
1 pound sunchokes, scrubbed clean and cut into ¼-inch dice (about 4 cups)
2 teaspoons kosher salt
¼ cup all-purpose unbleached flour
Freshly ground black pepper
Cayenne pepper
Roughly chopped flat-leaf parsley and celery leaves
Benne Seed and Country Ham Oyster Crackers (page 451)

Place a wire-mesh strainer over a medium bowl and drain the oysters, reserving the liquor. Inspect the oysters and remove any bits of shell and set aside.

In a medium saucepan, over medium heat, warm the milk and cream just until simmering. Turn off the heat and cover with a lid to keep warm. In a large Dutch oven over medium heat, melt 4 tablespoons of the butter until foamy. Add the onion, celery, sunchokes, and 1 teaspoon of the salt, stirring well to coat. Cook, stirring often, until the onion is tender and translucent, 8 to 10 minutes. Sprinkle the flour over the vegetable mixture. Cook for 2 more minutes, stirring well to cook the raw taste out of the flour. Slowly whisk in the warm milk and cream; bring the mixture to a low simmer, stirring often to keep it from sticking. Add the oyster liquor to the Dutch oven and continue to simmer until all the vegetables are tender. Be sure to taste a sunchoke to check for doneness.

In a large skillet over medium heat, melt the remaining 2 tablespoons butter until foamy. Add the drained oysters in a single layer. Sprinkle with the remaining 1 teaspoon of salt and a few grinds of black pepper. Cook just until the oysters begin to curl around the edges and the gills are exposed. Immediately transfer the oysters and any liquid to the Dutch oven and stir to combine. Remove from the heat, cover, and let stand for 10 minutes. When ready to serve, ladle the hot stew into each bowl and sprinkle each with a pinch of cayenne pepper. Garnish the servings with freshly ground black pepper, parsley, celery leaves, and oyster crackers.

BENNE SEED AND COUNTRY HAM OYSTER CRACKERS

Brought over by African slaves, the sesame plant took root well in the sandy coastal plains of the South. Benne, the Malinke word for sesame, is now considered an heirloom American ingredient and is prized for its nutty flavor and healthy oils. Laced with country ham and benne seeds, these crisp bites reference both my mountain and my low-country background. If you prefer to make a vegetarian version, substitute butter for lard, and replace the country ham with 1 teaspoon of fine sea salt.

2 cups crackers

¼ cup benne (sesame) seeds
1 cup unbleached all-purpose flour, plus more for working with dough
¼ teaspoon baking powder
¼ teaspoon kosher salt
4 tablespoons chilled lard
½ cup loosely packed, finely chopped country ham
¼ cup whole milk

Heat the oven to 300°F. Spread the benne seeds in a single layer on a baking sheet and place on the center rack of the oven. Toast, checking frequently and stirring occasionally, until the seeds turn golden brown, 15 to 20 minutes.

In a medium bowl, combine the flour, baking powder, and salt. Add the chilled lard and work it into the flour mixture with your fingers, until the mixture resembles coarse meal. Add the country ham and sesame seeds and stir to combine. Stir in the milk and mix until all the ingredients are fully incorporated. Turn the dough out onto a floured surface, and knead 4 or 5 times. Dust the dough with a sprinkling of flour, then cover the dough with plastic wrap and allow it to rest for at least 1 hour, refrigerated.

Heat the oven to 400°F. Return the dough to the floured surface and roll out with a rolling pin as thinly as possible. The dough will have become dense and hard and may be a little crumbly. With a small pastry cutting wheel, cut the dough into ½-inch squares. Transfer them with a spatula to a parchment-lined baking sheet and bake until crisp and lightly browned, 12 to 15 minutes. Serve as a garnish with oyster stew.

THERE IS A STILLNESS, A QUIETNESS IN WINTER, ESPECIALLY ON THE COAST. THE WIND WHIPS BY OUTSIDE WHILE ROOTS ARE BAKING AND STEWS ARE SIMMERING.

BREAD AND BUTTER
SUNCHOKES

The term "bread and butter pickles" applies to a style of sweet cucumber pickle that was popular during the Depression era. These easy-to-make home pickles were often sandwiched between two slices of buttered bread as an inexpensive lunch when cupboards were bare. Pickled sunchokes riff on the traditional method and flavor, but stay extra crisp, even after the hot brine covers them. They are fantastic with smoked meats, with charcuterie, or as an accompaniment to a winter vegetable plate. Some hearty bread and good butter on the side won't hurt.

1 quart

1 pound well-scrubbed sunchokes, thinly sliced (about 3½ cups)
2 tablespoons kosher salt
2 cups apple cider vinegar
¾ cup sugar
2 teaspoons mustard seeds
6 black peppercorns
½ teaspoon ground turmeric
1 sprig fresh thyme

Place the sunchokes in a medium bowl and sprinkle with 1 tablespoon salt. Mix well, cover, and leave at room temperature for 1 hour. Rinse off the salt and put the sunchokes into a sterilized quart jar.

Meanwhile, in a small saucepan, combine 2 cups water with the remaining 1 tablespoon salt, vinegar, sugar, mustard seeds, peppercorns, and turmeric. Bring to a boil and pour over the sunchokes. Add the thyme sprig and seal the jar. Store in the refrigerator for a minimum of 1 week before serving. They will keep refrigerated for up to 3 months.

ORANGE AND BRANDY MASHED PARSNIPS

Brandy, orange, and nutmeg elevate this rustic, hand-mashed root vegetable dish that sings of the holidays. Try it with any braised meat in place of the usual mashed potatoes.

6 to 8 servings

10 to 12 medium parsnips, peeled, trimmed, and cut into ½-inch pieces
  (about 6 cups)
Zest and juice of 1 orange
6 tablespoons unsalted butter
1 teaspoon kosher salt
¼ teaspoon freshly ground black pepper
¼ teaspoon freshly grated nutmeg
1 tablespoon brandy

Put the parsnip pieces in a saucepan and cover with water. Bring to a boil over high heat, then reduce the heat to a rapid simmer. Cook until tender, about 20 minutes, and drain well. Transfer the hot parsnips to a large bowl and add the orange zest and juice, butter, salt, pepper, nutmeg, and brandy. Mash well with a potato masher, and stir to combine. The mash will have a coarse texture. Taste for seasoning and adjust as needed.

PARSNIP, PEAR, AND ROSEMARY MUFFINS

The sweetness in these light, moist muffins comes naturally from the pear and parsnip, with just a little boost from sugar. I like to eat them for a healthy breakfast on the go, or as afternoon pick-me-up with coffee. The aroma of fresh rosemary will fill your kitchen as they bake.

12 muffins

Butter: 8 tablespoons (1 stick), melted; plus more, softened, for greasing muffin tin
1½ cups unbleached all-purpose flour
⅓ cup sugar
2 teaspoons baking powder
1 teaspoon fine sea salt
1 cup milk
2 large eggs
1 pear, peeled, quartered, cored, and grated (about ⅔ cup)
1 cup peeled, grated parsnip (about 1 medium)
1½ teaspoons finely chopped rosemary leaves

Heat the oven to 375°F. Lightly butter a 12-cup standard-size muffin tin.

In a medium bowl, whisk together the flour, sugar, baking powder, and salt. In another medium bowl, whisk together the milk and eggs. Add the dry ingredients to the wet ingredients. Stir in the 8 tablespoons melted butter, pear, parsnip, and rosemary. Distribute the batter evenly among the muffin cups. Bake until the tip of a knife inserted in the center of a muffin comes out clean, 20 to 25 minutes.

CARROTS AND SWEDE

Having two Englishmen on our staff at Miller Union, I've become well aware of some of the nostalgic dishes they long for. This golden-hued, orange-speckled root mash, traditionally served at Christmastime in Britain, is one of them. The cabbage flavor of the rutabaga (or "swede," as they call it) can be a turnoff to many, but carrots push this polarizing vegetable toward the sweeter side, making it a palatable introduction for any new rutabaga eater.

8 servings

2 medium rutabagas, peeled and cut into 1-inch cubes
4 medium carrots, peeled and cut into 1-inch pieces
8 tablespoons (1 stick) unsalted butter, room temperature
1 to 2 teaspoons kosher salt
½ teaspoon freshly grated nutmeg
½ teaspoon freshly ground black pepper

In a Dutch oven, combine the prepared rutabagas and carrots. Cover with cold water by 2 inches and bring to a boil, then reduce to a simmer and cook 20 to 30 minutes, or until the carrots and rutabagas are both tender.

Drain the vegetables in a colander at least 5 minutes. Return the vegetables to the Dutch oven and add the butter, 1 teaspoon salt, the nutmeg, and the pepper. Mash well with a hand masher. Taste for seasoning and adjust as needed.

BRAISED OXTAILS

Oxtails are hands-down my favorite cut of beef for braising. The rich beef flavor concentrates as it slowly cooks with the bones. If you cannot find oxtails, this recipe works perfectly well with short ribs or beef brisket. Just scale the cooking time according to the size of the cut of meat, as larger pieces take longer to cook. Serve with Carrots and Swede (opposite page), and some quickly roasted carrots and celery.

6 to 8 servings

1 head garlic, roughly chopped
3 tablespoons kosher salt
1 tablespoon black pepper
2 tablespoons roughly chopped thyme leaves
1 tablespoon roughly chopped rosemary leaves
1 tablespoon roughly chopped sage leaves
5 pounds oxtails, crosscut through the bone into 2-inch-thick pieces
2 tablespoons olive oil
1 bottle dry red wine
4 cups chicken stock
3 onions, quartered
2 carrots, cut into 2-inch-long pieces
2 ribs celery, cut into 2-inch-long pieces

Heat the oven to 300°F. In a small bowl, combine the chopped garlic, salt, pepper, thyme, rosemary, and sage. Mix together well and set aside. Lay out the oxtails in a deep roasting pan in a single layer. Rub the oxtails with the garlic mixture on all sides and set aside for 1 hour at room temperature.

In a large skillet over high heat, warm 1 tablespoon of the olive oil. Working in batches, brush off any excess herb mixture from the oxtails, and sear them on both cut sides until browned, about 5 minutes. Return the browned oxtails to the roasting pan while you work with the next batch. Add the red wine to the hot skillet and bring it to a simmer. Using a wooden spoon or spatula, scrape the bottom of the pan to loosen the browned bits that may be stuck. Pour the wine and loosened bits over the beef. Add the stock to the skillet and bring to a simmer. Pour the hot stock over the beef. Add the onions, carrots, and celery to the roasting pan, distributing them evenly.

Cover the pan with parchment and aluminum foil and place on the bottom rack of the oven. Cook for 4 hours, or until the beef is tender and falling off the bone. Remove the oxtails from the pan and strain the solids from the braising liquid. Skim off the fat from the reserved cooking liquid. Oxtails may be served on the bone or, for a more elegant presentation, remove the meat from the bone and mix with some of the braising liquid before serving.

RUTABAGA AND
TURNIP GRATIN

Turnips and rutabagas aren't at the top of most people's favorite foods list. But that didn't stop me from cajoling customers into trying them when they appeared on Miller Union's winter menus. I use these nutritious, overlooked roots in the same way potatoes might be layered in a gratin. Instead of using all dairy as the liquid, I use half cream, half stock, and barely any butter, to keep this on the lighter side of starchy.

4 servings

1 medium rutabaga
1 large or 2 small purple top turnip roots
1 tablespoon unsalted butter, softened
2 teaspoons kosher salt
1 teaspoon freshly ground black pepper
1 teaspoon fresh thyme leaves
1 cup bread crumbs from stale baguette
1 cup chicken or vegetable stock
1 cup heavy cream
2 tablespoons extra virgin olive oil

Heat the oven to 350°F. Peel the rutabaga and turnip, and then thinly slice each on a mandoline. Butter an 8-inch square baking dish. In a small bowl, combine the salt, pepper, and thyme leaves. Line the bottom of the dish with an even layer of the rutabaga slices, edges slightly overlapping. Sprinkle with some of the salt mixture. Top with a layer of turnip slices and season with some of the salt mixture. Repeat, alternating layers, until all the pieces are in place. Scatter the bread crumbs evenly across the top. Ladle the stock over the bread crumbs to moisten them. Then carefully pour the cream over all the crumbs. Drizzle the olive oil over the top, and bake until the crumbs are lightly browned on top and the gratin is bubbly, about 1 hour. Remove the gratin from the oven and test a corner to make sure the vegetables are tender. If not, return it to the oven. If the gratin starts to dry out, add a little more stock or cream.

Note: If the topping isn't sufficiently crunchy, return the dish to the oven and broil for a few minutes, until lightly browned and crisp.

ROASTED SUNCHOKES WITH LEEKS AND SHIITAKES

In many professional kitchens, sunchokes are typically peeled and diced so that you can't tell them apart from a piece of potato. This recipe is not that fussy. I just scrub the hell out of them to remove any clinging earth, pop them into the oven for a bit, and serve them, skin and all. Here I've paired them with leeks and mushrooms for a starchy side dish that I especially like with braised pork.

6 servings

2 leeks
½ pound shiitake mushrooms
1 pound sunchokes
Kosher salt
Freshly ground black pepper
5 tablespoons extra virgin olive oil

Heat the oven to 350°F. Trim away the root ends and dark green tops from the leeks and slice the leeks lengthwise. Rinse them well under cold running water to remove sand or dirt between the layers. Slice the leek halves into 1-inch-long pieces, and place in a large bowl. Remove the stems from the mushrooms, and if the caps are large, tear them into halves or thirds. (Reserve the stems to make a stock, page 131.) Transfer the mushroom caps to the bowl with the leeks. Season the leek and mushroom mixture with salt and pepper and drizzle with half of the olive oil. Spread the mixture in a single layer in a roasting pan. Place on the center rack of the oven and roast for 15 minutes. Remove from the oven and set aside.

With a vegetable brush under running water, scrub the sunchokes clean, making sure to remove sand and dirt from all crevices. Cut them into uniform 1-inch pieces.

Season the sunchokes with salt and pepper and drizzle with the remaining olive oil. Toss well. Spread them in a single layer in a large roasting pan, or 2 smaller pans. Place on the center rack of the oven and roast until the sunchokes are just tender. Depending on the age and size of the sunchokes, this could take from 30 minutes to 1 hour.

Combine the roasted sunchokes with the roasted leeks and mushrooms and reheat them together in the oven just before serving.

NEXT SPREAD
WINTER VEGETABLE FEAST (clockwise from top left): English Bloodhound; Sautéed Beets with Orange and Walnuts; Melting Pot Braised Pork; Celery, Apple, Pecan, and Watercress Salad; Orange and Brandy Mashed Parsnips; Bread and Butter Sunchokes; Roasted Sunchokes with Leeks and Shiitakes; Sea Island Red Pea Hoppin' John; (center of table, left to right) Kumquat and Pickled Beet Relish; Sautéed Baby Collards; Hot Sauce; Pickled Baby Carrots

These multipurpose doughs are called for in specific recipes and menus in this book, but they can be used in different ways throughout the year and easily adjusted to suit the seasons and the occasion.

PIE DOUGH

For the Radish Greens and Spring Garlic Quiche on page 63.

One 9-inch pie crust

8 tablespoons (1 stick) cold unsalted butter, cut into pieces
1¼ cups all-purpose flour, plus additional for work surface
½ teaspoon fine sea salt
1 teaspoon sugar
1 tablespoon apple cider vinegar

To prepare dough: Place the cut butter in the freezer to chill. Meanwhile, in a mixing bowl, combine the 1¼ cups flour, salt, and sugar. Get some ice water ready. Add the chilled butter to the mixing bowl and, with both hands, rub the diced butter between your fingers through the flour until the texture resembles coarse meal, with some pea-size chunks of butter remaining. Drizzle 3 tablespoons ice water into the flour mixture and mix with a large spoon or spatula until the dough just comes together. On a floured surface, turn out the dough and pat gently into a disk. Lightly coat the top surface with flour, cover the disk in plastic wrap, and refrigerate for a minimum of 1 hour before rolling out. The dough can be stored refrigerated for up to 2 weeks or frozen for up to 6 months.

To blind-bake a single crust: Roll between 2 sheets of parchment to a 14-inch circle. Place the dough and parchment in the freezer for 5 minutes, then peel the top sheet of parchment off the dough. Invert and center over a 9-inch pie pan; remove the second sheet of the parchment and gently ease the dough into the bottom and up the sides of the pan. Crimp the edges. Freeze for 30 minutes.

Heat the oven to 350°F. Remove the crust from the freezer. Line with a fresh sheet of parchment. Fill with a layer of pie weights or dried beans, making sure they fit snugly against the sides. Bake until the crust is set, about 20 minutes. Gently remove the parchment and weights and return the pan to the oven to bake until the crust is lightly browned, approximately 10 more minutes. Remove and let cool.

For the Rustic Apple Tart on page 250: Double the recipe above and follow the instructions for preparing the dough.

For the Rhubarb Turnovers on page 71: Double the recipe and then substitute 2 ounces of cream cheese for 4 tablespoons of the butter. Follow instructions for preparing the dough.

TART DOUGH

For Pecan-Caramel Chocolate Tart on page 336

One 10-inch tart crust

9 tablespoons unsalted butter, room temperature
4½ tablespoons granulated sugar
7 tablespoons confectioners' sugar
1 large egg
2 cups unbleached all-purpose flour, plus more for work surface
¼ teaspoon salt

In the bowl of a stand mixer combine the butter and both sugars and beat 2 to 3 minutes, or until well combined and light yellow. Stop to scrape down the sides of the bowl as needed. Add the egg and beat until fully incorporated. Mix together the 2 cups flour and salt, add in thirds, and beat until just combined after each addition. Cover in plastic wrap and chill 2 to 3 hours before rolling.

Preheat the oven to 350°F. Roll out the dough on a lightly floured surface to ⅛ to ¼ inch thick and to fit a 10-inch tart pan. Poke the crust with a fork all around and return to the refrigerator for 10 minutes. Par-bake the crust 15 to 20 minutes or until light golden.

PIZZA DOUGH

For the Spring Onion Pizza on page 52.

One 12-inch crust

1½ cups unbleached all-purpose flour (can substitute whole wheat flour for half of the all-purpose), plus more for the work surface
1 teaspoon fine sea salt
1 teaspoon active dry yeast
3 tablespoons extra virgin olive oil

In a large bowl, combine the 1½ cups flour and salt. In a small bowl, combine the yeast and ½ cup lukewarm water, and let sit for 1 minute. Gently stir 2 tablespoons of the olive oil into the yeast mixture, and add the liquid to the dry ingredients. Using a sturdy spoon, stir the dough until just combined. Transfer the dough onto a floured surface, and knead until a cohesive ball forms. If the dough is difficult to work with, place the large bowl over the dough for a few minutes and allow it to rest.

Pour the remaining 1 tablespoon olive oil into the large bowl. Roll the dough ball in the bowl to coat it with the oil. Cover the bowl with plastic wrap, and allow the dough to rise at room temperature until it has doubled in size, about 1 hour or more.

Put the dough back onto the floured surface and, with the palms of your hands, punch out the air from the dough. Re-form a ball and return the dough to the bowl. Cover and set aside for 20 to 25 minutes to rest. Return it to the floured surface one more time and roll it out. See page 52 for baking instructions.

POPOVERS

For the spring vegetable feast on pages 104–105.

6 popovers

1 tablespoon unsalted butter, melted, plus 1 teaspoon for greasing the popover pan
1½ cups all-purpose flour
1½ teaspoons kosher salt
3 large eggs, room temperature
1½ cup whole milk, room temperature

Heat the oven to 425°F.

Grease a 6-cup popover pan with the teaspoon of butter and set aside. Combine the tablespoon of butter, flour, salt, eggs, and milk in a medium bowl and whisk until well combined. Pour the batter into the popover pan, dividing equally among the cups. They will be about half full. Bake for 35 to 40 minutes until golden brown and puffed. Do not open the oven door during cooking. Remove from the oven and let cool. Note: To allow the popovers to hold their shape, poke a hole in the top of each popover with a paring knife to let the steam escape. Serve warm or at room temperature.

Variation: Add 2 tablespoons minced green garlic to the batter before pouring it into the pan.

CRACKERS

For the English Peas Hummus on page 90.

12 to 15 servings

1 cup unbleached all-purpose flour (or substitute half buckwheat flour for half of the all-purpose); plus extra unbleached flour for kneading and rolling out dough
2 teaspoons fine sea salt
½ cup walnuts (optional)
½ teaspoon freshly ground black pepper
About ½ cup buttermilk
Extra virgin olive oil for brushing the dough
Flaky sea salt for sprinkling the dough

In a food processor, combine the flour, salt, pepper, and walnuts (if using). Process until the walnuts are finely chopped and the ingredients are well incorporated. With the motor running, slowly pour in ¼ cup of the buttermilk. Stop the motor and scrape down the sides of the container with a rubber spatula. Turn the motor back on and slowly pour in just enough buttermilk to form a ball. Transfer the dough to a floured surface.

Heat the oven to 350°F. Line a rimmed baking sheet with parchment. Grease the parchment by lightly brushing it with olive oil. On a pasta roller, roll the dough into manageable-size sheets the thickness of fresh pasta. Transfer the dough to a hard baking sheet and brush the surface of the dough with more olive oil. Sprinkle lightly with salt and bake until crisp and lightly browned, about 8 minutes.

SHORTBREAD

For the Strawberries and Cream with Rose Water and Pistachios on page 100.

About 3 dozen 2-inch cookies

8 tablespoons (1 stick) unsalted butter, room temperature
½ cup confectioners' sugar
1 cup unbleached all-purpose flour, plus more for rolling
½ teaspoon fine sea salt
½ cup finely chopped pistachios or other nuts (optional)
1 teaspoon black pepper (optional)
Granulated sugar

In an electric mixer, cream the butter and confectioners' sugar 4 to 5 minutes, turning the motor off from time to time to scrape down the sides of the bowl. With the motor off, add 1 cup flour, salt, nuts (if using), and black pepper (if using). Turn the motor on at the slowest speed to incorporate and beat slowly. Turn the motor off and scrape the sides again. Beat slowly one more time until fully combined. Turn the dough out onto a floured surface. Flatten out the dough into a thick disk and dust with more flour. Cover in plastic wrap and refrigerate for at least 1 hour.

Remove the dough from the refrigerator, unwrap, and let sit for 30 minutes to soften. Heat the oven to 300°F. On a floured surface, roll out the dough to ¼-inch thickness. Use a cookie cutter to cut the dough into the desired shapes; place on a parchment-lined baking sheet. Leave at least ½ inch between cookies. Bake on the middle rack until lightly browned, 12 to 15 minutes. Sprinkle the cooled cookies with granulated sugar before serving.

MEASUREMENT EQUIVALENTS

Measurements should always be level unless directed otherwise.

⅛ teaspoon	0.5 mL	
¼ teaspoon	1 mL	
½ teaspoon	2 mL	
1 teaspoon	5 mL	
1 tablespoon	3 teaspoons	
2 tablespoons	⅛ cup	½ fluid ounce
4 tablespoons	¼ cup	1 fluid ounce
5 ⅓ tablespoons	⅓ cup	2 fluid ounces
8 tablespoons	½ cup	3 fluid ounces
10 ⅔ tablespoons	⅔ cup	4 fluid ounces
12 tablespoons	¾ cup	5 fluid ounces
16 tablespoons	1 cup	6 fluid ounces

OVEN TEMPERATURE EQUIVALENTS

250°F	120°C
275°F	135°C
300°F	150°C
325°F	160°C
350°F	180°C
375°F	190°C
400°F	200°C
425°F	220°C
450°F	230°C
475°F	240°C
500°F	260°C

INDEX

Page references in *italic* refer to illustrations.

Acknowledgments

Ben Tompkins, an extremely patient man

MILLER UNION

Neal and Carolyn McCarthy, business partners

Emily Hansford, chef de cuisine

Katherine Perry, sous chef

Denver Richardson, sous chef

Pamela Moxley, pastry chef

Julie Steele, dining room manager

The rest of the amazing crew at MU

COOKBOOK TEAM

Karen Rinaldi, publisher, Harper Wave

The hardworking staff at Harper Wave/Harper Collins

Amy Hughes, literary agent, Dunow, Carlson & Lerner

John Kernick, photography

Rizwan Alvi and Darrell Taunt, photography assistants

Erika Oliviera, art direction and design

Hollis Yungbliut, design assistant

Rebecca Harrigan, assistant/cookbook producer/all-around badass

Susan Puckett, writing coach/local editor/surrogate wife

Deborah Geering, recipe tester/production/voice of reason

Tamie Cook, recipe tester/production/fast hands

Kim Phillips, styling/props/sassiness

Thom Driver, styling/props/dance moves

Farmers, markets, foragers, and food wranglers: Brandon Smith, Watsonia Farm and Mercier Orchards. Nicolas Donck, Crystal Organics. Celia Cooper, Woodland Gardens. Cory Mosser, Burge Organics. Robby Astrove, Concrete Jungle. Patricia and Philip Bennett, Green Ola Acres. Michael Schenck, the Turnip Truck. Michael Hendricks, Indian Ridge Farm. Katie Hayes, Community Farmers Markets. Lauren Carey, Peachtree Road Farmers Market. Rashid Nuri, Truly Living Well. East Lake Community learning garden. Al and Mary Pearson, Pearson Farm. Will and Jenni Harris, White Oak Pastures. Mike McGirr. Ivy Creek Family Farm. Willow Springs Herb Farm. Anson Mills, Artisan Mill Goods. Mary Rigdon, Decimal Place Farm.

Locations: Denise and Diane, Mermaid cottages. Katrina and Amy, Tybee vacation rentals. Asha Gomez and Bobby Palayam, the Third Space. Steve and Marie Nygren, Serenbe community, Serenbe Farms, Bosch Experience Center. Seth Solomon, Tybee Island. Kathy Trocheck, Tybee Island. Steven and Kelley Wilkinson, Laughing Frog Estate, aka "Asheville Sanctuary." Joe Reynolds and Judith Winfrey, Love Is Love Farm.